THE ROMANCE
of the
EPISCOPAL CHURCH
in
WEST TENNESSEE

THE ROMANCE

of the

Episcopal

Church

in

West Tennessee
1832—1964

by

Ellen Davies-Rodgers

With Illustrations

Photographs and Reproductions
by
Nadia Price

PUBLISHED BY

The Plantation Press

BRUNSWICK

MEMPHIS, TENNESSEE

Manufactured by
McCowat-Mercer Press, Inc.
Jackson, Tennessee

Dedicated to
The Glory of God
and
in memory of
The Right Reverend Theodore Nott Barth, D.D.
Sixth Bishop of the Protestant Episcopal Church
Diocese of Tennessee
from
September 21, 1953 to August 22, 1961

———————

July 11, 1898, Mt. Savage, Maryland

August 22, 1961, Memphis, Tennessee

———————

A Beloved Bishop and a Friend of Great Affection

CONTENTS

ILLUSTRATIONS

PREFACE

The history and development of many things is of interest but the beginnings and growth of God's people is always an intriguing subject. Such is the case in this volume of "The Romance of The Episcopal Church in West Tennessee" which deals with people's yearnings to worship God and to bring up their children in the way they should go.

Every Churchman in this area and in this Diocese will be fascinated by the account of the struggle and persistence that went into the establishment of the Episcopal Church in West Tennessee. It is a story of love and loyalty to the Author of Life and to this branch of His Holy Apostolic Church.

That Ellen Davies-Rodgers has taken upon herself this task is cause for thankfulness and gratitude from all of us who endeavor daily to follow in His steps.

JOHN VANDER HORST
Seventh Bishop of Tennessee

INTRODUCTION

Someone once said that "there is nothing easier than not to read a book," and I'm sure that there's a great measure of truth in the allegation. However, it would seem to me that there is something easier than not to read a book, and that is not to write one!

The disciplined perseverance and infinite patience of the historiographer have always fascinated me. The separation of fancy from fact, the distillation of truth from the witch's brew of hazy recollections, wishful thinking, propaganda, faulty memory and pure guesswork requires a dedication and a perceptiveness vouchsafed to few.

Ellen Davies-Rodgers in this work on the development and growth of the Episcopal Church in West Tennessee, has placed us all deeply in her debt. Threading her way through a vast maze of source material, she has collated and set forth in unpretentious prose the annals of the comings and goings of those doughty champions of the Faith, both clerical and lay, who have staked out and built the foundations of our Church heritage in this portion of the vineyard.

It may be true that "there is nothing easier than not to read a book," but not to read this one will be to deprive the interested Churchman of a delightfully rewarding experience.

DONALD HENNING
Rector, Calvary Episcopal Church

"My golden spurs now bring to me,
And bring to me my richest mail,
For tomorrow I go over land and sea
In search of the Holy Grail;
Shall never a bed for me be spread
Nor shall a pillow be under my head,
Till I begin my vow to keep; . . . .
. . . .

'Lo, it is I, be not afraid! . . . .
Thou hast spent thy life for the Holy Grail;
Behold it is here, — this cup which thou
Didst fill at the streamlet for me but now;
This crust is my body broken for thee,
This water his blood that died on the tree;
The Holy Supper is kept indeed,
In whatsoever we share with another's need;
Not what we give, but what we share,
For the gift without the giver is bare;
Who gives himself with his alms feeds three,
Himself, his hungering neighbor, and me.'

Sir Launfal awoke as from a swound:
'The Grail in my castle here is found!
Hang my idle armor up on the wall,
Let it be the spider's banquet-hall;
He must be fenced with stronger mail
Who would seek and find the Holy Grail."[1]

---

[1] "The Vision of Sir Launfal," by James Russell Lowell.

AUTHOR'S PREFACE

The Romance of the Episcopal Church in West Tennessee—a title challenging, historical. A subject and a writing which it is hoped may find a place in the chronicles pertaining to the Protestant Episcopal Church.

Sometime after the title for this volume had been chosen, attention was called to a most worthy and interesting book, "The Romance of the Book of Common Prayer," by Francis G. Burgess. The opening paragraph attentively sets the pace for the volume:

> At the head of all English literature stands the English translation of the Bible. Next in rank stands that matchless volume, the "Book of Common Prayer." Of this book it has truly been said that its fortunes are the romance of history.

The story of the Western District of Tennessee as a fertile setting for the planting of the Protestant Episcopal Church is thrilling to layman and citizen alike. That the narrative is unique, legendary and romantic cannot be denied.

One hundred thirty-one years have passed since Mary Hayes Willis Gloster mounted her steed at La Grange, Fayette County, Tennessee and rode to Franklin, Williamson County, Tennessee! There she sought the able assistance of James Hervey Otey, teacher-minister, and received full cooperation. The singular interest of Mrs. Gloster was to establish a church of the Episcopal faith in the town of La Grange, to which she had moved in 1827. However, the devotion which she held for her Church caused her to broaden her request to include the sending of missionary-ministers to evangelize the whole Western District.

Therefore, a broad missionary spirit prevailed in the early work in the Diocese. It is difficult to speak conclusively of the building of any one church in the Western District without giving broad expression of the spreading movement which made a number of churches come into being. The account of the effort in traveling across the vast, scarcely populated District and in preaching to the people the faith of the Episcopal Church is indeed a moving, gratifying story. Truly, the results were made possible by the determined interest and sacrificial endurance of a devoted band of stout-hearted Christians, ministers and laymen, as well.

15

A look at the history of the Episcopal Church in America all the way from Jamestown, 1607, to the Western District, 1832, fails to reveal a more dramatic or more romantic episode than the one which characterized the coming of the Church to West Tennessee. Of course, a few accounts have been written in which Mrs. Gloster has been named as the woman who rode her horse on a church-journey! No source has been found where her full maiden name was used—Mary Hayes Willis—whose heritage was deeply rooted in the founding of our nation. Nor, has any reference been found which has indicated recognition and appreciation shown by a parish of West Tennessee, other than by Immanuel Church, La Grange, in behalf of Mrs. Gloster. Throughout the history of the Episcopal Church the names of stalwart Churchmen and Churchwomen have been revered, both in life and in memory, by appropriate citations. If there exists a Woman's Auxiliary, or a Chapter, which bears the name of Mrs. Gloster, such has not been found! Therefore, may one contribution of this piece of writing be that of recording more information concerning Mrs. Gloster, her family and her memorable deed fulfilled.

In the preparation of this volume contacts have been made with Rectors and in many cases with vestrymen, or communicants, concerning the history of each of the churches in West Tennessee. Gratifying cooperation has been experienced. Many of the churches have been visited. The Record Book of Christ Church, Brownsville was copied in full and certified. Much of the Vestry Book of Trinity Church, Mason has been copied. Similar books have been read at Immanuel, La Grange; St. Andrew, Collierville, and Calvary, Memphis.

Yet, with the many available sources of valuable information covering the influence of the Episcopal Church in West Tennessee, only a very few Churches own a written or printed history. In full measure, it is realized that the time is long overdue for the writing of the history of each Parish, where such has not been done. Records have been lost, older persons have passed on. In other words, time has taken its toll of sources of accurate information of the Church's life and of its people. It is believed that each church should bestir itself to be certain that all remaining bits of the Church's history are permanently recorded and placed in a vault for safe keeping, to become eventually the worthy heritage of generations yet to follow.

Therefore, may the CHART OF CHURCHES, 1832-1964, as compiled in this account, be used as an acceptable, brief historical record of the organization of the Episcopal parishes of the Western District.

Every parish in West Tennessee today stands as a salient factor in the history of the Episcopal Church. Every effort by every communicant is a significant part of the whole cherished opportunity to give, to worship. Every sermon preached, every lesson learned, every prayer invoked, every hymn intoned, every penny placed in the alms basin, is an expression of faith, of hope, of charity. Each is an achievement typical of church-fellowship. Each denotes a continuity in precept and in deed passed down through the years to the followers in the faith! In such manner, each parish shares the sacred, stimulating romance which appropriately signifies the movement peculiarly identified as the coming of the Church to the Western District.

May we, in conclusion, paraphrase a part of Lowell's denotative verse. Of Mrs. Gloster, Bishop Otey, the early ministers and all who were inspired by them in selfless deeds—wrought in the extension of the Episcopal Church from the area of the Tennessee River to the banks of the mighty Mississippi, —this may be said:

> *Each was fenced with strongest mail!*
> *They sought and found the Holy Grail!*

ELLEN DAVIES-RODGERS

Davies Plantation
Brunswick, Tennessee

July 28, 1963

THE ROMANCE
of the
EPISCOPAL CHURCH
in
WEST TENNESSEE

CHAPTER I

THE EPISCOPAL CHURCH IN THE AMERICAN COLONIES

Founding of Jamestown 1607
Types of Early Church-houses

The history of the Episcopal Church, from its beginnings in the Colonies and later in the United States, is unalterably tied to the history of the constitutional government of this republic. To fail to call attention to these closely coordinated facts would break a conspicuous continuity totally worthy of consideration. In other words, we must recognize the Church of today, as we know it and love it, as the product of a most rewarding religious, cultural and legal heritage.

It is evident that the Church of today, as in the past, has a two-fold duty. First, as prescribed in the Prayer Book, Churchmen are inheritors of the kingdom, heirs of God and joint heirs with Christ. To acknowledge this age-old inheritance, which belongs to the Church, is a duty. Coupled with such a duty is another which requires clear interpretation of this inheritance to this age. In such manner, in full, true faith those who come after may understand and bear witness to the bounteousness of their spiritual endowment.

Of historic and religious significance was the founding of Jamestown, Virginia, in 1607. It was there, as we know, with the establishment of the first permanent colony, that our nation's history began. Thus a new colony and an ancient Church came to the American continent simultaneously in 1607.[1] Their way of life and religion were inseparable in the minds and hearts of the Jamestown colonists and in their acceptable social structure, which by careful effort they fashioned and changed with great promise.

Prior to the colonization of Jamestown, it is known that on occasions English clergy had landed on the shores of America. One English minister came with John Cabot in 1497; another sailed with Sir Francis Drake in

---

[1] *The Founding of Jamestown and the Church*, by Jamestown 350th Anniversary Committee of the General Convention of the Protestant Episcopal Church with the assistance of the Old Dominion Foundation. (A pamphlet; National Council of the Episcopal Church)

1579—both, in reality, were ships' chaplains and held services ashore, while their vessels were anchored nearby.

Significant is the fact that Sir Francis Drake's famous voyage around the world touched the shore of California. Later, in commemoration of this historic event a large Celtic cross, known as the Prayer Book Cross, was erected in Golden Gate Park, San Francisco, on the highest elevation. The chaplain of the fleet, the Reverend Francis Fletcher, held services which marked the first Christian services on America's western shores.

It was in 1587 that a company of English people, sent by Sir Walter Raleigh, sailed to the coast of North Carolina and with them brought the Prayer Book. Virginia Dare, born in August of that year, became the first white child baptized in America.

It is appropriate that reference be made to the effort of the Reverend Richard Hakluyt "for stirring up in the minds of the Christian statesmen and people to the duty of finding out barbarous countries, in order to their conversion to the Christian faith." The Reverend Mr. Hakluyt's first writing in 1570 was a collection of accounts of voyages and discoveries. In 1587, this dedicated minister-historian republished Peter Martyr's history of the New World. To this he wrote a preface which he dedicated to the benevolent gentleman, Sir Walter Raleigh, who gave in 1588 one hundred pounds toward the furtherance of Christianity in Virginia.[2]

To be noted also is the fact that the Reverend Mr. Hakluyt was one who urged the colonization of Virginia "but sought and obtained the honour of being one of those to whom Virginia was consigned, by letters-patent from King James, that he might the more effectually labor for her welfare." Therefore, the early expeditions of 1603 and 1605 may be largely attributed to his effort.

The whole purpose of religious extension was expressed in the terms of the patent for Virginia in 1606. In the language of King James that "so noble a work may, by Providence of God, hereafter tend to the glorie of his divine majestie, in propagating of Christian religion to such people as sit in darkness and miserable ignorance of the true knowledge and worship of God, and may in time bring the infidels and savages (living in those parts) to human civility and quiet government." King James gave further admonition in his instructions of 1606, that "all persons should kindly treat the savages and heathen people in these parts, and use all proper means to draw them to the true service and knowledge of God."[3]

---

[2] *Old Churches and Families of Virginia,* by William Meade, D.D., Bishop of Virginia, 1854, Vol. 1, p. 62.
[3] Bishop Meade, Vol. I, p. 63.

History adequately records the account of the expedition which sailed on December 19, 1606 from Blackwell, England.[4] Because of unfavorable winds the vessels remained for six weeks afloat in sight of English shores. During this time, the Reverend Robert Hunt, the minister aboard, "was so weake and sicke that few expected his recovery. . . . Notwithstanding the stormy weather, nor the scandalous speeches of some few, little better than atheists, . . . of the greatest rank among us, suggested against him, all this could never force him so much as a seeming desire to leave the business, but preferred the service of God, in so good a voyage, before any affection to contest with his godless foes . . . so many discontents did there arise, had he not only with the water of patience and his godly exhortations, but chiefly by his devoted example, quenched those flowes of envy and dissention."[5]

This group of Englishmen which started in December 1606 to Virginia shores, brought the first minister to James City. As has been noted he was the Reverend Mr. Hunt. About him, Mr. Wingfield, the first President of the Colony stated: "For my first worke, which was to make right choice of a spiritual pastor, I appeal to my Lord of Canterbury, — his grace, — who gave me very gracious audience in my request. . . . And the world knoweth whom I took with me, truely a man, in my opinion, not any waie to be touched with the rebellious humour of a papist spirit, nor blemished with the least suspicion of a factious schismatic."[6]

The two personages of paramount importance on this voyage were, of course, the Reverend Mr. Hunt, the devout minister, and John Smith, the dedicated Captain. Aptly written of them by Bishop Meade — "two men who seemed to know no fear, but that of God."[7]

A sketch, descriptive of the religious character of Captain John Smith, important because of its relation to the history of the James City Parish, gives an interesting account of the first place of worship there:

"Now because I have spoken so much for the body, give me leave to say somewhat of the soul; and the rather, because I have been demanded by so many, how we began to preach the Gospel in Virginia, and by what authority, what churches we had, our order of service, and maintenance for our ministers; therefore, I think it not amiss to satisfie their demands, it being the mother of all our Plantations, entreating pride to spare laughter, to understand her simple beginnings and proceedings. When I went first to Virginia, I well remember, we did hang an awning (which is an old sail) to three or four trees, to shadow us from the sun; our walls were rails of wood,

[4] *Ibid.*, p. 64.
[5] *Ibid.*
[6] *Ibid.*
[7] *Ibid.*

our seats unhewed trees, till we cut planks, our pulpit a bar of wood nailed to two neighboring trees; in foul weather we shifted into an old rotten tent, for we had few better, and this came by way of adventure for new. This was our church, till we built a homely thing like a barn, set upon crotchetts, covered with rafts, sedge, and earth, so was also the walls. The best of our houses were of the like curiosity, but the most part far much worse workmanship, that could neither well defend wind nor rain, yet we had daily Common Prayer morning and evening, every Sunday two sermons, and every three months the Holy Communion, till our minister died, (the Rev. Mr. Hunt). But (after that) our prayers daily with an homily on Sundays, we continued two or three years after, till more preachers came, and surely God did most mercifully hear us, till the continual inundations of mistaking directions, factions, and numbers of unprovided libertines near consumed us all, as the Israelites in the wilderness."[8]

The Virginia Company of London, which founded Jamestown, performed its act primarily as a business enterprise. Religion was not the foremost concern of those who were the initiators and promotors of this historic experiment. Yet, as believers they were entirely capable of envisioning, at the outset, the possibilities of the potent missionary appeal to their English countrymen. This appeal was effectively set forth in a pamphlet entitled, *The Purpose and Ends of the Plantation Begun in Virginia,* which carried this statement as to purpose: "To preach and baptize into (the) Christian Religion, and by propagation of the Gospell, to recover out of the armes of the Divell a number of poore and miserable soules, wrapt up into death, in almost invincible ignorance, and to add our myte to the Treasury of Heaven."[9]

Truly, their expression of purpose was a form of advertising far in advance of modern practice. Literally thousands of Englishmen sent gifts of communion silver, Bibles, Prayer Books, and generously subscribed money to the Virginia Company. The psychological approach brought financial assistance sadly needed and thus the struggling settlement was aided in its survival. The response which resulted in England, following the circulation of this appeal, was tremendous.

To American shores, in the settlement of the Colony of Virginia, "England's children brought her choicest gifts across the sea."[10] Such gifts were her concepts of civil rights, of English common law and the right of representative government.[11] And one of her greatest gifts, that of the historic faith of her Church—the Church of England. Pertaining specifically

---

[8] *Ibid.,* p. 66.
[9] *The Founding of Jamestown and the Church* (a pamphlet, National Council of Episcopal Churches).
[10] *Ibid.*
[11] *Ibid.*

to this gift was the contribution of the Book of Common Prayer and, at first, the Bishop's Bible; later, by a few years, the magnificent King James version of the Scriptures.

James City Parish in Virginia was created by the Bishop of London. King James I, Defender of the Faith, gave approval and impetus to this religious progress. Thus the English colonists of 1607 came to America with the full intention of bringing to their new home, in this broad wilderness, their Church! Definitely, this was the opposite purpose of the Pilgrims to Massachusetts in 1620, who came to escape the influence and domination of the Church of England.

So, let us repeat: Jamestown was the first American parish of the Anglican Communion. Virginia had previously not been touched by Christianity. The Reverend Robert Hunt was the first Anglican pastor in the New World. It was on June 21, 1607, that the colonists received Communion from Mr. Hunt and thereby inaugurated the continuity of the Anglican Church in the Western Hemisphere. And from the crude church edifice of the historic Jamestown settlement was to grow the virile American Episcopal Church which has become our heritage of today.

The Church in Jamestown planted in 1607, originally completed in 1647, disappeared long ago. Records reveal that at least four wooden chapels were built on Jamestown Island before a substantial church-house was created—built of brick. From an architectural standpoint these frame houses of worship were of four types:

Cruck Church, 1607 (a Gothic building set on crucks or bent tree trunks.) "The crucks consisted of a pair of curved uprights put together, wishbone fashion. Two or more pairs of them were spaced, usually, sixteen feet apart to support a ridgepole. The result was a tent-like structure that was covered with rush or basket-work and sod!"[12]

Lord De la Warr's Church of 1610, 60' x 24', had two bells at the west end. The church was built of unhewn logs. There were few windows; each had wooden shutters. The communion table was of black walnut, the pews of cedar. Sir Thomas Dale came in 1611. In 1611, Pocahontas was baptized in this church and given the name Rebecca. Also there on April 5, 1614, she married John Rolfe, an Englishman.

Argall's Church of 1617, 50' x 20'. It is thought this may have been the type of church in James City in 1623 which had a "lattice gallery for women and for visitors."[13] Captain Samuel Argall arrived as governor in 1617. He found the colonists worshipping in a crude storehouse.

A church of 1636 situated near the Rev. Thomas Hampton's land. Authorities agree the brick church at Jamestown was built on the site

---

[12] *Old American Houses (1700-1850)*, by Henry L. and Ottalie K. Williams, 1957, p. 22.
[13] *The Architecture of the Old South (1585-1850)* by Henry Chandlee Forman (1948), pp. 80-82.

of the Argall's Church. Only the ivy-clad tower of this old church remains today.[14]

In 1907 the Jamestown Church originally completed in 1647, was reconstructed as Jamestown Brick Church, patterned largely after the Old Brick Church in Isle of Wight County, Virginia.

Old Bruton Parish, founded in 1674 at Williamsburg, whose church of 1710 stands today, is steeped in the history of the nation's founding as well as being a venerable church edifice.

In later years, when in Williamsburg on the business of Virginia, Bruton Parish was the "church home" of Thomas Jefferson, James Madison, James Monroe and later of John Tyler.

Three known examples of buttressed churches in Virginia were the Old Brick Church (St. Luke's) ;[15] the first Jamestown Brick Church and the demolished Second Bruton Church in Middle Plantation (Williamsburg).

Among the oldest churches in Virginia is Merchants' Hope Church, built in 1657, Prince George County. "Because of its excellent state of preservation and the details of its masonry, its exterior, which is so devoid of unnecessary adornment, represents the supremely classical example of ecclesiastical architecture in colonial Virginia."[16]

St. Luke's Church, the "Old Brick Church,"[17] in Isle of Wight County, near Smithfield, Virginia, is according to good authority the oldest existing church of the Protestant faith in America, with its original walls standing. The Church served as a place of worship soon after the founding of Jamestown. It was not unusual for an early church to have required eight or ten years in building. The "Old Brick Church" was originally completed in 1632. Tradition gives credit to a Captain Joseph Bridger for having built the church. It is located across the river from Jamestown and near historic Williamsburg.

St. Luke's (Old Brick Church) is "built of bricks, made of clay of the very best quality, found in its immediate vicinity, and put together with a mortar made from well burnt oyster shell lime and building sand, both of which can be found near by in great quantities, the sand being taken from the base of the hill upon which it rests, the mortar becoming almost as hard as flint, preventing the displacement of a brick without tearing away a part of those to which it is attached, baffling the incursions of the would-be despoiler, has assisted greatly in its preservation."[18]

---

[14] *Ibid.*
[15] Newport Parish Church.
[16] *Virginia's Colonial Churches,* by James Scott Rawlings (1963), p. 30.
[17] *A Sketch of the Old Brick Church, Isle of Wight County, Virginia,* by E. Virginia Hayden (1925) (Reprinted 1954).
[18] *Seventeenth Century Isle of Wight County, Virginia,* by John Bennett Boddie (1938), p. 117.

"It appears from the vestry-book that in the year 1737, — that is, one hundred and five years after it was first built, — the old Smithfield Church had a new covering of shingles put upon it. This was doubtless the first repair of this kind since its erection, for it was no uncommon thing for a well-built roof to last thus long."[19]

Truly, St. Luke's is a magnificent example of a well buttressed English Church fashioned after the type of church of much greater antiquity. "It has massive walls and a square set tower which can resist the ravages of time as well as when it was first built centuries ago. Even fire could destroy its wooden interior but the walls would stand. We can but look upon the builders of those days with admiration, as they built for eternity."[20]

Services in the Church were discontinued in 1832.[21]

About the year 1887, the Reverend David Barr, rector of Christ Church in Smithfield, discovered in passing the Old Brick Church that the roof had fallen in, caused by a windstorm on the night before. Thereby, Mr. Barr resolved to make every possible attempt by which funds might be raised and the old Church restored to its former grandeur. This movement was effective and definitely saved the Church from destruction at that time.

Of especial interest to all lovers of churches, which have played so great a part in our national culture, is the non-denominational corporation known as "Historic St. Luke's Restoration,"[22] Smithfield, Virginia, (chartered in 1953). Their purpose: "to acquire, preserve, restore and maintain St. Luke's; . . . all to the end that it may be a memorial to the Christian character of the American colonists, a shrine for religious worship, and a vital and significant sanctuary." The passage chosen as the Restoration's motto is from Isaiah 61:4, "And they shall build the old wastes, they shall raise up the former desolation, and they shall repair . . . , the desolations of many generations."

St. Luke's stands today beautiful within and without, and filled with memorials to those connected with its history and that of the Colony (of Virginia). Its stained glass chancel window eighteen feet by twelve, made in London, divided into twelve sections, each dedicated to some well known character prominent in Church or State, is a most striking piece of art. All of the windows are stained glass, of beautiful design, memorials to founders and communicants. Its carved altar and exquisite reading desk; its wine glass pulpit with its broad steps and high sounding board; its beautiful font, of the purest Carrara marble, made in England, are especially

---

19 Bishop Meade, p. 304.
20 Seventeenth Century *Isle of Wight Co., Virginia,* by Boddie, p. 178.
21 *Ibid.,* p. 180.
22 *Historic St. Luke's Restoration* (a pamphlet), pp. 10, 11, 12.

attractive. The pews are of original style, made of native heart pine. All these things impress the observer with a deep sense of solemnity."[23]

It is known that during the Revolutionary War the records of the "Old Brick Church" were taken from the church by a vestryman, Colonel Josiah Parker, to his home nearby. The British raided Colonel Parker's home, destroyed his personal papers and several of the church registers. The vestry books had been placed in an old trunk which was buried in the ground. The dampness of the ground penetrated the walls and the oldest book was deteriorated. In the Court House is the only remaining record book of the old church.

On May 18, 1957, a service of rededication was held at St. Luke's in commemoration of the complete restoration which had been chartered in 1953. Of great interest is the recent citation by the National Park Service in its designation of the "Old Brick Church" as a Registered National Historic Landmark. A presentation service was held on May 20, 1961.[24]

So, the Old Brick Church, an ancient house of worship, stands and continues through the years to give evidence of the spiritual strength which sustained one or more generations in their settlement of the American Colonies.

---

[23] Boddie, p. 179.
[24] *D.A.R. Magazine,* January 1962, "St. Luke's Church, Smithfield, Virginia," p. 127.

CHAPTER II

TIME POSTS OF PROGRESS TO 1789

The Declaration of Independence—1776
Consecration of the First American Bishop—1784
Two American Bishops Are Consecrated—1787

On July 4, 1776, within only a few hours after the Declaration of Independence had been made, the Vestry of historic Christ Church in Philadelphia met and passed this resolution: "Whereas the honorable Continental Congress have resolved to declare the American Colonies to be free and independent states in consequence of which it will be proper to omit those petitions in the Liturgy wherein the King of Great Britain is prayed for, as inconsistent with the said Declaration."[1]

Included here is a copy of the page given consideration from the Prayer Book. It was from this prayer that Dr. William White deleted, in his handwriting, all references to the King of England and Great Britain. He also made changes in the wording of the prayer in keeping with the spirit of the Declaration of Independence, so recently signed, and the resolution passed by the Vestry of Christ Church:

A Prayer for the King's Majesty
O Lord our heavenly Father, the high and mighty, Ruler of the universe, who dost from thy throne behold all the dwellers upon earth; Most heartily we beseech thee, with thy favour to behold all in authority, legislative, executive and judicial in these United States and so replenish them with the grace of thy Holy Spirit, that they may alway incline to thy will, and walk in thy way; Endue them plenteously with heavenly gifts; grant them in health and wealth long to live; strengthen them that they may vanquith and overcome all their enemies; and finally after this life, they may attain everlasting joy and felicity, through Jesus Christ our Lord.

Amen

With the Revolutionary War over, the independence of the Colonies was secured and jurisdiction by the See of London was eliminated. The

---

[1] *The Story of Christ Church in Philadelphia, Pennsylvania* (Booklet, copyrighted by Christ Church, 1953).

¶ A Prayer for the King's Majesty.

O Lord our heavenly Father, high and mighty, King of kings, Lord of lords, the only Ruler of princes, who dost from thy throne behold all the dwellers upon earth; Most heartily we befeech thee, with thy favour to behold our most gracious Sovereign Lord King George; and fo replenifh him with the grace of thy Holy Spirit, that he may alway incline to thy will, and walk in thy way: Endue him plenteoufly with heavenly gifts; grant him in health and wealth long to live; ftrengthen him that he may vanquifh and overcome all his enemies; and finally after this life, he may attain everlafting joy and felicity, through Jefus Chrift our Lord. *Amen.*

¶ *A Prayer for the Royal Family.*

Photostatic copy of the Prayer for the King's Majesty prior to Dr. White's changes

principles of freedom invoked by the Declaration of Independence were of common knowledge. Yet, let us not fail to recall that repeated attempts to secure the Episcopate for the Colonies ended in failure. The English Church remained unwilling to arrange for the grasping of such an opportunity by the Church in the American Colonies.

A full volume might well be written if an attempt were made to give a detailed account of the difficulties experienced by Samuel Seabury, Jr., in his effort to receive consecration by the English Church. However, eventually he was consecrated as the first Bishop of Connecticut and thereby the first to be elevated to the Episcopate in America.

Truly worthy is a sketch of the life and service of the presbyter, Samuel Seabury, Jr., who was advanced to the Episcopate.

Samuel Seabury, Jr., was born in Groton, Connecticut November 30, 1729, son of the Reverend Samuel Seabury, a minister of the Congregational Church. He was tutored for college by his father and graduated from Yale at nineteen, in 1748. He studied theology under his father's tutelage. In 1752 he went to England and studied medicine for a year at the University of Edinburgh. On December 21, 1753, he was ordained a Deacon by John, Bishop of Lincoln, in London and on December 23, 1753, he was made a Priest, also in London, by Richard, Bishop of Carlyle. Both of these Bishops were acting for the aged, infirm Bishop of London. He was licensed by the Bishop of London on May 25, 1754 and assigned by him to Christ Church, New Brunswick, New Jersey. On October 12, 1756 he married Mary Hicks; his father officiated.

During the difficult period of the American Revolution the Rev. Mr. Seabury on many occasions proved his loyalty to England.

It was in 1783 that ten clergymen of the Episcopal Church in Connecticut met for the purpose of choosing someone to go to England and to apply for consecration as Bishop of Connecticut. Two men were chosen— Jeremiah Leaning and Samuel Seabury, Jr. As Jeremiah Leaning declined to go, Samuel Seabury sailed from New York.[2]

In reviewing accounts by historians of the loyalty to England credited to Samuel Seabury, Jr., one becomes absorbed in several questions related thereto. Why was he chosen by his fellow clergymen to travel to London to seek consecration? Was their decision based solely on the conspicuous qualities of leadership and churchmanship displayed by their candidate? Was a psychological influence injected into their decision, based on their knowledge of Dr. Seabury's well-known loyalist sentiments? Were his sponsors hopeful

---

[2] *Historical Magazine of the Protestant Episcopal Church,* Sept. 1934 (Bishop Seabury Sesqui Centennial Edition 1784-1934).

that one of such loyalties would be more readily approved for consecration by the English Church?

Regardless of the reasoning, in reality or in conjecture, Dr. Seabury arrived in London, July 7, 1783. With him he took various letters of commendation and testimonials from his associates in America, so eager that he be consecrated a Bishop. Prior to his going, his associate clergyman had gone so far as to advise him that if the Bishops of the Church of England would not consecrate him that he should continue to Scotland and receive ordination from a non-juring Bishop. To secure "a free and valid episcopate for the American Church" was the full purpose of his mission.

Yet, to secure approval from the Church and the State, as then required in England, became an impossible mission when related to the approval of a bishop. Every conceivable reason was offered by the Church of England for not consecrating Dr. Seabury! Some of the churchmen were cordial, but non-commital; others approved the scheme but refused leadership; to others the whole matter was foreseen as offering great difficulties. Dr. Seabury conveyed to the ecclesiastical authorities the attitude of the State of Connecticut as he had been advised by letter; that the leading members of the House of Assembly of Connecticut saw no necessity to seek permission for a bishop to reside in the State. They wrote, "Let a bishop come and he will stand upon the same ground that the rest of the clergy do!"[3]

Numerous contacts ensued. The Church of England decided to apply to Parliament for authority to consecrate a bishop for the state of Connecticut. After fourteen days, Dr. Seabury was informed by the Archbishop that his request for consecration had been denied. The formal denial stated that the ministry had refused "and had declared peremptorily that they would not suffer a bill authorizing the consecration of a Bishop for any of the States of America to pass the House of Commons."[4]

In sure and certain haste contacts were made with the authorities of the Episcopal Church in Scotland. Bishop Kilgour, in Scotland, replied on behalf of the non-juring Bishops and expressed a sincere willingness—

> To clothe him with the Episcopal character, and thereby convey to the western world the blessing of a free, valid and purely ecclesiastical Episcopacy, not doubting that he will so agree with us in doctrine and discipline, as that he and the Church under his charge in Connecticut will hold communion with us and the Church here on catholic and primitive principles; and so that the members of both may with freedom communicate together in all the offices of Religion.[5]

---

[3] *Ibid.,* p. 148.
[4] *Ibid.*
[5] *Ibid.*

Interested were those in Scotland who knew of the clerical situation which existed. The son of a Scotch clergyman asked: "Can consecration be obtained in Scotland for an already dignified and well-vouched American clergyman, now at London, for the purpose of perpetuating the episcopal reformed Church in America, particularly in Connecticut?"[6] To this Dr. George Berkeley replied: "I have this day heard, I need not add, with the sincerest pleasure, that a respectable presbyter, well recommended from America, has arrived in London, seeking what, it seems, in the present state of affairs, he cannot expect to receive in our Church. Surely, dear sir, the Scotch prelates, who are not shackled by any Erastian connexion will not send this supplicant empty away."[7]

Indeed Dr. Seabury was not sent as a "supplicant empty away!" The great blessing of the Protestant Episcopate was conveyed by the "persecuted Church of Scotland" to a representative presbyter of the "struggling, persecuted Protestant Episcopalian worshippers in America."[8] A part of the official record of consecration read:

1784, Nov. 14. Dr. Samuel Seabury, Presbyter, from the State of Connecticut, in America, was consecrated Bishop at Aberdeen, by Bishop Kilgour, Primus; Bishop Petrie and Bishop Skiller.[9]

On June 20, 1785, Bishop Samuel Seabury landed in America and this item appeared in a Journal in Newport, Rhode Island:

June 20, 1785. Arrived in town via Halifax, from England, Dr. Samuel Seabury, lately consecrated in Scotland, Bishop of the State of Connecticut. The Sunday following, did the duties of the Church (Trinity Parish) and preached A.M., and P.M., to a crowded audience from Heb. XII, 1st and 2nd verses. Monday proceeded to New London by water, where he is to reside.[10]

In relating the return of Bishop Seabury to America this account from a Boston newspaper is found to be amusing: "Two wonders of the world, a Stamp Act in Boston and a Bishop in Connecticut!"[11]

Therefore, in such manner was elected and consecrated the first Bishop of the Protestant Episcopal Church in America. For the stout-hearted determination of Bishop Seabury and for the broad, vital, ecclesiastical concept conferred by noble Churchmen of Scotland, we of America, should be eternally grateful.

During the time in which Dr. Seabury was in England and Scotland, a very important conference was held in America in May 1784. The confer-

---

[6] *Ibid.,* p. 154.
[7] *Ibid.,* p. 199.
[8] *Ibid.,* pp. 153-155.
[9] *Ibid.,* p. 155.
[10] *Ibid.,* p. 157, quoted from *Gospel Messenger,* N. Y., December 21, 1849.
[11] *Boston Gazette,* May 30, 1785.

ence was attended by clergymen and laymen and steps were taken "to form a continental representation of the Episcopal churches."[12] At this conference it was resolved to hold a general convention of the Episcopal Church in Philadelphia in September 27, 1785.

The 1785 Convention, historically considered the first in America, was held in Christ Church, Philadelphia. Dr. William White presided.

Several years elapsed and the Church moved forward slowly but firmly. The whole effort of those of the Episcopal faith in America, eventually called to the attention of the English Church her duty to those of the same faith in America. How revealing in decision, how consistent, how benevolent —how magnanimous was the action which led to the amendment of English statutes, so that in the future the Episcopate might be "more readily conferred for the benefit of the daughter Church in the new nation across the seas!"[13]

So it followed, on February 4, 1787, in Lambeth Palace, London, that Dr. William White and Dr. Samuel Provost were consecrated. Dr. White was consecrated Bishop of Pennsylvania and Dr. Provost as Bishop of New York. Participating in the ceremony of consecration were the Archbishop of Canterbury, the Archbishop of York, the Bishop of Bath and Wells and the Bishop of Peterborough.[14]

The First House of Bishops in the United States was made possibly by the consecration of three Bishops: the Rt. Rev. Samuel Seabury, D.D., Bishop of Connecticut (of the Scotch succession); the Rt. Rev. William White, D.D., Bishop of Pennsylvania (of the English succession) and the Rt. Rev. Samuel Provost, D.D., Bishop of New York (of the English succession). The Protestant Episcopal Church in the United States, by action taken in forming its House of Bishops became free of English domination. Therefore, with its own organization, it could consecrate its own Bishops and ordain its own ministers. Never can the true greatness of these first American Bishops be evaluated.

In 1789 the most important Convention of the Church was held in Christ Church, Philadelphia. It is of interest that the first three sessions were held in the Church. However, the final session, at which the ratification of the Church Constitution took place, was in Independence Hall, where the Declaration of Independence and the Constitution of the United States of America were signed.

---

[12] *History of the Diocese of Tennessee* by Dr. Arthur Howard Noll, 1900, p. 40. Note: During the writing of this volume the author was the grateful recipient of a copy of Dr. Noll's rare book, a gift by Mrs. Helen Mangum Bedford, Collierville, Tennessee.
[13] *Ibid.,* p. 42.
[14] *Ibid.*

The Church was fully organized by the action of the 1789 Convention and became "The Protestant Episcopal Church in the United States of America."[15] A Constitution, a General Convention and a Prayer Book comprised the Church's ecclesiastical equipment and gathered together its liturgical privileges!

Because of his inestimable service in the great cause of Christianity in America, let us review the high points in the life of the remarkable and distinguished Churchman, the Rt. Rev. William White, D.D. He was born April 4, 1747, and was ordained a presbyter, April 25, 1772.

The many "firsts" experienced by Dr. White during his long, full years reveal his consecration in service. He was the first Chaplain of the Continental Congress and Chaplain of the United States Senate as long as Philadelphia was the seat of the Government. On July 4, 1782, he received a D.D. degree, the first person on whom this degree was conferred by the University of Pennsylvania. He presided at the first Convention of the Protestant Episcopal Church which began on September 27, 1785. Elected on September 14, 1786, he served as the first Bishop of Pennsylvania. He became the first Presiding Bishop of the Protestant Episcopal Church in the United States on July 28, 1789. The Philadelphia Sunday School Society was started in 1791; Bishop White was its president.

In 1794, through the influence of Dr. White, the Bishop's Council gave recognition to the first legally organized Negro Church in America. Absalom Jones' efforts were largely responsible for the founding of this church, — St. Thomas Protestant Episcopal Church, located at Fifty Second and Parrish Streets, Philadelphia. Dr. White officiated in 1804 at the service of ordination of Absalom Jones, the first Negro to be ordained a minister of the Protestant Episcopal Church.

In addition, in giving consideration to Dr. White's distinguished ministerial service, it is phenomenal to note the dates of his association with Christ Church, Philadelphia. On November 30, 1772, he was elected Assistant Minister and on April 15, 1779, he became Rector. In this capacity, covering a period of sixty-four years, he served until his death on July 17, 1836, in Philadelphia, the place of his birth.

As has been written, the Episcopal Church was so deeply rooted in the founding of our nation, its beginnings in this new free land cannot fail to be observed and evaluated. Significant in the role of sowing seeds of independence was historic Christ Church, Philadelphia, founded in 1695. The whole development of America was influenced by its founding. 'Twas there in 1776 that men entered to pray for strength to meet the exigencies

---

[15] *Ibid.,* p. 43.

of that difficult era in our nation's history. Today men enter to renew spiritual values, the bases of our way of life. Numbered among the Bishops consecrated in Christ Church was the Right Rev. James H. Otey, D.D., first Bishop of the Diocese of Tennessee. Appropriately, Christ Church is often called "The Nation's Church."

George Washington expressed the interdependence of religion and prosperity when he said: "Of all dispositions and habits which lead to political prosperity, religion and morality are indispensible supports. Reason and experience both forbid us to expect that national morality can prevail in exclusion of religious principles."

It is true that influences of the church of England are evident in many aspects of Church protocol. Natural and interesting is this background: "The Protestant Episcopal Church in the United States of America came into corporate existence . . . with . . . marks of the Catholic and Apostolic Church and . . . identified therewith by historic continuity."[16] Thus, the Episcopal Church in America today is in organization a free institution in a brave land, where freedom's price was great. Yet, freedom's debt was paid in full measure by the sacrificing of lives and fortunes of innumerable patriots of the American Revolution.

Thomas Jefferson once had this to say: "The God who gave us life, gave us liberty at the same time." "Life, liberty and the pursuit of happiness," — these three objectives are as much a part of the history of our faith as they are determining principles of the law of the land. These basic precepts, conceived by the Founding Fathers guided by a Supreme Being, were destined to cause to be created that "one nation under God, indivisible, with liberty and justice for all."

---

[16] *Ibid.*

CHAPTER III

THE EPISCOPAL CHURCH IN TENNESSEE, 1829

Original Constitution of Tennessee, 1796

Tennessee's First Diocesan Convention, 1829

Consecration of the First Bishop of Tennessee, 1834

Tennessee admitted on June 1, 1796, by Congress as the sixteenth State, to the great sisterhood of States was comprised of two grand divisions, East Tennessee and West Tennessee.[1]

It had been on the prior date of January 11, of that year, that fifty-five delegates had gathered in Knoxville for the purpose of drafting a constitution and seeking admission of the State into the Union.[2] Distinguished indeed was the personnel of this first Constitutional Convention.

A member of the Convention, also with James Robertson and John McNairy from Davidson County, was Andrew Jackson,[3] a young lawyer practicing in Nashville. He had a very influential part in the Convention and was a delegate destined to attain great fame in later years.

The task of drafting Tennessee's first Constitution was concluded on February 6, 1796. The delegates assembled had admirably expressed their purpose, spirit and mutual accomplishment in the preamble of the document.

We the people of the Territory of the United States, south of the River Ohio, having the right of admission into the General Government as a member State thereof . . . Do ordain and establish the following constitution or form of government and do mutually agree with each other to form ourselves into a free and independent State by the name of the State of Tennessee.[4]

The broad democratic concept that government is ever to be achieved by mutual compact, was fully embodied in Tennessee's first Constitution.

---

[1] The State Constitutional Convention of 1834 created three grand divisions in Tennessee—East, Middle, West. Tennessee State Constitutional Conventions have convened in the years 1796, 1834, 1870, 1953 and 1959. The author was a delegate from Shelby County to the 1953 and 1959 Conventions.

[2] Noll, pp. 55, 109.

[3] *History of Tennessee* by Stanley J. Folmsbee, Robert E. Corlew and Enoch L. Mitchell, 1960, Vol. I, pp. 209, 214, 217.

[4] *Constitutional History of Tennessee,* by Joshua W. Caldwell, 1907, pp. 130, 131.

Of the document, Thomas Jefferson said that it was "The least imperfect and most republican" of any adopted up to that time.

On April 8, 1796, George Washington submitted Tennessee's Constitution to the Congress. On May 31, following, the bill was passed admitting Tennessee into the Union. On June 1, President Washington affixed his signature and the great seal of his office to the measure and thereby granted full statehood to Tennessee.

Dr. Arthur Howard Noll gives, in his excellent "History of the Diocese of Tennessee," a full, descriptive account of the people who settled the State and the denominations which indicated their religious affiliations.

The early Tennesseeans were largely God-fearing, sturdy, intelligent people. More specifically, they were frontiersmen challenged by the joy of adventure. Among them were many determined characters "who held in no restraint the untamed and turbulent passions which they had inherited from their Scotch-Irish progenitors."[5]

Inspired by the good land of Tennessee for the growing of the crops of corn and tobacco, the early settlers who came were the Presbyterians. Very soon, ministers of the Presbyterian faith followed and began their effective labors toward the establishment of churches in the wilderness. Among these ministers were men of "deep learning and pure lives"[6] who "insisted upon dignified quietness in their congregations." Dr. Noll gives credit to the Presbyterian ministers and teachers for the early schools which were established by them as having set high educational standards for the State.

Ministers of other denominations came: between 1770-1780, "Baptists were on the ground" and in 1783 "Methodists reached the Holston."[7]

Among the early settlers in Tennessee were not only the staunch, law-abiding citizens possessed of religious fervor and with a dedicated purpose for better living at any cost, but others who were of questionable character. Such persons were disguised desperadoes, recognized fugitives and those of the pirate class! Of the pirate gang some remained in the Western District as late as 1834 and operated extensively along the Mississippi River and the Natchez Trace.

Tennessee's statehood, so recently achieved, placed her in a very vulnerable position to be caught in the movements which came in close succession. These movements have been labelled by writers of religious history as the "Great Awakening," originated in New England and the "Second Great Awakening," generally known as the "Great Revival of 1800." The last movement grew large in the Kentucky-Tennessee area, or Cumberland

---

[5] Noll, pp. 22, 23.
[6] *Ibid.*
[7] *Ibid.*

Country. So, Tennessee became a fertile field for the continuation of denominations previously organized, for variations within these faiths and for the coming of many, many other forms and sects.

Dr. Noll in writing about the coming of the Episcopal Church to Tennessee states: "It is no spirit of arrogance that the body whose progress in Tennessee it is the present intention to set forth, is termed 'The Church.'[8] That it is the body "which is mentioned in the creeds of Christendom as the One, Holy, Catholic and Apostolic Church."

In recounting the beginnings of the Church in Tennessee consideration is given to its background and purpose.

Deeply rooted is the heritage of the Episcopal Church. Characterized by ritualistic dignity, with qualities of prescribed form, classical content and depth of meaning, the service is religiously and historically distinctive. Its doctrine, ministry, discipline, worship and sacraments have attained for the Church a position in ecclesiastical annals. The Bible, The Book of Common Prayer and The Hymnal constitute its basic literature.

The fact that a church with its appointments, is a building which exists for the purpose of surrounding an altar, a place of prayer, must be appreciated. And, that upon the altar there is a Cross! This placement of the Cross signifies the sacrifice which our Lord offered on Calvary and now presents in Heaven — "And sitteth on the right hand of God the Father Almighty." Two candles on the altar give evidence that Christ "is the light of the world." The two candles also signify the Divine and the human, the two natures of Christ our Lord. The Chancel is divided into the Choir and the Sanctuary. When consecrated elements are present it is the sanctuary lamp which symbolizes the presence of God and is a constant reminder that silence and reverence should ever be present in God's House. "The Lord is in His Holy Temple, let all the earth keep silence before Him!"

Ornaments, appropriate to the appointments of the Church, are used for beauty and to adorn useful objects. Flowers, reminders of the purity, fragrance and beauty of a holy, good life, are placed on the altar to beautify the whole setting for worship. Three linen cloths are used on the top of the altar. The "fair linen cloth"—, the upper cloth—, is embroidered with five crosses, symbols of the five wounds of the Lord and also a reminder that before our Lord's body was laid in the tomb it was wrapped in a linen cloth. The frontal is a cloth, often of silk or lace, which hangs from the altar front.

---

[8] *Ibid.*, p. 37.

The extensive use of colors in the Church not only creates vivid effectiveness, but each color lends a peculiarly significant meaning. The choice of color is determined by either or both, the occasion or the season. Particularly is this true when related to the vestments of the minister and to the altar vestments. WHITE or GOLD denotes joy and gladness and symbolize the great festivals of the Church—Christmas, Easter, Ascension Day. RED, the color of blood and office, is used on Whitsunday and on Saints' Days. PURPLE bespeaks penitence and sorrow. It is used at Advent and the Lenten season, Ember and Rogation Days and at the Feast of The Holy Innocents.

Epiphany and Trinity seasons require the use of GREEN, the color of nature. BLACK commemorates the departed and is used on Good Friday and at funeral services.

The Sacred Vessels associated with The Lord's Supper are of either silver or gold. Namely, the chalice, paten and ciborium. Totally significant is the presence of the Cross, the American Flag and the Church Flag, whether in processional or recessional, or placed in their appropriate positions in the chancel.

The smooth functioning of the Church's service is dependent on a corps of stout-hearted, able, dedicated persons. The Rector; Associate Rector; Deacons; Organist or Choirmaster; Ushers; Acolytes—who serve as Crucifers, Flag Bearers, Servers; all contribute to the coordinated effort of a well ordered service of worship.

Into this religious environment, created around an altar dedicated to God, the people come. To this setting, human beings—God's children—bring their total personalities with facets of physical, mental, spiritual, emotional and social-moral development. Varying attitudes and purposes of the worshippers run the whole gamut of human relations. They come gratified by happiness, bewildered by insecurity, heart-broken by grief, burdened by worry, harried by want, shaken by fear or consoled by love. Patterns of behavior acceptable in religious service accompany the knowledge of a helpful formula for procedure in worship. "Kneel to pray, Stand to praise and Sit for instruction."[9] Faithful followers come with abundant gratitude for their splendid inheritance and with sincere prayers in their hearts that continued strength may be experienced in faith, in order and in the benefits of corporate devotion.

> Here see the Bread of life; see waters flowing
> Forth from the throne of God, pure from above;

[9] Calvary Episcopal Church, Memphis, Tenn. (Bulletin).

> Come to the feast of love; come ever knowing
> Earth has no sorrow but Heav'n can remove.[10]

Dr. Noll in his writing set forth this extensive challenge related to the Church in Tennessee:

> It is only so far as the Protestant Episcopal Church in the United States, is loyal to the Church's own conception of Christianity, and to the duties imposed upon her by that conception, that she is entitled to be called the Church; and it is only the Church in that sense whose history in Tennessee is here intended.[11]

The Diocese of North Carolina organized in 1817, was placed under the care of the Rt. Rev. Richard Channing Moore, Bishop of Virginia. In 1818 the Rev. John Phillips came as a missionary to North Carolina. In 1823, John Stark Ravenscroft, a minister of Virginia—, "Of the same sturdy Scotch-Irish stock as the early settlers of Tennessee," — was unanimously elected the first Bishop of North Carolina. "He was nominated by William Mercer Green, later Bishop of Mississippi.[12]

The Consecration of Bishop Ravenscroft marked a very noticeable step in Church history. As a result of this influence the Church was encouraged to venture into the neighboring state of Tennessee. Thus it was from Tennessee's sister state of North Carolina that the Church's first teacher-missionary came to Tennessee in 1821 in the person of James Hervey Otey. Unsuspected indeed was the destiny which centered around Mr. Otey's coming to this State. That he should in future years render such conspicuous service that to future generations he would be known as the "father of the Episcopal Church in Tennessee,"[13] was not evident at his coming.

Mr. Otey, a Virginian by birth, came to Tennessee and opened a school for boys near Franklin in Williamson County. He had recently graduated with honors from the University of North Carolina and was married.

Within his family had been churchmen; but he, personally knew very little about church ways. However, as principal of the school he deemed it necessary to begin the day with some type of religious experience. To aid Mr. Otey in meeting this need a gentleman from Columbia, Tennessee, Mr. James H. Piper, gave him a copy of the Book of Common Prayer. The full significance of such a gift was the influence which changed the course of the life-work of James Hervey Otey. "That Prayer Book in God's Providence, made Otey a Christian and a Churchman," wrote Bishop Thomas F. Gailor.[14] He remained in Franklin for eighteen months.

---

[10] The Hymnal. Hymn 483.
[11] Noll, p. 37.
[12] *Ibid.*, p. 49.
[13] *Commercial Appeal*, Centennial Edition, Jan. 1, 1940; Episcopal Church's Story in Tennessee for 110 Years, by the Rt. Rev. James M. Maxon.
[14] *The Tennessee Churchman*, Gailor Memorial Edition, 1926.

Mr. Otey was offered an appointment as principal of the Warrenton Male Academy, Warrenton, North Carolina. His acceptance of this position in Warrenton was one of the most decisive opportunities of his entire life. In Warrenton, he was to find the abundant encouragement which awaited him. His experience there was to be, in reality, a challenge to light his way toward life anew, with heights undreamed of in the field of religious service.

In Warrenton, Mr. Otey was enabled to renew a friendship with William Mercer Green which had begun at the University of North Carolina several years before. The Rev. Mr. Green had been only recently ordained a deacon and was in charge of Emmanuel Church in Warrenton. Events unfolded rapidly which destined James Hervey Otey's firm and consecrated devotion to the Church of his choice.

On May 8, 1824, Mr. Otey was baptized by his old friend, the Rev. Mr. Green in St. John's Church, Williamsboro, North Carolina, and confirmed by the Rt. Rev. John Stark Ravenscroft. Immediately he began preparation for Holy Orders.[15]

Here, let us review in brief the meaningful history of Emmanuel Church, Warrenton. This church wielded a peculiar and lasting influence on the beginnings of the Episcopal Church in Tennessee. Emmanuel, at Warrenton, was definitely the "Mother Church" of the Episcopal faith in the Western District, presently known as West Tennessee. At the 1820 Diocesan Convention in North Carolina, the Rev. Mr. Phillips reported more than thirteen communicants in Warrenton. Duncan Cameron, Esq., arose at the 1821 Convention and gave an interesting report on the organization of a Church in Warrenton. He stated that a congregation had been organized and a vestry appointed. He further stated that "want of time and other causes" had not permitted the completion of certificates of appointment; yet, that Mr. John Anderson had come as a delegate to the Convention. "These facts being known to the Convention, Mr. Anderson was admitted to a seat."[16]

Land in Warrenton was deeded[17] February 16, 1822 by Miss Hannah Maria Lees "for and in behalf of the religious congregation of Protestant Episcopalians," this property "to be for the use and benefit of the said congregation by such name as it may hereafter assume and be recognized by in said Church." Soon thereafter, John Anderson and George W. Freeman,[18] the building committee, contracted with Thomas Bragg[19] for the

---

[15] Noll, p. 55.
[16] Notes from accounts of history of Emmanuel Church, Warrenton, N. C., by Charles A. Tucker, Warrenton, 1961.
[17] Deed Book, 22, Warren County, North Carolina.
[18] George W. Freeman in 1844 became Bishop of Arkansas.
[19] Father of General Braxton Bragg.

sum of $2,050.00 to build the Church; this amount did not include the cost of plastering and painting. The report, made at the Convention in April, 1822, stated: "At Warrenton, particularly, it is gratifying to learn that an Episcopal Church is erecting and there is reason to believe that there will be at that place a very flourishing Congregation."

Emmanuel Church, Warrenton, North Carolina

Emmanuel Church, Warrenton was consecrated to Almighty God on Tuesday, August 1, 1824, by the Rt. Rev. John Stark Ravenscroft, assisted by the Rev. Mr. Green,[20] Rector. Of record in the Parish Register are the names of the Vestry who served Emmanuel Church at that time: Kemp Plummer, George Anderson, John Anderson and James H. Otey.

Bishop Ravenscroft made a visitation to Emmanuel Church and preached on August 28, 1825. The fact that he was pleased with the small new Church and its progress was expressed in his report to the Diocesan Convention held in Hillsboro in May 1826.

---

[20] William Mercer Green became Bishop of Mississippi in 1850.

Evidences of the history of Emmanuel Church are to be seen within and without the Church edifice. In the floor of the Chancel, near the Vestry door, there is a plaque marking the final resting place of Miss Lees, the donor of the original acreage for the Church lot, who also gave generous bequests by will to the Church.

The historical significance of Emmanuel Church in the marriage of Mr. Horace Greeley and Miss Mary Y. Cheney has been cited by the State of North Carolina in the placing of a marker near the Church. It was in Emmanuel Church, Warrenton, on Tuesday morning, July 5, 1836, that Mr. Greeley, editor of the "New Yorker," and Miss Cheney of Warrenton were married. The Rev. William Norwood performed the ceremony.[21] Miss Cheney, of Connecticut, was a teacher in Mrs. Harriet Allen's School in Warrenton at the time of her marriage to Mr. Greeley.

Another item of historic interest is a small tombstone which stands a few feet from the southeast corner of the Church. The stone marks the grave of Mary Turner, the daughter of Congressman Daniel Turner[22] and his wife, Anna Arnold Key, daughter of Francis Scott Key, the author of the "Star Spangled Banner."

The foregoing sketches related to the history of Emmanuel Church, Warrenton, are of especial interest in the weaving of the story in this volume. These facts of history are descriptive of the particular environment in which the founders of the Episcopal Church in Tennessee lived and served prior to their coming westward. It was there James Hervey Otey became identified with the Church and held his first official position, a vestryman of Emmanuel Church. It was there "the closely-knit lives during these years of the three men—Ravenscroft, Green and Otey—more than any other one thing, provided the devotion and dynamic force which was to spread the Episcopal Church throughout the whole middle and lower South."[23] Perhaps unique in the American Church was the close personal association of these three distinguished men-of-God,—eventually three Bishops serving the dioceses of North Carolina, Mississippi and Tennessee.

In old Warrenton, James Hervey Otey, through his Church experience made other lasting friendships with persons who were of most substantial personal and religious influence then and in future years. It is recalled that John Anderson was the first delegate to represent Emmanuel Church in a Diocesan Convention (1821). Also, the fact is repeated, serv-

---

[21] *The New Yorker,* July 16, 1836.
[22] Daniel Turner was a son of Polly Anderson and James Turner. Polly Anderson was a sister of George and John Anderson (who later settled in LaGrange, Tennessee). (Bible of Daniel Anderson, 1765.)
[23] *James Hervey Otey of Tennessee,* by Frank M. McClain (Builders for Christ Series, The National Council).

ing as members of the Church's first vestry with James H. Otey were the Anderson brothers—George and John—and Kemp Plummer.[24]

Mary Hayes Willis Gloster
(Mrs. Thomas Benn Gloster)

However, of all his associates, no one played a more significant role than a devoted churchwoman who acted as Mr. Otey's sponsor in baptism—Mary Hayes Willis (Mrs. Thomas Benn) Gloster. Mrs. Gloster was the wife of a prominent physician in Warrenton. Dr. Gloster and Mary Hayes Willis were married in Orange County, North Carolina, May 30, 1795.[25]

---

[24] Records of Emmanuel Church, Warrenton, North Carolina, courtesy of Charles A. Tucker.
[25] Marriage Records (1752-1868), Office of Register of Deeds, Orange County, N.C.

Dr. Thomas Benn Gloster

"Dr. Thomas Benn Gloster, son of Arthur and Catherine Gloster, was born in Limerick, Ireland, on September 16, 1763. He left Limerick on July 1, 1785, and arrived in Warrenton, North Carolina, one of the United States of America, on February 20, 1786."[26]

Dr. and Mrs. Gloster had two children: Elizabeth Willis Gloster, born September 25, 1796, and Arthur Brehon Gloster, born February 18, 1799. Elizabeth Gloster[27] married John Anderson on January 17, 1815, in War-

---

[26] Bible Records, Gloster Family, certified copy in possession of author.

[27] *Written for Her Children* 1822-1862, by Elizabeth Willis Anderson (Mrs. John Anderson) edited by Miss Mary Mae Anderson, 1947, El Paso, Texas. Copies in

renton. (George Anderson, a bachelor, brother of John, died in La Grange, Tennessee, January 1, 1844.) Arthur Brehon Gloster married Mary Hayes Willis, daughter of Plummer and Druscilla Willis in Fayette County, Tennessee, December 24, 1828.

The ancestors of Mary Hayes Willis Gloster were among the Founding Fathers of this nation. She was the daughter of John Willis (a farmer; an Episcopalian) b. 1744, at Beddingfield Hall, Brunswick County, Virginia, died Orange County, North Carolina, married, in 1769 in Virginia, Mary Hayes Plummer (more presently), born in Gloucester County, Virginia, died October 12, 1824, Warrenton, North Carolina.

John Willis was the son of John Willis, born 1719, White Hall, Gloucester County, Virginia, died 1766, Beddingfield Hall, Brunswick County, Virginia, and Mildred Smith (Willis) (more presently), born September 22, 1719, at Shooters Hill, Middlesex County, Virginia, married June 26, 1743, died 1769. John Willis was a vestryman, St. Andrew's Episcopal Church, Brunswick County, Virginia.

Mildred Smith was the daughter of Augustine Smith, born June 16, 1689, md. Nov. 9, 1711, Gloucester County, Virginia, Sarah Carver, born June 5, 1694, died March 13, 1726.

Augustine Smith was the son of John Smith, born 1662, Middlesex County, Virginia, died April 14, 1698; married February 17, 1680, Mary Warner, died November 12, 1700.

Mary Warner was the daughter of Augustine Warner, of Warner Hall, Gloucester County, Virginia, born June 3, 1642, died June 19, 1681; married 1665, Mildred Reade.

Mildred Reade was the daughter of Col. George Reade, born 1608, died 1671, and Elizabeth Martiau.

Col. George Reade was the son of Robert Reade, born in Likenholt, Hampshire, England, died 1627; married July 31, 1600, at St. Martins in the Field, London, Mildred Windebanke, died 1630. Mildred Windebanke was the daughter of Sir Thomas Windebanke and Frances Dymoke, died 1607.

Col. George Reade was a burgess, James City County, Virginia, in 1649 and in 1656. He became a member of the Governor's Council, March 13, 1657-58.

Mary Hayes Plummer (Willis), the mother of Mary Hayes Willis (Mrs. Thomas Benn) Gloster, was the daughter of William Plummer, born

possession of descendants of Mary Hayes Willis Gloster, among whom are Dr. Edwin T. Yancey, Germantown, Tenn.; Mrs. H. T. Adair, Ellendale, Tenn.; Mrs. E. W. G. Meers, Memphis, Tenn., and Mrs. Charles Wade, LaGrange, Tenn.

1748, North Carolina, died 1779, Gloucester County, Virginia, and his wife Mary Cecilia Hayes. William Plummer was the son of Wm. Thomas Plummer and Elizabeth Kemp. William Thomas Plummer was the son of William Plummer I, born about 1650.

The children of William Plummer and Mary Cecilia Hayes (Plummer) were: William, Jr., married Eliza (Elizabeth) Ransome; Mary Hayes, married John Austin Willis; Elizabeth, married Daniel Weldon; Hannah, married Nathaniel Macon; Anna; Kemp (II), born 1769, married Susan Martin.

Interesting indeed are the names of the grandchildren of Dr. and Mrs. Gloster.[28] The children of Elizabeth Willis Gloster and her husband, John Anderson, were: Daniel Beveridge Anderson,[29] Thomas Gloster Anderson, Mary May Anderson, Elizabeth Gloster Anderson, James Archibald Anderson, George Anderson, Arthur Gloster Anderson, John Gloster Anderson, William Walker Anderson. Arthur Brehon Gloster, their son, and his wife Mary Hayes Willis, named their children: Thomas Benn Gloster, Arthur Willis Gloster, Lucy Plummer Gloster, Plummer Willis Gloster, James Otey Gloster, Mary Druscilla Gloster, Elizabeth Willis Gloster, Emma Polk Gloster, Rose Lenore Gloster, William Mercer Gloster.

All of the grandchildren of Dr. and Mrs. Gloster were baptized in the Episcopal faith. The original Bible records[30] kept by those of the Gloster and Anderson families reveal names of ministers and places familiar in Church history. Daniel Beveridge Anderson, their first grandchild, was born in Warrenton, November 6, 1815. As this was before Emmanuel Church was founded (1821), the child at sixteen months of age was taken by his parents to Petersburg, Virginia, where he was baptized by "The Rev. Andrew-Syne of the Protestant Episcopal Church of North America."[31] Thomas Gloster Anderson was baptized at three weeks of age in Warrenton by the Rev. Bethel Jud, at the time Rector of St. John's Church, Fayetteville; Mary May Anderson, "On the 23rd day of her age was offered to her Creator in the holy rite of baptism administered by the Rev. John Phillips, Rector of Trinity Church, Tarborough."[32] Elizabeth Gloster Anderson was baptized in Emmanuel Church, Warrenton, by the Rev. William Mercer Green on April 11, 1824. James Archibald Anderson, born in 1826, was

---

[28] Gloster Family Bible, records copied by Charles M. Seymour, July, 1936.

[29] Bible of Daniel Anderson (dated 1765). John and George Anderson were sons of Daniel Anderson (b. May 28, 1748, Scotland; d. Jan. 25, 1813, Petersburg, Va.) and Maizy Beveridge.

[30] Gloster Family Bible. Anderson Bible Records—"Daniel Anderson was buried at the east end of the brick church in Blanford by the side of his first wife." Petersburg, Virginia.

[31] Gloster Family Bible.

[32] *Ibid.*

also baptized by the Rev. Mr. Green in Emmanuel Church, Warrenton. The next two children, born in 1829 and 1831, "in Fayette County, Western District of Tennessee" had died by early January 1832. John Gloster Anderson "was baptized by the Rev. Thomas Wright of the Episcopal Church, and William Walker Anderson, born 1836, was baptized by the Rev. Samuel G. Litton in 1837.

Likewise, the children of the only son of Dr. and Mrs. Gloster, Arthur and his wife, were baptized by ministers of the Church. Of especial mention is this record: "James Otey Gloster was born August 23, 1839; baptized by the Rev. James H. Otey in LaGrange, Tennessee, on October 9, 1839. He was killed December 31, 1862, at the Battle of Murfreesboro, Tennessee."[33]

Elsewhere in this volume we shall find more about Dr. and Mrs. Gloster, their children and the Anderson brothers and their constant devotion to the Episcopal Church.

Let us return to James Hervey Otey and seek to know more about his rich experiences as they are revealed by the fullness of his life and of his service.

After ordination by Bishop Ravenscroft on October 16, 1825, Deacon Otey returned to Tennessee. In 1827 he went again to North Carolina, where he became a Priest, "on Sunday the seventeenth day of June in St. Matthew's Church, Hillsboro (North Carolina) on testimonials from Christ Church, Nashville, in the State of Tennessee."[34]

In 1825, Mr. Otey reopened his school, Harpeth Academy, near Franklin, Tennessee. Patient, diligent teaching and careful, thorough preaching followed on his return to the State. He gained the distinction of being one of the greatest educators in Tennessee's early history. His success as a minister often seemed futile. He was ever fearless in speaking the truth and many were the times he felt that he was as "a voice crying in the wilderness."

Bishop Ravenscroft came to Nashville in June 1829, at the urgent request of Mr. Otey. Truly the Bishop from North Carolina was the man most beloved by his close friend, Mr. Otey. Many came to hear and to see a Bishop! He explained the doctrine, discipline and worship of the Church.

At this time there were approximately fifty communicants of the Church in Tennessee. Therefore, by reason of the number of delegates present at the first convention the "representation of one delegate for less than every five communicants"[35] was larger than in any succeeding Convention. The

---

[33] *Ibid.*
[34] McClain, p. 5.
[35] Noll, p. 65.

meeting was held in the Masonic Hall, Nashville, and Bishop Ravenscroft presided. Three clergymen were in attendance: "the Rev. Mr. Otey, the Rev. Dr. Stephens and the Rev. Mr. Davis, and six lay delegates."[36]

At this Convention on July 1 and 2, 1829, the organization of the Protestant Episcopal Church began in Tennessee. A Constitution and canons were adopted. The following parishes were recognized as parts of the newly organized diocese: Christ Church, Nashville; St. Peter's Church, Columbia; St. Paul's Church, Franklin, and St. John's, Knoxville (though not fully organized).[37] Yet, not one of these organized congregations had erected a house of worship!

Soon thereafter, however, Church buildings began to be created. On July 2, 1831, Bishop William Meade of Virginia laid the cornerstone of St. Peter's Church, Columbia,[38] and on July 6, he consecrated Christ Church, Nashville.[39] St. Peter's Church, Columbia, was completed and consecrated in 1834. St. Paul's Church, Franklin, was also completed in 1834 and consecrated in 1835. St. Paul's had been started by the Rev. Mr. Otey and was the first organized parish in Tennessee.

The education of Christian young women was a very special objective of the religious program of Bishop Otey. The gratification of this interest was realized in the establishment of the Columbia Female Institute[40] in 1838. The original concept of the institution implied no diocesan affiliation. However, the school in reality became church sponsored and for many years was in "the very front ranks of Southern schools."[41]

The first church building erected in West Tennessee was built by the Alston family[42] on their plantation near Randolph. Bishop Ravenscroft of North Carolina had long been a friend, prior to their coming to Tennessee. Therefore, appropriately this first church-house in the Western District, consecrated by Bishop Otey on October 23, 1836, was named Ravenscroft Chapel.

Previously in this chapter, consideration has been given to some of the most decisive movements which signified the beginnings of the Protestant

---

[36] *Ibid.*, James Hervey Otey, Daniel Stephens, John Davis. Six lay delegates: Thomas Claiborne, George Wilson and Francis B. Fogg, Nashville—representing Knoxville.

[37] *Ibid.*

[38] *Ibid.*, p. 68.

[39] *Ibid.*, p. 67.

[40] Linnie Lee Davies, b. March 15, 1863, at Davies Manor, Brunswick, Tennessee, attended Columbia Institute. Daughter of Logan Early and Frances Anna Vaughn Davies; granddaughter of William Early and Sarah Hadley Davies; a great-grand-daughter of Zachariah Davies, and of Ambrose Hadley of the Revolutionary War and a great-great granddaughter of Christopher Bustin, a patriot of the American Revolution. Her brother was Gillie Mertis Davies, father of the author.

[41] Noll, p. 212.

[42] Alston family came from Warrenton, North Carolina.

Episcopal Church in the United States of America. Now, as the beginnings of the Church in the Diocese of Tennessee are summarized it seems of value to give attention to the background of the Church's influence.

In 1833-1834 Tennessee was one of the twenty states, of the twenty-four then in the American Union, wherein the Episcopal Church had been organized. At that time there were fifteen Bishops, two of whom were assistant Bishops. Therefore, it was quite evident the body had not yet reached full stature as an organized national "unit of ecclesiastical government in the Church of America."[43]

Admitted to the diaconate on June 29, 1832 were John Chilton and Samuel George Litton as the first ordinations in the Diocese of Tennessee.[44] Bishop Levi S. Ives of North Carolina administered the ecclesiastical rites to these two able men who were destined to serve brilliantly in the advancement of the Church within the State.

Eight clergymen were at work in Tennessee in 1833. The great need of a Bishop was keenly felt. To carry forward this effort due notice was given of a convention of the diocese, called to meet in Franklin on June 27, 1833. Nine parishes comprised the organization. The Rev. Dr. Stephens presided at the Convention and Mr. Godfrey M. Fogg served as secretary.

The election of a Bishop was the chief business of the Convention. James Hervey Otey received the votes of all the clergy on the first ballot, except two which were cast for the Rev. William Mercer Green and the Rev. Henry Anthon.[45] By unanimous vote by the nine laymen present, Mr. Otey's election was confirmed. Of interest indeed are the names of the men who signed the testimonial of the Bishop-elect: "The Rev. Daniel Stephens, D.D., the Rev. George Weller, D.D., the Rev. Albert A. Muller, D.D., the Rev. John Chilton, the Rev. Samuel G. Litton; Messrs. John C. Wormley and George C. Skipwith, of Columbia; William G. Dickinson, B. S. Tappan and Thomas Maney, of Franklin; Matthew Watson, Godfrey M. Fogg and Francis B. Fogg, of Nashville, and John Anderson of LaGrange."[46]

Church history records the difficulties which arose because of objections to the consecration of Tennessee's Bishop-elect. South Carolina objected to the consecration of Mr. Otey, stating that Tennessee had an insufficient number of parishes and presbyters to elect a Bishop, according to canonical number. Maine, New Jersey and Georgia required time to weigh the issue.

---

[43] Noll, p. 75.
[44] *Ibid.*, p. 69.
[45] Jl. of 1833 Convention (p. 14).
[46] Noll, p. 78. John Anderson, Warrenton, N. C., moved to La Grange, Tenn., 1827.

However, consent of a majority of the dioceses was obtained within several months.

Mr. Otey, prior to this time, had travelled only in Virginia, North Carolina and Tennessee. It now became necessary that he go to Philadelphia during very cold weather to receive consecration. In Christ Church, Philadelphia on January 14, 1834, James Hervey Otey was consecrated the first Bishop of the Protestant Episcopal Church in Tennessee. The Presiding Bishop, Dr. William White was assisted in the ceremony by the Bishops of Pennsylvania, New York and New Jersey. Bishop Doane preached the consecration sermon which was in part:

> There is a common notion that Bishops are stately persons, and that large salaries, noble edifices and splendid equipages are somehow an essential appendage of their office. But here is a Bishop who has never had a Church to preach in, and has never yet had a living at the altar, but has been obliged to labor for his children's bread in the laborious, though most honorable vocation of teaching; spending five days out of seven in a school, and for years has not had a month's relaxation.[47]

At the time of consecration Bishop Otey was almost thirty-four years of age, and with two exceptions the youngest Bishop, up to that time, consecrated in the American Church. "He became the thirtieth in the line of the American Episcopate and raised the number of Bishops then living to sixteen."[48]

A Virginian by birth, a North Carolinian by appointment and a Tennessean by choice, Bishop Otey began with abundant vigor, great physical stamina and dedicated religious precepts his magnificent work for the Church in the state. As he carried the message and gave opportunities "to hear the church"[49] the settings varied. Court houses, community halls, homes and in some towns, Presbyterian or Methodist Churches were graciously loaned as places wherein services were held. He was totally fearless in preaching the truth, based on his keen knowledge of the Bible and of the Book of Common Prayer. Bishop Otey once said "that an amount of prejudice, ignorance and prepossession prevailed in this diocese respecting our communion, unequalled in any other State of the Union."[50]

One form of effort to improve this bespoken ignorance and prejudice was the organization in 1858 of the Diocesan Book Society. The project was an idea of the Rev. Charles Todd Quintard, M.D., destined to succeed Bishop Otey to the Episcopate of Tennessee. Depositories, or book stores, for

---

[47] *Ibid.*, p. 80.
[48] *Ibid.*, p. 81.
[49] *Ibid.*, p. 85.
[50] *Ibid.*, p. 91.

the sale of Church books and literature were established, first in Memphis, and later in Nashville and Knoxville. Today these worthy projects continue within the State, and each is known as the "Episcopal Book Store."[51]

For thirty years the first Bishop of Tennessee "toiled in poverty."[52] Nevertheless, in his time he was gratified by staunch faith in believing that his labors had not been in vain. Bishop Otey had firmly established "the educational character of the diocese"[53] of Tennessee. His leadership was strong in that he was a "Catholic, Prayer-Book Churchman of the old school."[54] Truly he had "laid the foundation of the Church of Apostolic Truth and Order in Tennessee."[55]

---

[51] Episcopal Bookshop, 672 Poplar Avenue, Memphis, Tennessee.
[52] Noll, p. 225.
[53] *Ibid.*, p. 196.
[54] *Ibid.*, p. 167.
[55] *Ibid.*, p. 148.

CHAPTER IV

THE WESTERN DISTRICT OF TENNESSEE

Chickasaw Purchase, 1818
Twenty-One Counties Formed 1819-1875

Thrilling and interesting to the layman and non-Churchman alike are the hard-wrought beginnings of the Episcopal Church in America. Both vicissitudes in effort and glorious rewards in accomplishment characterize the founding of the Church in the colonies, in the United States and later in the State of Tennessee.

Therefore, we approach the last phase of the story of the Church's beginnings to be covered in this volume. Last, yes, but by no means least in religious significance nor in romantic concept. The settlement of the Western District of the great State of Tennessee and the Church's coming to this section, typify a movement of extensive proportions, in fact and in deed—a story of life and religious endeavor to be carefully and enthusiastically related.

The vast area, lying between the Tennessee and the Mississippi Rivers, known as the Chickasaw Country contained some of the richest, most desirable land in the great new west. In 1818 the Legislature of Tennessee requested Congress to appoint commissioners to negotiate a treaty with the Chickasaw Indians, whereby the Chickasaw Country might be acquired. Therefore, General Andrew Jackson of Tennessee and Governor Isaac Shelby of Kentucky were appointed by Congress and negotiations began. After twenty days spent in discussions, the treaty was signed on October 19, 1818.[1]

Several titles were accorded this historic action: Jackson-Shelby Treaty, the Jackson Purchase or the Chickasaw Purchase. Whatever the name, the results were that on January 7, 1819, the treaty was proclaimed by President James Monroe. The text of the treaty begins:

> To settle the territorial controversies, and to remove all ground of complaint or dissatisfaction that might arise to interrupt the peace and harmony which have so long and so happily existed between the

---

[1] *Historic Madison,* by Emma Inman Williams, 1946, p. 26.

United States of America and the Chickasaw Nation of Indians, James Monroe, President of the United States, by Isaac Shelby and Andrew Jackson, of the one part, and the whole Chickasaw Nation, by their chiefs, head men, and warriors, in full council assembled, of the other part, have agreed on the following articles, which when ratified, by the President and Senate of the United States of America, shall form a treaty binding on all parties.[2]

Descriptive of the land acquired by the Chickasaw Treaty is the following:

> Art. II. To obtain the object of the foregoing article, the Chickasaw Nation of Indians cede to the United States of America (with the exception of such reservations as shall be hereafter mentioned) all claim or title which the said nation has to the land lying north of the south boundary of the State of Tennessee, which is bounded south by the thirty-fifth degree of north latitude, and which land, hereby ceded, lies within the following boundary, viz: Beginning on the Tennessee River, about thirty-five miles by water; below Colonel George Colbert's ferry, where the thirty-fifth degree of north latitude strikes the same; thence due west, with said degree of north latitude, to where it cuts the Mississippi River at or near the Chickasaw Bluffs; thence up the Ohio River to the mouth of the Tennessee River; thence up the Tennessee River to the place of beginning.[3]

It must be noted here that by this cession, the Chickasaw Treaty, the tribe of Chickasaw Indians gave to the United States all of West Tennessee as well as their lands in Kentucky and Alabama. So it was, that the stage had been legally set for the coming of the white man to the Western District and the beginning of his settlement in this vast new area.

Early in 1819, the great movement westward began as pioneers from the Carolinas, Virginia, from East Tennessee and elsewhere ventured into the Western District. Of this area—the Western District—John Haywood, an early Tennessee historian wrote:

> In going from Jackson, in the Western District of Tennessee, through the states of Mississippi and Alabama, and thence to Florence, near the Tennessee line, the alluvial land of the Western District cannot fail to attract the attention of the traveller. There are marshes on the banks of every stream, dangerous quicksands, sluggish waters, and a sound made by the hoof of the horse when it strikes the ground. The falling of a tree at some distance will produce a tremulous motion of the earth to the distance of several hundred yards; and here are frequent shocks of earthquakes. In the banks of rivers, and under high bluffs, sticks or logs of wood are found sometimes petrified. And in digging wells through the sand, leaves and sticks of wood are often found; and also fire coals and pieces of pottery. Along the ridges dividing the headwaters of Sandy River from the waters of Hatchie

---

[2] *The Chickasaw Nation,* by James H. Malone, 1922, p. 314.
[3] *Ibid.*

River, immense beds of marine shells on the top of the ground are presented to view. No fossil or mineral substance is found in what may be supposed to have been its primitive state. They all seem to have been acted upon by heat and moisture. The Chickasaw Old Towns furnish a great variety of marine substances. Calcareous limestone is found in that section of country, a few feet underground, and the small streams are soon sunk or absorbed. Springs are scarce.[4]

From the standpoint of travel facilities within the Chickasaw Indian Territory, historians have given varying accounts. It has been written that the Western District at that time was a "pathless wilderness."

The trails or traces of the Indians extended hundreds of miles in all directions and they crisscrossed each other over the whole continent, and over these the Indians constantly traveled on continuous trips thousands of miles. The Chickasaws were great travelers, and thought nothing of going to the far West, over their trails.[5]

Their trails or traces were far superior to any the white man could locate, and the early use by white pioneers of these Indian trails was a constant source of friction, for the Indians resented that use. As soon as state governments were organized, roads were laid out over these traces; and the United States government made these trails available. Thus, the Chickasaw had a trail leading from about where Natchez, Mississippi, now is, on to the Cumberland River where Nashville is now situated, and the trail led thence onward to the Atlantic seaboard, over which the Chickasaws traveled.[6]

Over the trails and traces traveled the caravans of those adventurous persons who came as early settlers to the Western District. The trek started in 1818-1819, continued steadily through succeeding years. In 1825 the movement was described in this manner by the editor of the *Jackson Gazette:*[7]

Few sections invite emigrants equal to the Western District. In many instances of from twelve to fifteen hundred weight of fine quality cotton can be grown. Lands can be bought for less than their value because of the scarcity of money.

Truly no better description of the detailed preparation and intimate perils in travel of the early settlers to West Tennessee can be found than has been recorded by Joseph S. Williams in his "Old Times in West Tennessee," now a rare volume. The wording of the dedication of his work in 1873 gives stamp of meaning to the content covered:

Respectfully dedicated to the surviving pioneer settlers, whose brave hearts and strong arms subdued the Wilderness of West Ten-

---

[4] *Natural and Aboriginal History of Tennessee,* by John Haywood. Edited by Mary W. Rothrock, 1959, p. 364.
[5] Malone, p. 57.
[6] *Ibid.,* p. 58.
[7] Williams, *Historic Madison,* p. 43; *Jackson Gazette,* February 19, 1825.

nessee, and made it the fitting abode for refined, civilized enjoyment and their immediate successors.

Early in his account, Mr. Williams writes of "the land of the Chickasaws and Davy Crockett—the Obion, Forked Deer and the Big Hatchie country—when in the cradle of the wilderness."

Glimpses of the eventful journey from Mississippi territory are taken from the colorfully related account.

The fatigue and peril of moving a large family of white and black, through a savage wilderness, with all the paraphernalia of comfortable living, in those days of rude travel, was an undertaking requiring almost superhuman endurance and inflexible will, but my father proved himself equal to it. . . .

Through the lonely vistas of the pine woods was seen a long train of movers. In front rode my father, on his faithful and sure-footed dapple-gray mare, with heavy bolsters swinging across the pommel of his saddle, with their black bear skin covering. . . . Following close behind was a large black carryall, containing mother, grandmother and the young children. The carryall, . . . my father had made in North Carolina, with an eye single to its usefulness as a sleeping apartment, as well as a traveling vehicle; long and broad, deep sides and high back, with heavy leather curtains, lined with thick, green baize, when closely buttoned down and bed made up in it, was comfortable enough for an emperor's wife. It was the traveling and sleeping apartment of my mother, grandmother and three young sisters.

Provident in arrangement my father . . . had purchased a year's supply of everything requisite to a comfortable living in the wilds of the Big Hatchie—coffee, tea, rice, sugar, flour, spices and medicines; card, cotton and spinning-wheels; every variety and kind of seeds; implements of husbandry; carpenter and blacksmith tools, and assorted nails, not forgetting an ample stock of powder, lead and shot; selecting twenty head of choice milch cows with their calves and yearlings, and about the same number of stock hogs.

My mother contributed her share in the necessary preparation for the journey; every one, both black and white, were properly and comfortably clad in home-spun clothes—stout overcoats for the men and long jackets for the women. The seats and knees of her boys' pants she padded with dressed buckskin. . . .

We made some days as much as ten miles, oftener, however, not more than six or eight. . . .

Reaching the Chickasaw territory, the Choctaw guide was relieved, my father making him many presents for his faithful services, sending presents to his chief. A Chickasaw guide was engaged, and the course of travel decided upon. . . .

The country through which we traveled was slightly rolling, wood principally oak and hickory, devoid of tangled undergrowth. Traveling for days . . . we reached the thickly settled portion of the nation, . . . the principal village, at which the chief resided. It was on a Friday;

man and beast needed rest, and the order was given that we would lay over till Monday. No travel was done on the Sabbath.

The author continues to relate in full the incidents of the journey and the eventual settling of their new home.

Buried, as it were, in the wilderness, beyond the outskirts of busy civilized life, we lived in Quaker simplicity. The schoolmaster and the preacher had not yet arrived in the land. . . .

My father, the Fall of the first year he settled in the wilderness, surveyed out and cut a road through the Hatchie bottom, and established the first ferry on the Hatchie, below McGuire's, in Haywood. There was then a continuous road from Brownsville to Covington, and became the principal road of travel between the two places, and my father's house the only habitation on the road, which of necessity became a "house of entertainment."

The incident is described wherein a half dozen well dressed men rode to the house one night and asked to "stay all night." The home made cheerful by the blazing fire and the aroma of food was comforting indeed to the weary travelers.

Word was soon conveyed to my Mother that they were real, nice, broadcloth gentlemen. . . . The servants and everybody spread themselves in preparation. My Mother got out her best damask. The new tea tray and china . . . preserves, in glass dishes . . . a fresh cake of butter was fixed . . . in pineapple shape . . . the last two sperm candles, stuck in the tall silver candle-sticks, were lighted, and the guests invited in to supper. My Mother, . . . had taken her seat at the head of the table, behind the new tea-tray and glittering service. The party entering the dining room (a shed room boarded up with clapboards) was led by a tall and stately silver-haired gentleman . . . he paused . . . with a fixed gaze at my mother . . . . A mutual recognition followed . . . she exclaimed, "Colonel William Polk, of North Carolina" and extended her hand. . . . My dear Madam, this is the most joyous meeting since I left our native State. . . . Colonel William Polk,[8] (father of

---

[8] Colonel William Polk (son of Thomas Polk), b. July 9, 1758, Charlotte, N. C., d. 1834, Raleigh, N. C., md. 1, Grizel Gilchrist, two sons: Thomas G. Polk and Dr. William Polk. Md. 2, Sarah Hawkins, nine children: Lucius J., md. 1, Mary Eastin (a great niece of Rachel Donelson Jackson); 2, Mrs. Ann Pope; Leonidas, b. April 10, 1806, Raleigh, N. C., md. May 6, 1830, Frances Ann Devereaux, he died June 14, 1864; Mary, md. George E. Badger; Alexander Hamilton, d. unmd.; Rufus King, md. Sarah Jackson; George Washington, md. Mary (Sally) Hilliard; Susan S., md. Kenneth Rayner; Andrew Jackson, md. Rebecca Van Lear; Charles J., d. 1830 in childhood. (Ref., General Leonidas Polk, C.S.A., The Fighting Bishop, by Joseph H. Parks, 1962.) (Ref., Records of Jones County, N. C., 1779-1868, Vol. I, by Zae Hargett Gwynn, 1963, pp. 764-765; Frances Ann Devereaux Polk, daughter of John and Frances Devereaux, Raleigh, N. C. Property settlement, July 3, 1839.) (Mrs. Gwynn is a member of Zachariah Davies Chapter N. S., D.A.R.) Colonel William Polk located numerous land grants in the Western District. He bought large tracts of land in Middle Tennessee. The splendid homes established by his sons on plantation acreage in Maury County, near Columbia, were: *Hamilton Place*, home of Lucius Polk (presently the home of Mr. and Mrs. Trezevant P. Yeatman); *Ashwood Hall*,

the late Right Reverend Bishop Polk)[9] and my mother were . . . acquainted in their young days. Their meeting was most unexpected to both of them.[10]

In this fashion the Western District was settled by people of energy, courage and ingenuity. They experienced, unquestionably, great hazards and decided inconvenience in travel. After treacherous mountain passes, they crossed fordable streams and throughout the wilderness territory these early travelers were subjected to the danger of lurking wild animals.

Prior to the post-roads of 1829 numerous ideas had been proposed concerning the need of improved travel facilities for the District. The first concern was that of making navigable the rivers, along which settlement had begun.

The keel-boat was the type of water-craft best suited to survive the hazards of the undredged, narrow rivers of that time. Down the Tennessee, the Cumberland and Ohio Rivers came such boats and into the navigable streams of the Western District. In 1821 three keel-boats came down the Forked Deer River. Up the Hatchie River supplies were carried to the first stores in Brownsville by boat. The Hatchie was navigable to Bolivar and the Obion River was a waterway in the northwest section of the District. Groceries, dry goods, flour, wheat, cotton, corn and whiskey were usual items of the cargoes transported to or from the area.

As the result of a request to the Legislature, of 1825, for improvement of all rivers, a Navigation Board was appointed for the Western District. A lottery was authorized by the Assembly for the benefit of the Forked Deer River, although there is no record that it was ever held. Effort was made to get a canal cut from the Tennessee River to the Hatchie, which did not materialize. However, in 1834 Memphis operated the first steamboat on the Mississippi River and in 1837 a steamboat was on the Hatchie at Bolivar.

Internal improvements were keenly needed by all, yet were sought diligently by only a few public-spirited citizens. Attention became diverted from rivers as waterways to improved roads, with bridges, as a more nearly desirable means of general travel. Therefore, the wilderness trail, no more than a bridle-path, became a road and in many cases an eventual turnpike.

---

built by Leonidas Polk; *Westbrook,* home of Rufus King Polk; *Rattle and Snap,* built by George Washington Polk; *Willsgrove,* home of Andrew Jackson Polk.

[9] The Right Reverend Leonidas Polk, Bishop of Louisiana, a General in the Confederate Army during the Civil War. To him a friend once said, "What you a bishop, throw off the gown for the sword!" General Polk replied, "No, sir, I buckle the sword over the gown."

Four Polk brothers, Lucius, Leonidas, Rufus and George, built St. John's Episcopal Church, Ashwood.

[10] *Old Times in West Tennessee,* by Joseph S. Williams, 1873, pp. 8, 9, 10, 11, 12, 47, 48, 49.

It is of interest to note that by 1830, facilities of travel had both increased and improved. Steamboats and bridged roads—over which stage coaches traveled—contributed immeasurably to the general well-being of the early settlers of the vast west of Tennessee.

Counties were rapidly organized and settled in the Western District. The formation of counties, their dates of creation by the Legislature and the chief towns which are their county seats, are of historical value in providing a background for the organization and advancement of the Episcopal Church within their borders. The names of the counties which comprise West Tennessee follow:

Counties of the Western District[11]

Name	Date Formed	Parent County	County Seat
Hardin	11/13/1819	Western District	Savannah
Shelby	11/24/1819[12]	Hardin	Memphis
Madison	11/ 7/1821	Western District	Jackson
Henderson	11/ 7/1821	Western District	Lexington
Henry	11/ 7/1821	Western District	Paris
Carroll	11/ 7/1821	Western District	Huntingdon
McNairy	10/ 8/1823	Hardin	Selmer
Hardeman	10/16/1823	Western District	Bolivar
Dyer	10/16/1823	Western District	Dyersburg
Weakley	10/21/1823	Western District	Dresden
Gibson	10/23/1823	Western District	Trenton
Obion	10/24/1823	Western District	Union City
Tipton	10/29/1823	Western District	Covington
Haywood	11/ 3/1823	Western District	Brownsville
Fayette	9/24/1824	Shelby, Hardeman	Somerville
Benton	11/24/1835	Henry, Humphreys	Camden
Lauderdale	11/24/1835	Dyer, Tipton, Haywood	Ripley
Decatur	11/ /1845[13]	Perry	Decaturville
Lake	6/ 9/1870	Obion	Tiptonville
Crockett	3/ 9/1872	Dyer, Madison, Gibson, Haywood	Alamo
Chester	3/ 1/1875	McNairy, Hardeman, Madison, Henderson	Henderson

[11] Listing verified by Dr. Robert H. White, State Historian, State Library and Archives, Nashville, Tennessee.

[12] Legislative Acts, Tennessee, 1819, Chap. 146.

[13] Day not given in Act.

CHAPTER V

TOWNS GREW

Between 1821 and 1840 a network of post and stage routes developed throughout the Western District.

The picturesque, stage coach was destined to enter and continue as a rough but ready mode of early travel. The entire equipage was unique—the cinderella-type carriage set on wheels capable of the greatest speed of the age was drawn by nattily groomed, prancing horses harnessed usually in tandem fashion. And seated over all, an able driver keen of eye and swift in emergencies, equipped with a whip to urge the horses onward and a conch shell to blow in announcement of an approaching stop. Such stops were usually at a wayside inn and were most welcome interludes for passengers and horses alike. There, travelers found food and refreshment and horses were changed for the onward journey.

History records, that in 1829 post roads were established leading from Memphis by way of Raleigh, Morning Sun, Somerville, Bolivar and Jackson; also one from Memphis by way of Randolph, Covington, Brownsville and Jackson was in operation.[1]

The Western District, during the succeeding years, began to assume the character of a stimulated, thriving civilization. Obscure trading posts became settlements and remote, sparsely inhabited villages developed into towns of trade and culture. Indeed, many of the populated centers were seemingly destined from their beginning to become patterns of growth and influence in the settlement of the vast new area.

In the sketches[2] which follow, a sincere attempt is made to give particular coverage of the towns to which missionary-ministers of dedicated mind and purpose came and where the Episcopal Church was established between the years 1832 and 1964. In such manner, the Church found a place in the hearts and minds of the people of sprawling, receptive west Tennessee.

Let us in faithful retrospect see the settlement of the section of the Western District known as Madison County, and as well, the creation of the wonderful town of *Jackson,* — ever thriving since birth, — called by some-

[1] *History of Tennessee* (Shelby County) by Goodspeed, p. 810.
[2] The order in which the sketches appear follows closely the itinerary of the first missionary ministers of the Episcopal Church who came to West Tennessee.

one, and most appropriately, "The beautiful dimple of West Tennessee." On keel boats down the Forked Deer River and over Indian trails came the pioneers to this area. Cotton Grove and Alexandria, which was the county seat for two years, were the first settlements in the County. At the time the future site of Jackson was a farm belonging to Dr. William E. Butler and Thomas Shannon.

Named for Andrew Jackson, later the seventh President of the United States, Jackson in Madison County, Tennessee, became the capital of the Chickasaw Purchase. It was on September 17, 1822 that the new log courthouse had been completed at a cost of $135.00.[3] In that year "the County Court allowed bounties of money for wolf scalps; granted permits for the building of five sawmills and gristmills; issued a license for a hotel; and arranged for a permanent county seat."[4]

To the area of Jackson in 1822, there came from the Cumberland Settlement, Stokeley Donelson Hays. He was a lawyer and a surveyor and did much toward opening new roads in the community.

Among the members of the first board of commissioners for the government of the town of Jackson were Stokeley Donelson Hays and Dr. William E. Butler.[5]

As has been stated, the negotiations, which resulted in the 1818 treaty with the Indians, had been carried forward largely by General Andrew Jackson. Therefore, may we here speak of his fearlessness, his patriotic fervor, his abundant integrity and his devotion to law. All these were among the character traits of the statesman which he was. Such were the qualities which won for him great admiration and the respect of the rugged individuals of his time. These persons were the stalwart pioneers, in many cases his neighbors and his friends, who struggled diligently to create from a wilderness a safe, civilized abode—a great free land of pride and promise.

In the summer of 1825, a group of citizens of Jackson, Tennessee, invited General and Mrs. Jackson "to visit the Western District before he departed for Washington."[6] The invitation was accepted. In the introductory remarks given in presenting the General to his audience, reference was made to the debt of gratitude owed by the people of the Western District to General Jackson concerning his part in the negotiations of the Chickasaw Treaty.[7] To this expressed appreciation the General replied:

It is true that I was fortunate enough to conclude that treaty of 1818 which gave to our South the fertile and prosperous country which

[3] *Historic Madison,* by Emma Inman Williams, p. 35.
[4] *History of Tennessee,* by Silas E. Scates, p. 235.
[5] *Beginnings of West Tennessee,* by Samuel Cole Williams, 1930, p. 137.
[6] Williams, p. 3.
[7] *Ibid,* p. 4.

you occupy. The execution of this important trust had been assigned to me in connection with an esteemed man, Gov. Shelby of Kentucky. We spared no pains and left no effort proper to be used untried to effect the purpose of our mission. To me an inestimable satisfaction is derived from the evidence now offered that the haunts of the Savage man have been exchanged for the cultivated farm. You are yet young in years but press on; practice industry, and economy and soon you will claim in the State that prosperity to which the fruit of your soil and your already refined population abundantly entitles you.[8]

Brownsville was named for General Jacob Brown, who served in the War of 1812. The town was located on fifty acres of land donated by T. M. Johnson.

Commissioners appointed in March 1825 to make a survey, lay out the town and sell the lots were: Laurence McGuire, Charles White, Nicholas T. Perkins, William H. Henderson and Thomas G. Nixon.[9]

The town's first store-keeper and first inn-keeper was Hiram Bradford[10] from New Orleans and was present for the sale of lots in the new town in fertile Haywood County. At the sale he bought lot No. 1. Soon thereafter he felled a large oak tree on the corner of the lot, split it into slabs and built the first store-house in Brownsville. For many years he was a leading merchant in the town and a business man of the county.

In 1828, the Red Rover navigated the Hatchie to Brownsville and it is said to have been the first steamboat up the Hatchie to the Brownsville landing.[11]

Not even a brief sketch of Brownsville and the County of Haywood would be complete, without naming certain pioneer citizens who contributed noticeably to the settlement of the community and whose descendants have continued to make permanent homes within the area. The Taylor family was memoralized several years past by a roadside marker placed by the Tennessee Historical Commission. The plaque bears this inscription: "4D, 24 Tabernacle, 1.8 mi: This community was settled in 1826 by the Rev. Howell Taylor and his five sons. Haywood County's first schoolhouse was there; it also served as a church. The Taylor Kinfolks Camp Meeting was held here annually for over a century." The five sons were Allen, Howell, Richard, John Y., and Edmund Taylor.[12]

Dr. Allen J. Barbee, David McLeod, Daniel Cherry; John W. Strother and Major William R. Hess, lawyers; Valentine Sevier, F. S. Cox; also

[8] *Historic Madison,* Emma Inman Williams, p. 4.
[9] *Beginnings of West Tennessee,* by Samuel C. Williams, p. 150.
[10] *Old Times in West Tennessee,* by Joseph S. Williams pp. 239-243.
[11] *Ibid.,* p. 256.
[12] *The Taylors of Tabernacle,* Tabernacle Historical Committee, Brownsville, Tennessee, 1957.

Doctors Whitelaw, Johnston, Charles Boyd, Robert Boyd and J. C. Jones, were early settlers.

Among other family names long identified with Brownsville and Haywood County are those of Ashe, Bond, Burgess, Cannon, Claiborne,[13] Collins, Craig,[14] Currie,[15] Davie,[15] Dickinson, Evans,[15] Folk, Gray, Haywood, Holloway,[15] Johnson, Jett, King, Mann, Owen, Peete, Powell, Sheppard, Short, Thomas, Thornton, Wood.

In 1833 "almost four-twelfths of the people are Presbyterian, four twelfths Methodist, two-twelfths Baptist, and two-twelfths nondescript!"[16]

In March 1909, the David Craig Chapter D.A.R. was organized in Brownsville.

LaGrange early became a thriving, attractive settlement in Fayette County. The town was the business rival of Jackson in Madison County and enjoyed, as Bolivar did, a lucrative trade with the Chickasaw Indians of North Mississippi.

The flow of immigration was rapid as stories spread of the potentialities of the new community. The *Jackson Gazette* of Nov. 26, 1825 commented: "Immigration into the District is on a large scale; and no port faster settled than the south boundary line of the State. It is of a respectable class, bringing no small portion of wealth."[17]

The *Tennessee Gazeteer* published in 1834[18] lists LaGrange as follows: "thriving post town in the southeast corner of Fayette County, on Wolfe River. In 1828 it contained 60 houses, 240 inhabitants, four stores, two taverns and a dozen mechanics. . . ." LaGrange was incorporated January

---

[13] Claiborne—In *History of Zion (Christ) Church,* Brownsville, is this record: July 12, 1907—Baptism by Bishop Gailor, Rebecca Louise Claiborne, child of Henry J. and Teresa Claiborne. Sponsors: Parents, Miss Minna Wendel and R. F. Johnson. Rebecca Louise Claiborne, b. Sept. 19, 1905, the daughter of Theresa Lurleen Davie and Henry J. Claiborne, md. Dec. 30, 1903, J. William Roper (with *Nashville Tennessean*). Her sister, Rhea Sorrelle Claiborne, b. Sept. 7, 1916, md. April 19, 1941, John Gilliam Wynne; one child, John Claiborne Wynne, b. Aug. 1, 1944.

[14] Craig—Descendants of Capt. David Craig of the Revolutionary War from Orange County, N. C., settled early in the Brownsville area. The David Craig Chapter N.S., D.A.R., bears his name. Among those who have joined the Chapter on Captain Craig's record are: Virginia Short (Mrs. John C.) Gately (Nat. No. 413669) and Myra Collins Short (Mrs. D. D.) McBride (Nat. No. 203371). They are daughters of Myra Collins (Mrs. L. M.) Short, long an active D.A.R., and a Colonial Dame.

[15] Currie—Rosa Lee Evans (Mrs. Edward N.) Johnston, born in Haywood County, is descended from the Currie, Davie, Evans and Holloway families. Her parents were Dee Witt Clinton Evans and Kitturah Susan Davie Evans. Mrs. Johnston is a member of the Zachariah Davies Chapter N.S., D.A.R., on the records of ancestors: John Currie, James Currie and John Holloway (Nat. No. 356466). A sister, Rona Evans Kirk, and her three daughters are members of this chapter. Miss Mary Evans is a member of David Craig Chapter.

[16] *Beginnings of West Tennessee,* Williams, p. 151.

[17] *Ibid.,* p. 157.

[18] *Commercial Appeal,* 1936. An article entitled "Frederick Cossitt Who Gave the Library to Memphis," by A. H. Holden (compiled by Eastin Morris).

5, 1836. It is thought that this town in Fayette County was named for "La Grange," the home of the distinguished Frenchman, Marquis de La Fayette, near Paris, France.

Beautiful old homes and historic Immanuel Episcopal Church cause La Grange to be a pilgrimage town.

Even before Tennessee existed as a territory and long before the Chickasaw Purchase, land near the Chickasaw Bluffs was sold by North Carolina. A number of grants of considerable size were sold, a customary price being "two shillings per acre or ten pounds per one hundred acres."[19]

On parts of two adjacent North Carolina land grants, among the entries of 1783-86, each for five thousand acres laid out by John Rice and John Ramsey, *Memphis* was located. The laying out of Memphis began soon after Shelby County was established by the General Assembly in 1819. The three founders of Memphis have been accredited as Andrew Jackson, John Overton and James Winchester.

Historians are not in agreement concerning the proponent of the name "Memphis," so majestically borne for more than a century by the queen city of Shelby County and of the Mid-South. Both General Jackson and James Winchester are credited as having said:[20]

It shall be named Memphis for the famous city of Egypt, similarly situated on the Nile, for the new Memphis will rival the old in greatness.[21]

In 1819, fifty-three persons comprised the population of the small community.[22] By 1827, five hundred citizens were inhabiting the young village. The populace increased from 33,592 in 1880 to 64,586 in 1890. The number of the city's residents passed the 100,000 mark in 1900 and the 1960 census placed the population of Memphis, within the city limits, at 497,524.[23]

First in many fields of commercial and civic endeavor, Memphis stands today. In each of these coveted positions, Memphis ranks as the world's largest: Spot Cotton Market, Hardwood Market, Cottonseed Products, Hardwood Flooring, Interior Cotton Warehousing System and Artesian Water Supply System. Memphis has been accorded several cherished national titles: America's Quietest City, America's Cleanest City and America's Home of the Cotton Carnival. From the standpoint of achievement among other cities of the South, Memphis ranks as the largest Hospital and Medical Center, Wholesale Market, Trade Area, and Center of River, Rail, Highway, Bus and Motor Transportation.

---

[19] *History of Memphis,* Keating, Vol. 1, p. 132.
[20] *Beginnings of West Tennessee,* by Samuel C. Williams, 1930, p. 126.
[21] *History of Tennessee,* by Silas E. Scates, pp. 231, 233.
[22] *History of Memphis,* by J. M. Keating, Vol. 1.
[23] *Meet Memphis* (a pamphlet) by Memphis City Government, 1960, p. 11.

A Mayor and four Commissioners, elected by the citizens every four years, constitute the City Commission, responsible for the management of the government of Memphis. The present officials are: Mayor Henry Loeb, Commissioner of Administration and Health; Claude A. Armour, Commissioner of Fire and Police; William W. Farris, Commissioner of Public Works; John T. Dwyer, Commissioner of Public Service, and James W. Moore, Commissioner of Finance and Institutions.[24]

The degree of satisfaction found in the type of government enjoyed by Memphis citizens has been well expressed by the present City officials in a pamphlet compiled by them:

> In meeting the test of time, the Memphis Plan has proved it incorporates the three essentials of good government—continuous and intelligent citizen interest, official capability, and an effective Charter providing a simplified plan of organization.[25]

A great future was predicted for the town, so beautifully situated on the advantageous Chickasaw Bluffs—the banks of the mighty Mississippi!

Verily, brilliant historical and dramatic episodes contributed to the greatness of the town in its growing to city-hood! Indians, Spaniards and Frenchmen left their imprints in the warp and woof of the early community. Yet, Memphis' heritage is basically the result of the effort of the staunch, stout-hearted pioneer American citizens who founded a village and nurtured it to become a magnificent place—a city of good abode.

"This is Memphis on the Mississippi where the sweet magnolias grow, Where the roses bloom forever—Where your heart has longed to go!"[26]

Randolph, at the mouth of Big Hatchie and the Mississippi River ranked in importance as a shipping port for all of West Tennessee.[27] The town, laid out in 1828, was named for John Randolph of Roanoke, Virginia.

In 1830 Randolph became a flourishing center and continued as such for more than a decade.[28] It is said that in one year during the thirties 40,000 bales of cotton were shipped from Randolph. The town enjoyed a large wagon trade as well as a river trade and the added advantage of stage coach service made the location desirable for homes as well as businesses.

Because Dr. Charles Todd Quintard, after ordination as a deacon, went immediately to Tipton County and served Ravenscroft Chapel on the

---

[24] Officials elected on November 7, 1963 were: Mayor William B. Ingram, Jr.; Claude A. Armour, Pete Sisson, Hunter Lane, Jr., and James W. Moore, Commissioners.

[25] *Meet Memphis,* p. 2.

[26] From an old song, author unknown.

[27] *History of Memphis,* by Keating, Vol. 1, p. 131.

[28] *History of the Diocese of Tennessee,* Noll, p. 19.

Alston Plantation and St. Paul's at Randolph, this story is appropriately shared.

As known, St. Paul's Church at Randolph was one of the first five churches organized in the Western District in 1832 and was admitted to the Diocese of Tennessee at the 1833 Convention. The Church owned a beautiful silver communion service which was inscribed: "St. Paul's Church, Randolph."

During the Civil War, the well established town of Randolph was the object of repeated attacks by the Yankee forces stationed in Memphis, down the Mississippi River. During one of the raids, only a few weeks before Easter, the communion silver was stolen. In the absence of the silver chalice a glass tumbler was used for the wine and a china plate held the bread. These were used at the Easter service.

A gunboat landed at Randolph early that Easter Sunday morning. Later, the commanding officer, a General, with his Staff went up the hill to St. Paul's and received communion. The General had previously attended a communion service at Randolph and knew of the silver vessels.

The story is told that after the Easter Day service, the General asked a lady parishioner what had become of the communion service. She replied: "It was taken away by some of your soldiers!"

After a few days a package was received from Memphis by the lady and it contained the lost chalice and paten. That night, several women of the Church took the sacred silver pieces and buried them in the ground near a large tree—a safe and secret hiding place, known only to them.

Within a short while another attack by the Yankee forces practically destroyed the town of Randolph. St. Paul's Episcopal Church was burned during the raid and was never rebuilt after the War.

Two factors determined the eventual downfall of the thriving town. Had a proposed canal been constructed from above Hamburg, on the Tennessee River and connected with the Hatchie River at the Tuscumbia Creek junction, trade would have been assured. The removal of the Chickasaws to the West in 1831-1834, who settled later on fertile lands in north Mississippi, resulted in greater trade with Memphis than with Randolph. As a tragic result for the community "the merchants of Randolph drifted with the current of prosperity and landed at the mouth of the Wolf. . . ." Thus Memphis became a metropolis and Randolph faded to a place of deserted, majestic bluffs and haunted hollows at the River's edge! Today, there is no more beautiful setting in West Tennessee for the revival of a picturesque town than the site of old Randolph Landing. Good roads make the whole area quite accessible. And, of course, the Mississippi River is navigable. To witness a sunset at Randolph is an experience never to be forgotten!

Perhaps, in time, a builder possessed of vision, creativeness and adequate finance may look favorably upon this exquisite setting and Randolph may be restored as a place of beauty, of business and hospitality. If and when such may occur, we pray for the rebuilding and reconsecration of St. Paul's Episcopal Church.

Henry County, organized at the house of Peter Wall in December 1821, was named for the distinguished American patriot, Patrick Henry. Early, the county showed evidence whereby it was to become one of the most thriving of the counties of the Western District and thereby attracted a superior type of settler.

Paris, the county seat, was laid out in 1823. The area was a site in a thick forest on a ridge between the Obion and Sandy Rivers. The Commissioners appointed to locate the town were Sterling Brewer, James Fentress and Abraham Murray. In honor of General LaFayette, the town was named Paris in its charter of 1823, at the time of incorporation.

The population of Paris grew steadily; in 1833 there were eight hundred citizens and in 1837 twelve hundred comprised the population of the town.

It is a matter of record that the largest military warrant issued by North Carolina was to the heirs of General Robert Howe for sixteen thousand acres of land. The land was entered to the north and west of Paris.[29]

Among those associated early with Henry County and Paris were: John B. House, Joel Hagler, John Stoddard, James Williams, who came about 1819; and later Samuel McCorkle, Dr. T. D. Porter, Hugh Dunlap, Isham G. Harris, William G. Blount, Col. Richard Porter and John W. Crockett.

Since the organization of garden clubs in Tennessee the Paris Garden Club has been among the most active in the Tennessee Federation of Garden Clubs following the Federation's organization in 1926.

On the lands of Major William Ramsey, Hatchie, the county seat of Hardeman County was first located. Later the seat was changed, about one mile south of the location first chosen, to land belonging to Colonel Ezekiel Polk and to Major Ramsey. In 1825, in the act of incorporation, the name, *Bolivar,* was given to the town of Hatchie, in honor of Simon Bolivar, known as the liberator of South America.

---

[29] *Beginnings of West Tennessee,* by Williams, p. 134.

Lot sales in the town amounted to six thousand dollars, a fund used in the building of a court house and jail. The commission in charge of the town's creation was composed of Thomas Jones Hardeman, John H. Bills, Nathaniel Steel, West Harris and John Cochran. In addition to these, the first commissioned as justices of peace were Andrew Taylor, William Polk, Jacob Pirtle, Wm. P. Robertson, and John Rosson. The first court was organized in 1823.

Soon after the town was created it was predicted that Bolivar would become an important community because the Big Hatchie River nearby was to have been connected with the Tennessee by a canal, in order to make an adequate waterway for travel from East Tennessee to New Orleans. The early merchants of Bolivar sent loaded flat boats down the stream to the thriving Louisiana city.

First, a small trading post, the town later enjoyed for many years abundant trade with the Chickasaw Indians of North Mississippi. Great commercial integrity was practiced by the merchants of Bolivar.

The first settlers of Hardeman County associated with the town were such names as Polk, Leonidas Bills, Pitser Miller, E. P. and A. T. McNeal, Wood and others.

Through the years, Bolivar has been known for her well preserved old homes and churches.

A Chapter of the Daughters of the American Revolution organized in Bolivar bears the name "Hatchie Chapter."

The Hardeman County Court House in Bolivar is distinct in its architecture. The center section, built in 1868, was designed by Fletcher Sloan and built of brick made in the town.

The county was named in honor of Col. Thomas Jones Hardeman, who married Mary Polk, daughter of Col. Ezekiel Polk in Maury County, Tennessee. Col. Hardeman was one of the fourteen children of Thomas Hardeman and Mary Harding Perkins Hardeman, both natives of Virginia. Thomas Hardeman was a soldier in the Battle of King's Mountain during the Revolutionary War[30] and served with the Watauga Riflemen (1780-1790) of North Carolina under Capt. William Beene.

A roster of Tennessee lawyers in 1834[31] reveals these names associated as the "Bolivar Bar": Roger Barton, Edward R. Belcher, David Fentress,

---

[30] Among the descendants of Thomas Hardeman for whom his Revolutionary War record has been accepted for membership in the N.S., D.A.R., are Lora Ellis (Mrs. William Clay) Rodgers; her daughter, Martha Rodgers (Mrs. William F.) Reitz and granddaughter, Miss Nancy Rodgers Reitz. All are members of the Zachariah Davies Chapter.

[31] *Beginnings of West Tennessee*, Williams, p. 220 (*Tennessee Gazeteer*, by Morris, 1834).

Volentine D. Barry, Pendleton G. Gaines, Austin Miller and William C. Dunlap. Presently, a distinguished gentleman of the legal profession who has made his home in Bolivar for many years, is The Honorable Alan M. Prewitt, Chief Justice of the Supreme Court of Tennessee.[32]

Among the notable troops of West Tennessee was a company from Bolivar commanded by Captain Rufus Polk Neely, which in 1838 was called to Fort Cass in East Tennessee and aided in the removal of the Cherokee Indians to their reservation beyond the Mississippi River.

Settlement began in the area of the present town of *Somerville* between 1822 and 1823.

The home of Robert G. Thornton, on the north fork of Wolf River twelve miles southeast of Somerville and seven miles northwest of LaGrange, was the setting in which was held on Monday, December 6, 1824, the first County Court of Fayette County. The county had been named for Marquis de La Fayette, a distinguished visitor to the nation in 1824.

In February 1825, the site of the "permanent seat of justice" was located on lands owned by George Bowers and James Brown. Each donated to the county a tract of about twenty-five acres. The county seat was first called "Bowers Town." However, later the name was changed to Somerville, in honor of Lieutenant Robert Somerville, killed in the Creek War in 1814.

The court appointed William Owen, Daniel Johnson, Hamilton Thornton, Henry Kirk and John T. Patterson as commissioners to lay off the town lots and to sell the lots at public auction. The money derived from the lot sale was to be used in the erection of a temporary log court house, jail and other necessary public buildings. One hundred ninety-two lots were recorded on the original plat. The first public sale took place on September 14, 1825.

A Mr. Anderson was the first store-keeper in Somerville. He was sent to the village in 1825 by David Deaderick, a merchant of Jonesboro, Washington County, Tennessee. Also, during that year a tavern was opened by Henry M. Johnson.

"The Somerville Reporter," established by William Lewis in March 1837, was the town's first newspaper.

In the proceedings of the Grand Lodge (of Masonry) in Tennessee for 1826, there is a reference of November 11, 1825, to the "La Fayette Lodge No. 56, in Fayette County."[33]

---

[32] Funeral services for Judge Prewitt were held on Tuesday, February 19, 1963, Methodist Church, Bolivar, Tennessee.
[33] History of Somerville Lodge No. 73, F. and A. M. (a manuscript) by J. B. Summers, 1929.

Thus it is concluded that the Somerville Lodge No. 73 is the oldest chartered Lodge in Fayette County and one of the oldest in Tennessee. The first Master of the Lodge was Richard Cleere, a tailor, born in 1799, in Spottsylvania County, Virginia, and died in Fayette County, Tennessee, in 1846. Other first officers of the Lodge were W. S. Gray, M. Lynch and Josiah Higgason.

About Fayette County an early writer made this comment: "Settled by men of enterprise, intelligence and wealth, it early took a stand among the most favored counties in the District, noted for the refined, cultivated taste and good morals of its citizens."[33a]

Mason is the gateway to the County of Tipton to those who travel east on Bristol Highway (70). The old town lies thirty-six miles northeast of Memphis and thirteen miles south of Covington.

In 1858 James Mason donated four acres of land to the Memphis and Ohio Railroad, now the Louisville and Nashville system. The land was given as a site for a depot and for track right-of-way, with the definite understanding that the station located thereon should be named for the donor. The town was first called Mason's Depot.

In 1861 a hotel had been opened by M. Stevens and between 1866 and 1885 Mrs. O'Conner operated a hotel in the town.

The first merchants in Mason were Richard T. Brodnax,[34] Joseph A. Green and Maben Stevens.

Mason was incorporated in 1871. J. S. Walker was the town's first mayor. The present mayor of Mason is J. A. Whitaker. Aldermen chosen by the town's last election were: Doyle R. Morris, Neville R. Seay, C. E. Nash, Thomas Yarbrough, Wilkins Williamson, Jr., and J. N. M. Taylor, Jr. About five hundred citizens comprise the town's population.

[33a] Beginnings of West Tennessee by Williams (p. 157). Note: Willie Pearl Inman (Mrs. Fred T.) Fowler, Somerville, is a member of the Zachariah Davies Chapter, D.A.R. (Nat. No. 381544) on the Revolutionary War record of George Cherry, b. Antrim County, Ireland, about 1755, d. near Camden, South Carolina, 1799. Robert Cherry md. Letitia Leach, b. Antrim County, Ireland.

[34] Col. George T. Taylor (an uncle of George Anderson Taylor, reared him) was a founder of Holy Trinity (old Trinity-in-the-Fields). He married Mary Goodloe Somervill and had one daughter, Frances Taylor, who married her first cousin, James Taylor, and had two daughters: (1) Sally, married Richard T. Brodnax; their children were George T. Brodnax and Mary Brodnax. (2) Mollie Bett, married William Brodnax, no children.

George Taylor Brodnax, b. April 9, 1869, Mason, Tennessee; md. June 20, 1894 Miss Lucy Watkins (daughter of Dr. Thomas Richard and Sue Common Watkins); died Feb. 19, 1917. Children: (1) Sue, married first Andrew Krecker Jobe, children Andrew Jobe and Margaret Jobe; married second, Wilkins Williamson; (2) Frances Margaret; (3) George Taylor Brodnax, Jr.; (4) Lucy Virginia Brodnax, married first, Albert Biggs II, second, Dr. Sam Raines.

George T. Brodnax was associated for three years with C. L. Byrd Co., Jewelers, Memphis, prior to founding the present George T. Brodnax, Inc., Jewelers, Main Street, Memphis, Tenn.

The first local physicians were Drs. Mason, Read, Clement, Pettus, Tarwater, Phillips, Maclin, and Elcan.

Among family names long associated with the town of Mason are Taylor,[35] Brodnax, Somervill,[36] Nash, Williamson, Forgey, Maclin, Seay, Marshall,[37] and Poindexter.

A number of civic advantages and services are offered by the town to its residents. There are two schools. Fire protection is provided and two deep wells afford an adequate supply of water. All types of stores necessary to meet citizens' needs are to be found in Mason—grocery, dry goods, variety, drug and general store. Also there are garages, equipment and supply houses and a gin.

A very popular eating and meeting place in Mason for a number of years has been Bozo's. The present sizable restaurant has grown from a roadside stand made famous by its delicious old-fashioned pit barbecue. Located on Highway 70, it is owned and operated by Allen Williams and his sisters, Misses Iris and Helen Williams, whose father, Thomas Williams, started the business.

A unique and original idea with the business people of Mason was the Trade Day Association, which began April 7, 1936. For many years on the

---

[35] James Nathaniel Maclin Taylor and George Anderson Taylor of Mason were sons of John Young Taylor and Florence Taylor Maclin (her father was James Nathaniel Maclin, brother of Eliza Maclin, who married William Brodnax, his second wife). John Young Taylor was the son of George Anderson Taylor and Jane Frances Somervill Taylor. George Anderson Taylor was a Lay Reader, Trinity Church, Mason, Tennessee, for many years. J. N. M. Taylor married Aline Smith; their children are J. N. M. Taylor, Jr., and Mary Taylor (Mrs. Guy) Yoe.

[36] William Alexander Somervill, b. Sept. 13, 1862, d. Oct. 12, 1832 (buried—Old Trinity, Mason), md. Feb. 4, 1885, Maude Caroline Bailey, b. Sept. 12, 1866, d. Sept. 9, 1959. Their children: Bennett Augustine, b. April 16, 1887, md. Blanche Stuart; George Alexander, b. Nov. 18, 1890, md. Jo Somervill Nash; Jerry Joseph*, b. Dec. 31, 1892; Mary Charlotte, b. Nov. 9, 1894, md. John Wm. Dickinson; William Alexander, b. Apr. 12, 1896, d. Oct. 23, 1918, in Battle of Chateau Thierry; Charles E., b. Mar. 26, 1898, md. Elizabeth Walker; Ellen Maude*, b. July 27, 1902, md. Benton Terry; Helen*, b. Nov. 27, 1905, md. Lyle T. Rafferty; Elsie, b. May 17, 1907, md. James R. Kellam, Jr.
*Trinity Church, Mason.
William Alexander Somervill was the son of Augustine Claiborne Somervill and Mary Bennett Somervill (daughter of Joseph John Somervill and Ellen Geraldine Hill). Augustine Claiborne Somervill was a son of William A. Somervill I (a brother of Joseph John Somervill, sons of John Somervill, III, and Frances Anderson Taylor) and Helen Rosina Claiborne. Frances Anderson Taylor was a daughter of Col. Joseph Taylor of the American Revolution (a son of John Taylor of Caroline Co., Va., and Catherine Pendleton).

[37] Mary Ethel Marshall (Mrs. Winford) Clark, and John Marshall, Jr., Mason, are the children of Bess Poindexter Marshall and the late John McClanahan Marshall. John McC. Marshall was the son of John Zachary Taylor Marshall (1848-1920) and Laura McClanahan (1849-1939), md. Nov. 28, 1867. John Z. T. Marshall was the son of Wm. J. Marshall (b. Va. Feb. 2, 1807, d. April 24, 1886) and Sarah A. Thompson (b. N.C. Feb. 3, 1827, d. March 12, 1888) md. June 10, 1847. Laura McClanahan was the daughter of John Drew McClanahan (b. Ky. June 17, 1805,

first Saturday in each month farmers brought their horses and mules to be traded. It was a big day for the townspeople, for Tipton County and for the neighboring counties of Fayette and Haywood. The business-men of Mason participated generously by offering cash prizes to those with lucky tickets. Trade Day continues, even though there are neither mules nor horses to be traded. Too few of these reliable beasts of burden and of beauty have survived the onslaught of the rapid machine age!

The Bank of Mason through the years has been and continues a most substantial institution in banking history. Herbert McCraw,[38] of Braden, is president of the bank and J. N. M. Taylor, of Mason, is vice-president.

Nine churches are located in the town of Mason. They represent several Protestant denominations.

One of the first historical markers[39] placed by the Tennessee Historical Commission to memoralize a church in Tennessee was the marker to Holy

---

d. Feb. 9, 1890) and Margaret Ann Robinson (b. N.C. Feb. 8, 1822, d. July 6, 1903) md. Nov. 23, 1840. Margaret Ann Robinson was the daughter of Wm. B. Robinson (b. N.C. March 12, 1795, d. Jan. 28, 1867) and Elizabeth Boykin (b. N.C. Dec. 16, 1796, d. Feb. 14, 1872) md. Dec. 5, 1816. Wm. B. Robinson was the son of James Robinson (b. N.C. Jan. 16, 1766, d. August 10, 1830) and Margaret Ray (b. N.C. June 27, 1767, d. Oct. 27, 1837) md. May 1, 1788. James Robinson was the son of Michael Robinson (b. 1732, d. Orange Co., N.C., 1807) and Mary Ray. Md. 1753. Michael Robinson was a patriot of the American Revolution. He furnished supplies for the Continental Army. His place of residence during the Revolutionary War was Orange Co., N.C. Mrs. Clark (N.S., D.A.R., No. 466278) is a member of the Zachariah Davies Chapter. The late Mary Alice Marshall (Mrs. Luther F.) Jones (N.S., D.A.R., No. 466275), Brunswick, Tennessee, born in Mason, was also a member of this Chapter.

[38] The McCraw family of Braden is descended from Francis McCraw (b. Powhatan Co., Va., May 9, 1760, d. Buckingham Co., Va., Sept. 28, 1834), a soldier of the American Revolution. He was a son of Francis McCraw. Hervert McCraw is the son of James W. McCraw and Dora E. Lee McCraw (McCraw); grandson of Thomas Miller McCraw, who married Mary Ballon; great-grandson of Thomas Wood McCraw and his wife Martha Agee Bondurant and great-great grandson of the Revolutionary War ancestor, Francis McCraw, and his wife, Mary Harrison Word. Miss Ethel McCraw is a member of the David Craig Chapter N.S., D.A.R., Brownsville. The late Miss Sarah Hanby McCraw was a member of Zachariah Davies Chapter (Nat. No. 439725). Both joined the D.A.R. on record of Francis McCraw. Their niece Sara Elizabeth McCraw (Mrs. Henry Henderson) Swope, Nat. No. 424035, ancestor, Francis McCraw—and her mother, Mary Shore (Mrs. Chester) McCraw, Nat. No. 439721—ancestor, Kader Riddick, N. C., are members of Zachariah Davies Chapter.

[39] *Tennessee Historical Markers,* issued by Tennessee Historical Commission, Nashville, Tenn. (1958), "U. S. 70, Tipton Co., northeast of Mason; 4 E 11—Trinity in the Fields," p. 41.

Other residents of Mason or of nearby Covington who are members of Zachariah Davies Chapter NS., D.A.R. Ancestor, Michael Robinson, N.C.—Annie Bond McClanahan (Mrs. Albert Sidney) Witherington, Nat. No. 466284; Mary Drew Witherington (Mrs. Thomas W.) Griffin, Nat. No. 466285; Katherine McClanahan (Mrs. George D.) Gracey, Nat. No. 466279; Elizabeth McClanahan (Mrs. John S.) McBride, Nat. No. 467403; Mrs. Nell Elizabeth Wright Lara, Nat. No. 467403; Kate McClanahan (Mrs. John C.) Witherington, Nat. No. 466283, and Nell Beddingfield (Mrs. Solomon Isham) Wright, Nat. No. 467402. Ancestor, Col. Farlin Ball, Va., Bernice Ball (Mrs. John Henry) Forgey, Nat. No. 473755.

Trinity Episcopal Church (or Trinity-in-the-Fields), located between Mason and Charleston. The church is often called "Old Trinity," in order to distinguish it from Trinity Church, built later in the town of Mason. Trinity-in-the-Town was inspired by the coming of the railroad. The decision was made by the congregation of Old Trinity to build a lasting and beautiful brick church in Mason. Pure in architecture, Trinity Church stands in excellent condition as one of the most beautiful churches in the Diocese.

Among the oldest organizations in the county is the Mason Woman's Club. Through the years the programs of the group have won acclaim for having high cultural standards.

The more than a century-old town of Mason, typified by an atmosphere of traditional culture and good-will, continues to make a worthy contribution toward the steady development of thriving Tipton County.

The town of *Covington,* propitiously located in Tipton County, was laid off, and lots sold at public sale in April, 1825. The town was incorporated in 1826.

The County was given its name by legislative act in memory of Captain Jacob Tipton, killed in 1791 while serving in a company under General Arthur St. Clair in defense of the northwest against the Indians. Colonel Jacob Tipton, his son (first named Armistead Blevins Tipton, changed after his father's death)[40] came to the county in 1821 as one of the earliest settlers.

The first County Court was organized and held on December 1, 1823, in the house of Nathan Hartsfield, approximately two miles from the present site of Covington. The court was organized and conducted by the first magistrates appointed for Tipton County by Governor Carroll: Nathan Hartsfield, John T. Brown, Jacob Tipton, Andrew Greer, John C. McKean and George Robinson.

The site of the county seat was donated by John C. McLemore and Tyree Rhodes.

Early the county became known for its excellent facilities for education and culture.

"No town or village in the Western District had better schools at that time than Covington. . . .

Among the citizens of wealth and personal merit, who early settled in the vicinity of Covington were those of the families of Tipton, Dunham, Garland, Brown, Roberson, Hill, Harper, Pryor, Lauderdale, Coward, Cotton, Taylor, and many others whose names are identified with the early settlement of the Big Hatchie Country . . . ."[41]

---

[40] *Beginnings of West Tennessee,* Williams, p. 154.
[41] *Old Times in West Tennessee,* J. Williams, Chap. 7, p. 149.

On March 30, 1957, the Tipton Chapter N.S., D.A.R., was organized in Covington.[42]

Ripley was named in honor of General E. W. Ripley, who distinguished himself in the War of 1812. It is the county seat of Lauderdale County, established by the Legislature in 1835 and named for Colonel James Lauderdale, who distinguished himself in the Battle of New Orleans, also in the War of 1812.

A large spring in a ravine near the public square was the natural attraction which caused the site of the town to be selected. On February 24, 1836, about sixty-two acres of land were purchased from Thomas Brown by the commissioners and the town of Ripley was laid out by Abel H. Pope.[43] A log court house was built during that year.

J. N. Smith conducted the first mercantile business in a log cabin.[44]

"Old Times in West Tennessee" was written in Ripley when its author, Joseph Williams, was a lawyer in the town.

Ripley was first chartered in 1838.

The home of Joseph Wardlaw, built on what is now "Sugar Hill," was the first frame house in the town.

Eylau Plantation consisting of 10,000 acres comprised the famous estate of Dr. Samuel Oldham, located eight miles east of Ripley and about twelve miles from Brownsville in Haywood County. The splendid colonial mansion on the land was completed in 1835. Often the house was the scene of abundant hospitality extended by Dr. and Mrs. Oldham to friends from Memphis and towns nearby.

There is worthy evidence of Dr. Samuel Oldham's devotion to the Episcopal Church. In 1839, the Rev. John Chilton reported to the Diocesan Convention, as recorded in the "History of Christ (Zion) Church," Brownsville, that his time had been divided between St. Gregory's Chapel and Woodville, near the northwest corner of Haywood County. "This town was in the neighborhood of 'Eylau,' the well known residence of Dr. Samuel Oldham, a communicant and faithful supporter of the Church." In 1841, "Mr. Sheppard, M. Ashe, Egbert Sheppard and Dr. Samuel Oldham were delegates from the Parish (Zion Church, Brownsville) to the Convention held in June at Columbia." In 1844, Bishop James Hervey Otey reported to the Convention that he "visited the Parish (Zion) and held services on October 10, and preached in the Presbyterian Church . . . . On the 11th . . . etc. Left next A.M., for Dr. Oldham's at 'Eylau' near Woodville."

---

[42] Nina Early (Mrs. William A.) Shoaf was the Organizing Regent.

[43] *Lauderdale County From Earliest Times,* by Kate Johnston Peters, 1957, Chap. 5, p. 72.

[44] *Beginnings of West Tennessee,* Williams, p. 163.

1846, "The report of the Parish includes the family of Dr. Oldham, of "Eylau" . . . . 1849, "Dr. Robert H. Oldham, a delegate to the Convention." 1850, "Zion was in charge of the Rev. Cyrus Waters . . . who was also in charge of congregation at Ripley, County seat of Lauderdale and 20 miles from Brownsville." The Parish Register (Zion) signed by the Rev. Mr. Waters November 1849 lists: "Samuel Oldham, M.D., Mrs. Cornelia C. Oldham, Robert Oldham, M.D., Ripley." Recorded under "Marriages: October 9, 1880—Laura Cornelia Oldham to John H. Owen." Under list of communicants from date of organization of the Parish (Zion), August 25, 1832 are "Samuel Oldham, M.D., died at Eylau, Haywood County; Mrs. Cornelia C. Oldham, died at Eylau, Haywood County; Robert Oldham,[45] M.D., died at Ripley, Lauderdale County."

Lauderdale County records show that when town lots were sold in Ripley that Samuel Oldham bought lot 40 for $190.00.[46] It is not known that this was the same lot given for the Episcopal Church in Ripley, named "Immanuel." However, in Goodspeed's History of Tennessee is found: "The Episcopal Church erected in 1858 was of frame and cost $1,500. It was standing upon a lot donated by Dr. Samuel Oldham."

Of peculiar interest is the unusual call which is a part of the town charter. This unique feature has received national comment. In Chapter 223, House Bill 692 this is recorded:

. . . thence North 85 degrees East to a black gum marked with a cross and with mistletoe on the top, and with a blue bird sitting on a limb, ...[47]

With this description included, this charter was approved April 3, 1901, by Benton McMillin, Governor of Tennessee.

Gibson-Port was the name given first to the present town of *Trenton* in Gibson County.

The first house erected, before the location of the town, was built of logs by Col. Thomas Gibson and was used as a small store prior to 1821. It was in honor of Colonel John H. Gibson, an older brother of Colonel Thomas Gibson, and a gallant soldier, that the County of Gibson was named.

A Commission appointed in 1824 to choose a site for the County Seat of Gibson County was composed of James Fentress, Benjamin Reynolds, William Martin and Robert Jetton. The total land allocated for the town

---

[45] Dr. Robert Honeyman Oldham, son of Dr. Samuel Oldham, married Laura Partee; their daughter, Laura Cornelia Oldham married John Hobson Owen. Among their children were Cornelia Owen, who married Judge Davie Edington, and Elizabeth Owen, who married Dr. W. A. Alexander. (Notes by Rosa Lee Evans [Mrs. Edward N.] Johnston, Brownsville and Memphis.)

[46] *Lauderdale County From Earliest Times,* by Kate Johnston Peters, 1957, Chap. 5, p. 73.

[47] *Ibid.,* p. 76.

covered fifty-six and a quarter acres. The acreage was donated by James Whitaker, John Hogg, Jesse Blackburn, James Caruthers and Frank McGavock.[48]

By Legislative Act it was provided that the first County Court sessions should be held at the house of Luke Biggs, about four miles from the present town of Trenton. Later, on May 24, 1824, Judge John C. Hamilton held Circuit Court at the home of William C. Love. A log court house was completed soon thereafter.[49]

On the committee appointed to lay out the town and to sell the lots were: J. B. Hogg, William C. Love, John W. Evans, Robert Tinkle and John P. Thomas. The commission placed the following advertisement in the *Jackson Gazette* on June 4, 1825:

> Lots in Gibson-Port, Gibson County, will be sold July 20, 1825, on a credit of 12 months. From a test of a few years' experience, no doubt will be entertained with regard to health; the town is free from many causes destructive to health. Adjacent to the site are four never-failing springs. The river is now navigable within about seven miles of the town at all seasons of the year for keelboats of the largest size. The distance from the Mississippi to this landing point will not exceed one-half the distance from the Mississippi up South Fork to Jackson. Roads have already been marked out from Gibson-Port in all directions through the county and will soon be cut.[50]

When it seemed advisable to change the name of the town from Gibson-Port, Tennessee's Governor Carroll influenced the choice of the name of "Trenton." The name was changed to Trenton in 1825 and the town was incorporated in 1826.

The Elizabeth Marshall Martin Chapter N.S., D.A.R., of Trenton was named for a patriot of the American Revolution. She was the wife of Abram Martin and was the mother of Capt. Matt Martin, born 1763, a soldier in the Revolutionary War.

Trenton is a town deeply rooted in the traditions and culture of the old South. The Gibson County Fair held annually in Trenton is the oldest in the South. The first Fair was held October 22, 24, 1856. Fine horses continue to be an outstanding feature of the Fair. For many years the Trenton Bar was considered among the finest in Tennessee because of the quality of the local men of the legal profession who were its members. Today, Trenton is also modern in progressive business and thriving industry.

---

[48] *Gibson County Past & Present,* by Frederick M. Culp and Mrs. Robert E. Ross, 1961, p. 69.

[49] *Beginnings of West Tennessee,* by Samuel Cole Williams, p. 144.

[50] *Gibson Co.,* by Culp and Ross, p. 69.

Among family names familiarly identified with Trenton's history are: Adams,[51] Biggs,[52] Birmingham,[53] Cooper, Deason, Fielder, Fite, Freed, Harrison, Harwood,[54] Herron, Hillsman, Hogg, Inman, Jetton,[55] Keenan, Landrum, Lea, Love, Marshall,[54] McCaul, McRee, Neil,[56] Oppenheimer, Raines, Ross, Scrape, Seat, Smith, Taylor,[57] Tyree, Whitaker, Williams, Wilson,[54] Dance, Elder.

Carved from the extensive plantation acres, the property of Gen. Samuel Jackson Hays in Shelby County, is a town of three names. Located on the Louisville and Nashville railroad, built in 1856, is the incorporated town of *Arlington,* first known as Haysville and later as Wythe Depot.

---

[51] Judge Harry M. Adams, Memphis, was born in Trenton. He graduated from Fitzgerald School, Trenton, 1908, and from Central College, Fayette, Missouri, 1912. In college he starred in athletics. In 1915-1916, he was principal and coach at Arlington High School, Arlington, Tenn. He studied law at Washington and Lee University. He was in the Navy, 1917-1919. He married Miss Grace Harris, Norfolk, Virginia, and returned to Memphis, where he has been a successful lawyer. He retired Sept. 1, 1958, after having been for twenty-four years Judge of the Circuit Court, Division I. Judge and Mrs. Adams are communicants of Calvary Episcopal Church, where he has served faithfully as Senior Warden.

[52] Dr. Zack Biggs (son of Luke Biggs) married Julia Ella Raines (daughter of Mr. and Mrs. Edward Raines). Their children: Albert W. Biggs, who married Margaret Pharr; Latta Biggs, who married J. Preston Jetton.

Mr. and Mrs. Albert W. Biggs were the parents of Albert W. Biggs, II, who married Virginia Brodnax (daughter of George T. Brodnax). Mr. and Mrs. Biggs, II, had a son, Dr. Albert W. Biggs, III, presently of Memphis, who married Merry Spaugh. Albert Biggs, II, died when his son was a small boy. Virginia Brodnax Biggs married Dr. Sam Raines of Raines Station (Whitehaven).

[53] Dr. William F. Outlan, Collierville, Tennessee, is the son of Arch Booth Outlan and Hazelle Birmingham (Outlan). She was a daughter of William E. Birmingham and Emma Duncan Birmingham of Trenton. Dr. Outlan married Miss Lucia Chandler. Dr. and Mrs. Outlan are communicants of St. Andrew's Episcopal Church, Collierville.

[54] Elizabeth Marshall Wilson was born in Trenton, the daughter of Harwood and Charlotte Virginia Grizzard Wilson. She married Jan. 20, 1930 James Jackson. They have one daughter, Charlotte Jackson, who married Dr. Lewis Lunsford, Jr., and they are the parents of Lewis Lunsford, III, born Oct. 7, 1960. Mrs. Jackson is a member of the Zachariah Davies Chapter N.S., D.A.R., admitted on the Revolutionary War record of Matt Martin, South Carolina (Nat. No. 424027).

[55] Robert Jetton was descended from the Jetton family, which settled early in Davidson, North Carolina on land presently occupied by Davidson College. A relative, Mary Jetton (daughter of John Jetton), married John Thomas, Ensign, Revolutionary War, from North Carolina.

[56] The spacious colonial home of the late Judge and Mrs. M. M. Neil in Trenton stands today beautifully preserved and occupied by their two daughters, Mrs. R. L. (Florence Neil) Jordan and Mrs. Harwood (Virginia Neil Elder) Wilson. Mrs. Jordan is listed among Gibson County's outstanding native citizens. She is a musician of unusual ability and has been prominently identified with music, literary and historic-patriotic groups in Memphis. (Mrs. Wilson died in 1963.)

[57] Matthew Hillsman Taylor, born in Trenton August 4, 1884, married Miss Katherine Baird Taylor (a daughter of Governor Bob Taylor, no relation). Mr. Taylor, named for a distinguished Baptist minister of Trenton, Dr. Matthew Hillsman, was the son of Col. Robert Z. and America "Mettie" Clementine Ivie Taylor, and a grandson of Basil Manly Taylor. The children of Mr. and Mrs. Taylor are: Robert, Sally (Mrs. Millsaps Fitzhugh), Betty (Mrs. Duncan Dobson) and Matthew Hillsman,

Doubtless, the first plat of Haysville was sketched between 1857 and 1860. The streets in the town were named largely for members of the Hays family, for early settlers, for persons prominent in the civic, social and political life in Jackson, Tennessee, and for leaders of the State and of the Episcopal Church. Among the names of the streets in Arlington are those of: Battle, Brown, Campbell, Chester, Cuningham, Deaderick, Douglas, Forrest, Garrett, Greenlee, Griffin, Jackson, Karr, Marley, Motte, Polk, Preston, Quintard[58] and Walker.

As early as 1828 a trading center had begun. From Virginia, North Carolina, Georgia and South Carolina families came during the succeeding years. A community of splendid citizens was settled.

Arlington boasts the second oldest[59] continuous general mercantile business in Shelby County, the S. Y. Wilson Company, established in 1893.

The Memphis District High School, sponsored by the Methodist Church Conference, established at Wythe Depot opened in January 1884. One hundred students had enrolled by 1885 and each paid a tuition fee of $4.00 per month.[60]

The churches of Arlington, with their dates of organization, follow: Cumberland Presbyterian, built the first church-house in Haysville in 1871; land was given for a Methodist Church in 1881; the Episcopal Church—The Church of The Holy Innocents[61]—was built in 1882 and on land given to the Diocese of Tennessee by Ephraim E. and Sarah Butler Greenlee; the Presbyterian Church dates from 1909; the Baptist Church was organized in 1947 and the Church of Christ was built in 1959.

Collierville, named for pioneer Jesse Collier, was one of the early settlements of Shelby County in 1820.

Chartered in December 1835, the Memphis and LaGrange railroad was the first railroad chartered by the Legislature of Tennessee.[62] This railroad ran from Collierville to Colonel Epp White's plantation, a stop which became known as White's Station. In 1842[63] the completion of the line made possible the first train trip in Tennessee. In 1850, the charter of the Memphis-LaGrange line was purchased by the Memphis and Charleston

---

Jr., called "Peter." Mr. Hillsman Taylor has been for a number of years a prominent attorney in Memphis.

[58] The street bears the name of the Right Rev. Charles Todd Quintard, Second Bishop of the Protestant Episcopal Church, Diocese of Tennessee.

[59] The oldest continuous general mercantile business in Shelby County is that of James H. Barret and Sons, established in 1856 at Barretville, Tennessee.

[60] *History of Arlington Methodist Church* (1881-1956), Mabel Williams (Mrs. L. W.) Hughes, 1956.

[61] *The Church of The Holy Innocents, Episcopal, 1856-1929,* Ellen Davies-Rodgers, 1963.

[62] *History of Tennessee* (Shelby County) by Goodspeed, p. 343.

[63] *Ibid.,* p. 810.

Railroad Company. An event worthy of record was the shipping of three bales of cotton, grown by Andrew Taylor of Collierville to Memphis by rail on October 30, 1852.[64] By 1857 the road was completed and opened for regular traffic.[65]

In Memphis, the completion of the railroad was highly publicized and hailed as a master accomplishment because the road made travel possible from the Mississippi River to the Atlantic Ocean.

Quoted from a guide book given to the first passengers on the trains is the following:

Collierville twenty-four miles from Memphis occupies a high position on the ridge. The town contains about 250 residents and sustains a number of stores and produce houses; several mechanical shops. There are also Male and Female High Schools (academies) and a mixed (boys and girls) school for juveniles. The Methodists, Baptists, Camp-settlers and Cumberland Presbyterian Congregations comprise the religious denominations. Passengers alight here for Macon, Tennessee, as there is a stage triweekly.[66]

Collierville was incorporated by an Act passed February 17, 1870.

The Civil War took its dastardly toll of the population of the village, leaving it a most desolate place with few houses and businesses standing, poor dirt roads and unsanitary conditions.

Collierville is today a healthful, thriving, attractive community with a supply of pure water. The town offers adequate fire protection to its residents. Eight new industries have been established within the area during the past ten years. The present population of Collierville is about two thousand persons. A. G. "Chip" Neville is Mayor of the town.

Named in honor of Colonel Robert Henry Dyer, a North Carolinian of military prowess and associate of General Andrew Jackson, Dyer County has as its chief city, *Dyersburg*. First known as McIver's Bluff, in 1834, the town was laid out and lots sold in 1825.[67]

A two-story log court house was built in Dyersburg in 1827. The town boasted 100 inhabitants in 1833 and in 1836 it was incorporated.

Key Corner Chapter, Daughters of the American Revolution, is an active hereditary-patriotic group in the community, organized April 2, 1940.

The name *Woodstock,* by which a small community in northwest Shelby County is known, is colorful, literary and historic. Samuel Rembert II chose the name, according to tradition, for two reasons.

---

[64] Commerce Title Record, Mid-South Title Co., Memphis, Tenn. (1961), p. 21.
[65] *History of Collierville*, by Elizabeth Baker (Mrs. W. D.) Parr, 1949. Mrs. Parr is a member of Zachariah Davies Chapter N.S., D.A.R., Brunswick, Tennessee.
[66] *Commercial Appeal* (clipping), 1940, from Scrap Book of Alice Cartwright (Mrs. Milton K., Sr.) Mann, a member of Zachariah Davies Chapter N.S., D.A.R.
[67] *Beginnings of West Tennessee,* by Williams, p. 143.

In 1875 the Illinois Central railroad was established from Memphis to Covington. The line passed through the area already settled by several pioneer families with plantation acreage. Trains of that period required as fuel both wood and water. The wood by which the engines were fired was cut and piled as cord-wood[68] at necessary intervals along the railroad right-of-way.

Therefore, a stop for wood and for water was made simultaneously. So this particular train-stop began to be called "Wood-Stop," where Benjamin Hawkins supplied both wood and water for the engines. However, Samuel Rembert II in his wide reading, which included the works of Sir Walter Scott, had found the English name "Wood Stock." Thus with a stock of wood awaiting a train stop, the name became colloquial and the words were combined as *Woodstock*.

Two Revolutionary War claims were filed for all of the land on which Woodstock is presently located and for about two miles to the north. These were grants No. 561 for 2,000 acres in favor of William Alston[69] lying on the north side of Loosahatchie River and adjoining grant No. 465 of 2,000 acres, a claim by James Robertson. William Alston died before the Chickasaw Purchase of 1818 and his heirs sold the grant to Andrew Rembert.

With his young wife, Mary Sayre, and their infant son Samuel Rembert II, Andrew Rembert came to Shelby County, Tennessee, from Georgia early in 1820. A "double log" house[70] was built near the northern boundary of the property and he began with diligence to hew a plantation from a wilderness. Cool springs with abundant water prevailed in the area. Persons traveling between Randolph and Memphis often stopped at the watering place which became known as Rembert Town or Rembert Town Springs.

Several years after the settling of Andrew Rembert and his family, Samuel Rembert, Andrew's father, a son, James, and several daughters came. The senior Rembert acquired 5,000 acres of land adjoining the lands of his son, Andrew, to the east near Lucy. Soon a log-house, commodious for its time, was erected on a well-chosen site on the vast acreage.

In 1832 Samuel Rembert was one of the ten founding-members of Calvary Episcopal Church, Memphis, Tennessee. On the occasion of Bishop

---

[68] A rack of wood which measures 8 feet long, 4 feet high and 4 feet wide.

[69] Lieut. Col. William Alston, Warren County, N.C., b. Dec. 25, 1736, d. Elbert County, Georgia, about January, 1810. Married Charity Lillington Alston (a first cousin), b. North Carolina, d. Elbert County, Georgia, 1823. Their daughter, Nancy, married William Henderson Tait. Descended from Col. Alston are these members of the Zachariah Davies Chapter, N.S., D.A.R.: Mertice Norris (Mrs. Paschal) Foster (Nat. No. 424022); Vadis Norris (Mrs. T. Walker) Jeter (Nat. No. 424024); Mertice Vinton Jeter (Mrs. David) McGehee (425026); Vadis Norris Jeter (Mrs. Joe Charles) Hester, Jr. (424025).

[70] Two log rooms built with an open passageway between, commonly called a "dog-trot."

Otey's first visit to the Western District he arrived in Memphis on December 19, 1834. He visited the home of Samuel Rembert and also went to Randolph. At Ravenscroft Plantation he confirmed Phillip W. Alston, who became, five years later, rector of Calvary. Bishop Otey came again in 1836 and "found the road to Memphis thronged with Indians."[71] He spent the night of October 14 just outside Memphis with the Samuel Rembert family where he received "a cordial welcome."[72]

After the death of his wife in 1838, Samuel Rembert sold his property[73] to John Wesley Ward, a Virginian, and returned to his plantation in Georgia. The property became known as Walnut Grove Plantation, Lucy, Tennessee.[74]

One of the first frame houses erected in the Woodstock area was started in 1844 by Andrew Rembert. The house of hewed timbers and bricks made of native clay for the giant chimneys, remained unfinished in 1845 at the time of Andrew Rembert's sudden death. His son, Samuel II,[75] inherited the plantation and completed the house.[76]

Thus the area of Woodstock became populated by descendants of the Rembert family: Benjamin Hawkins, a Confederate soldier who married Miss Nancy Ward, an heir to part of Walnut Grove Plantation, had built a house and Colonel Henry Lee Douglass, with his wife, the former Miss Lucy Little of Littleton, N. C., came from Fayette County, Tennessee, in 1871 and bought 1,153 acres. And others came to make the community of Woodstock their home: Thomas Branch, who married Eliza (Lyde) Saunders—a daughter of Dr. David Saunders; Dr. William Henderson, who married Margaret Steele; Andrew Ward; the Wynn family and John Molder.

St. Ann's Episcopal Church,[77] Woodstock,[78] was built on land given by Benjamin Hawkins. Among the early organizers of the church were members

---

[71] *St. Mary's Cathedral,* by John H. Davis, p. 14.
[72] *Ibid.*
[73] Sold land in early 1840's.
[74] The land has been owned by descendants of the Ward family to the present time. For a number of years it has been the home of Mr. and Mrs. James Phipps (Fanny George) Chase.
[75] Samuel Rembert II married Miss Anne Duncan, daughter of Benjamin and Nancy Ross Duncan of "Big Creek," Shelby Co., Tenn. They had twelve children, several of whom died young. Andrew Rembert, killed at Shiloh; Samuel, III, married Nancy Brown; Henry married Alice Lewis; Margaret married Robert Steele; Virginia married Terrell Goldsby, and Ruth married William H. Williams, were the other children.
[76] The Rembert House, also known as "Seven Hills," is presently owned by a great-granddaughter, Miss Anne Charlotte Williams, who makes her home there.
[77] See Chart of Churches, Western District, Chapter 3.
[78] Research for this account was done by Rembert H. Williams, Jr., Lay Reader, St. Ann's Episcopal Church, Woodstock, and by Nancy Cocke (Mrs. Wayne A.) Lester.

of the families of Douglass, Henderson, Saunders, Rembert, Steele, Hawkins and Barrom.

Samuel Rembert II had the first store in Woodstock, yet the store in operation longer than any other in the community was "Hawkins Store." Other stores in the area were owned and operated by Dave Bolton, R. H. Williams, M. E. Branch and J. C. Carter.

There is an active Baptist Church in the community.

Since 1900 several incidents of importance have been experienced by the village of Woodstock and the area surrounding. The opening of a medical clinic by Dr. Lon C. Johnson was a step of great value in community progress. Dr. Johnson, with Mrs. Johnson at his side, continues to serve the people in his helpful humanitarian manner, made possible by his broad knowledge of medicine.

One of the first local airports was the one built at Woodstock by Mr. and Mrs. Vernon Omlie.[79] The eighty acre field was dedicated on Armistice Day 1926. Mrs. Phoebe Omlie became a foremost aviatrix of the nation and was a warm friend of the noted Amelia Earhart. On this field, Charles Lindbergh landed sometime after he had been acclaimed a famous flier. Mrs. Omlie is today an able authority on air travel.

Today industrial plants own hundreds of acres of the fertile farm land of the area. Yet, with the many recent citizens, new jobs, different noises and the unusual odors (from the chemical plants) the Illinois Central trains, powered by oil burning engines, pass swiftly through the village of Woodstock, whose name was in part created by the needs of the locomotive of long ago.

The original two hundred blocks which comprised the town of *Union City* were laid out on February 22, 1854. General George W. Gibbs, then president of the Hickman Railroad, provided the site for the town on his farm which was located at the junction of the present L. and N., and G. M. and O. railroads.[80]

Obion County, because of its heavily timbered acres and the excellent hunting available within its bounds, was among the last counties in West Tennessee to be developed.

During the Civil War, Union City was made a camp of instruction by Confederate authorities, because of the town's excellent railroad facilities. At that period the town was occupied on occasions by numbers from 5,000

[79] W. Percy McDonald, one of Memphis' first aviation enthusiasts, had much to do with the development of this airport and of the Memphis Municipal Airport, built later. Mr. McDonald is a prominent Memphis lawyer and is Chairman of the Shelby County Board of Education.

[80] Bulletin, Chamber of Commerce of Union City, Tennessee (Brief Historical Sketch).

to 20,000 men. Twice, General Nathan Bedford Forrest with a small number of Confederate soldiers kept the Federals away, however, the town was in Federal hands at the close of the War.

By 1870, with a growing population of 1,000, Union City was a lumber market engaged in recovering from the ravages of the Civil War and in making progress toward prosperity for its citizens. This progress has been continuous through the years and today Union City is a modern agricultural and industrial center.

Union City became the County seat of Obion County in 1889.

The Reelfoot Chapter D.A.R., was organized in Union City, April 18, 1932.

Established on the route of Shelby County's first railroad, the Memphis and Charleston (now the Southern) was *Germantown*. Early, a number of German families chose this high land, thus the name. However, during World War I the town's name was temporarily changed to "Nashoba."

Business was there as early as 1830—the first merchant was Mr. Rash. By 1834, Col. G. P. Shepard had laid out town lots and streets in Germantown. The town's first incorporation by act of the Tennessee Legislature was on December 28, 1841.[81]

A traveler's guide around 1857 spoke in glowing terms of the town,

". . . with two hotels, three churches, a cotton gin, a school for boys and one for girls, and, just east of the town, the Shelby Classical and Military Institute of which Col. A. M. Rather was superintendent." It is noted that residents of the town of Germantown patronized "three nearby resorts in evergreen groves, Nashoba, White Sulphur and Brunswick Springs. The inhabitants are generally moral, intelligent and a reading people . . ."[82]

Among other family names long associated with Germantown are those of: Bennett, Brooks, Callis,[83] Garner, Hanks, Harrison, Kimbrough, Kirby, Messick, Moliter, Moore, Neely, O'Neill, Pettus, Richmond, Strickland, Walker, Ware and Yancey.[84]

---

[81] Commerce Title Record, p. 20.

[82] *Ibid.*, pp. 20-21.

[83] Descendants of Major William Overton Callis, of Virginia, settled in Germantown. Three members of the Zachariah Davies Chapter N.S., D.A.R., were accepted on the record of Major Callis: Carrie Callis (Mrs. Phillip) Sullivan (Nat. No. 479365) and her two daughters, Adelaide Sullivan (Mrs. Stuart McGinnis) Dean and Caroline Sullivan. Franky Jones (Mrs. Joseph W.) Callis is also a Chapter member on the record of Michael Robinson, N.C. Mrs. Sullivan and Joseph W. Callis were brother and sister. Their mother's maiden name was Florence Moore.

[84] The Yancey family of Germantown has been for several generations identified with the Episcopal Church. Dr. Edwin Thomas Yancey, presently a citizen of the town is the third Dr. Yancey to bear the full name. Through his paternal grandmother, Mary May Anderson, he is descended from Mary Hayes Willis (Mrs. Thomas Benn) Gloster, the founder of the Episcopal Church in West Tenn., and through Mrs. Gloster, the lineage goes to the Revolutionary War ancestor, Corp. William

One of the beautiful old houses of Germantown which stands in an excellent state of preservation with original boxwood hedges is one known as the Esq. George W. Thomas House.[85] The land around the house originally consisted of one hundred fifty acres. For many years Mr. Thomas was an enterprising merchant of Germantown. Mr. Thomas was born in North Carolina May 23, 1837, the son of Lewis Washington and Anne Iredell McCulloh Thomas. He was a grandson of Ensign John Thomas, who served in the Revolutionary War from North Caorlina and a great-grandson of Jacob Thomas, an original landowner of Iredell County in that state.[86]

The present splendid school in Germantown, built in 1911, proudly bears the name "Mabel C. Williams High School" in honor of Mabel C. Williams (Mrs. Louis Wearen) Hughes,[87] a life long resident of Arlington, Tennessee, and one of the nation's distinguished educators. She, too, is descended from Ensign John Thomas and Jacob Thomas of North Carolina.

The largest unincorporated town in Shelby County is the thriving community of *Whitehaven* through which sweeps the Hernando Road.

Colonel Frank Marion White of Como, Mississippi, moved to the area on which the present Whitehaven Schools are located and settled there. He was influential in building the old Mississippi and Tennessee Railroad, which ran from Grenada to Memphis and became in 1880 the Illinois Central. In honor of Col. White the stop along the railroad was given in 1846 the name "White's Haven." With the establishment of a post office in 1871 the name became *Whitehaven*.[88]

Plummer of North Carolina. Lotta Lee Yancey (Mrs. H. T.) Adair (Nat. No. 489201), a sister of Dr. Yancey, III, and her two daughters, Nancy Adair (Mrs. Devereaux) Cannon and Kathryn Adair (Mrs. Morgan) Zook are members of the Zachariah Davies Chapter, N.S., D.A.R., on the record of William Plummer. Dr. and Mrs. Yancey, Mr. and Mrs. Adair are communicants of St. George Episcopal Church.

[85] Present owners of the Thomas Place are Mr. and Mrs. Enoch Brown.

[86] Annie Laurie Thomas (Mrs. Henry Wheatley Davis), a daughter of George W. Thomas and Mary Frances Scott Thomas, and her granddaughter, Helen Davis (Mrs. Christopher W.) Harlow were organizing members of the Zachariah Davies Chapter, N.S., D.A.R. (1935). Frances Ann Davis and Christopher W. Harlow, Jr., great-great grandchildren of George W. Thomas were organizing members of the Old Stage Road Society C.A.R., and Wheatley Davis, a great-grandson, was an organizing member of the Shelby Chapter, S.A.R. Each was accepted for membership on the Revolutionary War record of John Thomas, Ensign, N.C. The record was accepted first for the membership of Frances Ina Stewart (Mrs. Gillie M.) Davies (N.S., D.A.R., Nat. No. 352906), a member of Zachariah Davies Chapter. The record of Jacob Thomas was accepted first for membership by the Daughters of the American Colonists for Mrs. Davies (Nat. No. 14950).

[87] See *Who's Who of American Women* (1958-59): Mrs. L. W. Hughes, Supt. of Shelby County, Tenn., Schools 1909-1915; President, National Congress of Parents and Teachers, 1946-1949; Regent, Zachariah Davies Chapter N.S., D.A.R., 1948-1950.

[88] A History of Whitehaven (a manuscript) by Kathryn Farrow, 1950. The Whitehaven Press, Sept. 15, 1960 (Sketches on the history of Whitehaven).

Whitehaven has as its boundaries Tchulahoma Road on the east; State Line Road on the south; Brooks Road on the north and the old Horn Lake Road on the west. With a population of more than 55,000 persons, the community is located within seven miles of Memphis' Court Square.

Someone has unwittingly remarked: "Whitehaven has no character!" To one whose knowledge of and association with the people of this community has covered many years, this statement seems ridiculously lacking in factual content. Definitely there is character! Its character is truly that of a sprawling, overgrown country town, steeped in quaint home-folksy charm and neighborliness. Yet, there are flashing modern features which embody convenience and progress. Its citizens are busy. They are appreciative and the refinements of living are everywhere conspicuous in this growing community totally representative of the true spirit of Shelby County.

Extensive accounts could be written in relating the history, the legends and the "tall" tales of adventure long associated with the south-lands of Shelby County merged in great closeness to the northern border of the beloved, neighboring state of Mississippi. That two Indians owned the land on which Whitehaven is located is a matter of record. Toby Tubby and Luke Measles were the names of the Indians. The need of a sure way to travel to the Chickasaw Bluffs from Hernando made necessary an improved road. Therefore, a road once an Indian trail and over which wagons and stage coaches came from the East became a major thoroughfare. Plantation owners along the route decided in 1853 to charter the Memphis and Horn Lake Road. It became a plank road, financed by stockholders, for which a toll was charged. In 1885 the planks were removed from the road and it was surfaced with gravel. The route became the Hernando Road, now Highway 51 South.

Other roads, as created in the community, have taken names of citizens and places identified with the area. For example—Tchulahoma (an Indian name); Holmes, Hale, Raines, Farrow, McCorkle, Scaife, Brooks, Swinnea, Palmer,[89] Graves, Craft, McClure, Chambliss, Hollyford (now Airways), Davis Cove and others.

Among the earliest settlers who came to the community were:[89a] Benjamin Hildebrand, 1819; Dr. Kelsey Nelson, 1830; John Elam, 1833; Dr. Alfred Eldridge, 1836; Tinsley Davis, 1838; Monroe Roberson, 1843; John H. Van Hook, 1845; William Henry Hudgens, Wash and Marion Isbell, Lemuel Farrow and Finlay Holmes in 1849.

---

[89] The Palmer family gave the land for the first Christ Episcopal Church, Whitehaven (See Chart of Churches, Chapter 9).

[89a] A History of Whitehaven (a manuscript) by Kathryn Farrow 1950.

Dr. Eldridge brought with him from Virginia his daughter, Anne Eliza Eldridge. There came also two young doctors who were "reading-medicine," under his tutelage, as such was called in those days. One was Dr. William Nathaniel Raines. He married Anne Eliza Eldridge in 1844. Through the years descendants of these pioneer citizens have been prominently identified with the Raines and Whitehaven Communities.[90]

Businesses have grown during the years. Early, Benjamin Hildebrand had a mill and general store at the corner of Millbranch and Capleville Roads. In 1880, Willis Dean built a store on Hernando Road at Capleville Road. In 1894 the store was taken over by his son-in-law, J. W. Hale, and has since been known as J. W. Hale and Son. The "son" was the late, distinguished E. W. Hale, who began service as a member of the Shelby County Commission in 1912. Mr. Hale served as chairman of the Shelby County Commissioners from July 17, 1922, until he retired on December 31, 1955. The firm continues to be listed thus today, address—4671 Highway 51 S.

No account of the Whitehaven area should be written without reference to several of the old homes which remain and to others which have suffered the ravages of time. Of interest today are Cottage Home (Raines-Meux house); Faronia;[91] Spottswood Manor; McManus (or Powell) House; Eason House (or Plunkett Place) and East Lothian (Elam home). Former houses of interest were West Lothian, once the home of Edward Dozier Bray, who gave in 1866 the original acreage for Otey Memorial Chapel and Lambert Logs, destroyed by fire a few years ago.

Many, many new houses line the roads, new and old, throughout the community. Every type of architecture may be seen in houses costly and in those of cheaper construction. Though not new and yet not old, these three houses are named: Haledale,[92] Greenlawn[93] and Graceland.[94] Each is of interest in the community in a very special way.

---

[90] Miss Anna Leigh McCorkle of Whitehaven, daughter of Lena Raines (a daughter of Dr. Wm. Nathaniel Raines and his wife, Ann Eldridge) and Joseph Harris McCorkle, has compiled a history of the Raines-Eldridge-McCorkle families.

[91] *Faronia*, built in 1869, is the ancestral home of four generations of the Farrow family. The six children of George Ferdinand Farrow (son of Lemuel Farrow) and his wife, Catharine Gooch Farrow, were born in the house: Allen G.; May (md. E. A. Edmundson); Walter Dunn; Irene (md. Ford N. Taylor); Elizabeth (md. Robert Calvin Richey) and Kathryn Tate Farrow. Catharine Richey (Mrs. J. Karr) Hinton, Collierville, Tennessee, was born at Faronia. Mrs. Hinton is a member of the Zachariah Davies Chapter N.S., D.A.R. (Nat. No. 382879), on the record of Joseph Morton, Va., as was the late Miss Kathryn Farrow (Nat. No. 236257).

[92] *Haledale*—home of the late E. W. and Emma Kimbrough Hale. Presently owned by David and Madge Madden Harrison.

Miss Emma Kimbrough was born at Cotton Plant, south of Germantown. When a young lady, "Miss Emma"—as she was affectionately known by countless friends throughout her long, good life—went to teach school in Whitehaven. She met and

And what type of pioneer citizen came to the area later to be known as prosperous, plenteous (strong churches, good schools, fertile soil) prideful Whitehaven? Those who settled the community were largely of Scotch-Irish and English descent. People who were intelligent, morally strong, independent and thrifty. They were men of education and refinement, many of whom had come of families of wealth and influence in their native Virginia and North Carolina. To the "newly opened wilderness" they came, bringing with them their families and slaves to make a home. To buy and to sell Indian land, so recently inhabited by the Chickasaws, and to grow cotton were of prime concern to these industrious settlers. These able founders and their deeds of achievement lastingly wrought are Whitehaven's significant heritage.

Martin, a thriving town in Weakley County, was named for William Martin, who came from Halifax County, Virginia, to the County in 1832. He settled near the spot on which the town is located. About the same year, Thomas Martin, the father of William, also moved to the area.[95]

Not until 1873, however, was the town of Martin founded by Marshall P. Martin and his brother, sons of the original settler, William Martin.

The yellow fever scourge of 1878 resulted in many deaths in the community.

Of particular interest to the town and to the surrounding area of West Tennessee is the Branch of the University of Tennessee located in Martin. In this Branch of the University, courses in Agriculture and Home Economics are given especial emphasis.

---

married Mr. Hale. They had two children—E. W. (Will) Hale, Jr., and Alberta Hale (Mrs. Russell) Lyle.

The inspiration of Mrs. Hale's selfless service as a public-spirited, Christian lady lingers with all who knew her. She was beloved for her tireless interest and boundless energy exerted in behalf of the many causes by which she aided mankind toward a more abundant life. Cherished by the author are her great examples of leadership through which she bestowed affection, courage and confidence.

[93] *Greenlawn*—or the Hoyt Wooten house, was built in 1939. Mr. Wooten, formerly of Coldwater, Mississippi, is owner of WREC radio and television station, Memphis, Tennessee.

[94] *Graceland*—is the home of Elvis Presley, a favorite star of motion pictures and television.

Mrs. Ruth Brown Moore sold the house and acreage about 1952. An aunt of Mrs. Moore, Grace Toof, had owned the land since about 1880. The place bears her name.

S. C. Toof had three daughters: Belle, md. John G. Little; Grace; Ruth, md. Battle Manassas Brown. Mr. and Mrs. Brown had three children: Ruth Brown, md. Dr. Thomas Moore; S. Toof Brown and Bates Brown.

The only child of Dr. Thomas and Ruth Brown Moore was Ruth Marie Moore, who married Charles P. Cobb, son of Mr. and Mrs. Oliver P. Cobb of Whitehaven. Mr. and Mrs. Charles P. Cobb have four children: Thomas Oliver Cobb, Elizabeth Toof Cobb, Oliver Perry Cobb, III, Charles Pittman Cobb, Jr.

Ruth Moore Cobb is a concert harpist of rare ability.

[95] Letter from John M. Martin, Martin, Tennessee, a great grandson of Thomas Martin.

Camden, the county seat of Benton County, was surveyed in December 1836 and lots sold. The town was located on land of John Jackson.

The first settlement in the area had been made in 1819. Through Benton County passed an early Indian Trail on which settlers to the west later traveled.

Camden's first dwelling was erected by Irwin B. Carnes. Thomas H. Burton built the first store-house and Allen C. Presson taught the first school in 1822-1823.[96]

Humboldt in Gibson County is an interesting, busy town with a population of approximately 8,500 persons.

An early settler was John C. Gillespie, who came from North Carolina to the area (now Gibson County) in 1822. He was a farmer and in 1850 built a small store-house, which by 1857 had become something of a community center. In 1857 the Mobile and Ohio Railroad was built through the settlement and Mr. Gillespie became the first depot agent.[97]

John A. Taliaferro and W. A. Allison started a saw mill and a grist mill, which aided greatly in the development of the town.

Humboldt received its first charter of incorporation in 1866. The charter has been amended several times, as the town's government has improved. The first mayor was the Rev. Moses E. Senter, a Baptist minister.

A post-office was established in Humboldt in 1858.

The West Tennessee Strawberry Festival, organized in 1934, has brought national recognition to the town.

Raleigh, known for many years as Raleigh Springs was prior to this period of its fame, the county seat of Shelby County in 1827.

On December 1824, four Commissioners were appointed by the Legislature to select county seats for the organized counties of West Tennessee— James Fentress, Benjamin Reynolds, William Martin and Robert Jetton. The site chosen for Shelby County was at Sanderlin's Bluff on fifty acres of land owned, almost equally in amount, by Wilson Sanderlin and James Freeman. Lots were sold and public buildings constructed.

Shelby County's first Circuit Court Clerk, was Joseph Graham, a native of Raleigh, North Carolina. Thus the name "Raleigh" was chosen in consideration of Mr. Graham's former home-town.

The first settler of the area was a Mr. Tapp, who came in 1816.[98] Commonly known as Tapp's Hole—"where Raleigh's first white resident

---

[96] *Beginnings of West Tennessee,* Williams, p. 164.

[97] *Gibson County Past and Present,* by Frederick M. Culp and Mrs. Robert E. Ross, Trenton, Tennessee, 1961.

[98] *History of Memphis,* by Keating, Vol. I, p. 135.

trapped his game,"[99] — a seemingly bottomless pit was "a place containing some peculiar natural physical features, the source of some excellent medicinal springs whose virtues were accidentally discovered by Dr. Coleman in 1842."[100] The Raleigh Springs were four in number, each was distinct in its own particular chemical analysis and were classified as "Marble Spring, Freestone Spring, Box Spring and Beach Spring."[101] In the 1870's Raleigh Springs became a resort of wide patronage. The building of the Raleigh Inn and of the Raleigh Springs Electric Line were both valuable improvements to the town.

Among other early residents of Raleigh were: Dr. David Coleman, Benjamin McAlpin, James Wilson, W. P. Reeves, Elias Pharr, J. R. King, Dr. Benjamin Hawkins, E. H. Porter, Jefferson Messick, Samuel McMurray Allen,[102] Benjamin Duncan, John Only, Abram Bayless and William Battle.

The very old Raleigh Cemetery—atop precipiced Sanderlin's Bluff—where sleep the pioneers, continues to erode and cave into oblivion at the Bluff's base. Samuel H. Rembert and Wilson Sanderlin are among those interred in the old spot.

The historic name "Sanderlin's Bluff" was chosen for a chapter of the Daughters of the American Revolution headquartered at Raleigh and organized May 18, 1959.[103]

Among the homes at Raleigh, three are of particular interest: "Epping Forest Manor", estate of Mr. and Mrs. Berry Brooks, which contains a rare collection of objects of art and history; "Goodwinslow," immortalized by the late Anne Goodwin Winslow in *The Dwelling Place,* now the home of Mrs. Winslow Chapman. In the old brick jail house of Raleigh's county-seat days, Mr. and Mrs. John T. Willins have lived for fifty-five years.

---

[99] "The Three Lives of Raleigh," by Loula Green Mallory, *West Tenn. Hist. Quarterly,* 1959, Vol. 13, p. 78.

[100] Goodspeed, *History of Tennessee,* p. 911.

[101] The Springs have been owned for several years by Mr. and Mrs. Julian Fulenwider. Their daughter, Joan Fulenwider (Mrs. Raymond) Strong, is a member of the Zachariah Davies Chapter N.S., D.A.R., on the record of John Fulenwider, N.C. (Nat. No. 459230).

[102] Samuel McMurray Allen, b. 1805, North Carolina, d. 1878; md. 1826, Sarah Caroline Pharr, b. 1807, North Carolina, d. 1835. Sarah Caroline Pharr was a granddaughter of Walter Pharr (Farr), b. 1741, Ulster, Ireland; d. Dec. 22, 1799, Mecklenburg Co., N.C.; md. Jan. 1767, Sarah O'Brien, b. June 14, 1750, d. Dec. 1832. Walter Pharr was a soldier of the American Revolution. Three members of the Zachariah Davies Chapter D.A.R., who claim descent from this ancestor are: Mabel Williams (Mrs. L. W.) Hughes (Nat. No. 294732) and her granddaughter, Claire Allen Hughes (Nat. No. 479861) and Charl Ormond Williams (Nat. No. 210620).

[103] The Organizing Regent of Sanderlin's Bluff Chapter, N.S., D.A.R., was Ruth Malcolm (Mrs. James S.) Fleming.

CHAPTER VI

MRS. GLOSTER AND HER HORSE-RIDE

The foregoing sketches of history concerning those towns in West Tennessee, which contributed in great measure to the development of the vast new area, provide a fertile, picturesque geographical background for the beginnings and growth of the Episcopal Church in the Western District of the State. As written, the events having great bearing on potential progress in the State and in the Western Division as related to the religious, legal, social and cultural needs of the people were: the signing of the State Constitution by George Washington, June 1, 1796; the Chickasaw Treaty of 1818; the first Diocesan Convention of the Episcopal Church in Tennessee in 1829 and the consecration in 1834 of the Reverend James Hervey Otey as the first Bishop of the Diocese of Tennessee.

Throughout the preceding chapters a determined effort has been followed that the stage should be set historically, for the recording of the story of the coming of the Episcopal Church to the Western District. In reiteration, the effort has been and continues in nature two-fold: to consider the growth of the Episcopal Church in America, to tie with the whole movement the progress of the Church in West Tennessee, as a link in the puissant, ever lengthening chain of church history.

Therefore, let us here relate some facts of importance pertinent to the coming of the Church to the several communities to which we have already given consideration. Innumerable circumstances of livelihood and travel characterized the period dating from the Chickasaw Treaty, of 1818, and the coming of the Episcopal Church to the Western District in 1832. One of the most widespread migrations at the time was from the neighboring state of North Carolina.

The "Raleigh Register," Raleigh, North Carolina, on December 10, 1825, carried the following:

> There are nearly an hundred families in Orange, Chatham, Davidson and Rowan who are moving to the Chickasaw Purchase this fall. The emigration is astonishing.[1]

---

[1] *Beginnings of West Tennessee,* by Samuel C. Williams, p. 117.

Earthen jug carried by Mary Hayes Willis Gloster tied to her side-saddle
when she rode from La Grange to see Mr. Otey, 1832.
Photograph, courtesy of Dorothy Seymour (Mrs. R. C.) Harnden, Memphis, Tenn.

It is said that a severe drought in North Carolina in 1826 almost caused
near famine. Logs were burned that were obstructions in streams or
waterways.

In 1827 a correspondent from North Carolina stated that during
the last four months the flow of emigration through Asheville has
surpassed anything of the kind the writer has ever witnessed. It was
not uncommon to see 8, 10 or 15 wagons and carts passing in a single
day . . . wending their way to the more highly favored climes of the
West.[2]

[2] *Ibid.,* p. 118.

Among the many families who came to the Western District, during this period from several of the states, not one came imbued with greater zeal and affection for the cause of the Episcopal Church than did the Gloster-Anderson family from Warrenton, North Carolina. Thrilling and of historic value is the story of their coming!

"We removed to Fayette County in the Western District of the State of Tennessee from North Carolina in the Fall of the year 1827," wrote Elizabeth Willis Gloster (Mrs. John) Anderson.[3] The group of Church people which came from Warrenton to LaGrange consisted of Mary Hayes Willis (Mrs. Thomas Benn) Gloster, widow of Dr. Gloster; her son, Arthur Brehon Gloster; her daughter, Elizabeth Willis Gloster and husband, John Anderson and their five children,[4] and George Anderson, John Anderson's brother. Truly, they were a family of stout-hearted Christians and staunch supporters of the Episcopal faith.

An unusual record of the departure of Mrs. Gloster and her family from Warrenton and from Emmanuel Church, Warrenton, follows:[5]

The public ordinances were as well attended as on former occasions. In the Warrenton congregation the administration of the Lord's Supper was rendered peculiarly affected by the circumstances, that the appointment was requested at this particular time to meet the desire of the most numerous and influential family belonging to the Church in that place, for the last time to unite with their brethren in that Holy Ordinance previous to their removal to the Western Country. This family, Mr. and Mrs. John Anderson and five children moved to Fayette County, Tennessee.

"Sketches of Old Warrenton, North Carolina"[6] written by a communicant of Emmanuel Church, Warrenton, Mrs. Lizzie Wilson Montgomery, relates the story of the removal of the Gloster-Anderson family to the West. The account is quoted by Mrs. Montgomery from a letter dictated by Mrs. Ellen Mordecai at the age of ninety-five to her daughter:

I could not have been more than seven years old when the family moved to the Western Country, the vague name for what then seemed the remote region, now Tennessee. I can never forget the starting; when the whole village came to say good-bye. The looks of the big covered wagon, loaded with all their belongings. The stamping of the big-footed horses and all the bustle incident to such an occasion. The vehicle for the family was made strong for the needs of a long journey, which took weeks to accomplish. Warrenton was a friendly, unconventional little place then."

---

[3] "Written for Her Children" by Elizabeth Willis Gloster Anderson (unpublished booklet), p. 12.

[4] The names of the Anderson children are listed elsewhere in this volume. Chap. 3.

[5] *Diocesan Journal*, North Carolina, 1928, p. 17.

[6] Published 1924.

So, it was in the Fall in 1827, that the widow, Mrs. Gloster, with her son, Arthur B. Gloster; her daughter, Elizabeth Willis Gloster (Mrs. John) Anderson; her son-in-law John Anderson; her Anderson grandchildren and George Anderson, a brother of her son-in-law, arrived in LaGrange, Fayette County, Tennessee. The town was at that time a growing community characterized by wealth, education and culture.

At the time of LaGrange's incorporation, in 1828, there were 240 inhabitants, 60 houses, 4 stores, 2 taverns and a dozen mechanics! Yet, not one church had been established within the borders of the town![7]

The absence of a house of worship in LaGrange greatly disturbed Mrs. Gloster and the members of her family, who had brought with them lasting memories of their devout religious experiences while communicants of Emmanuel Church and residents of Warrenton, North Carolina. They were church people who sorely felt the absence of church privileges. Seemingly, to these newcomers, LaGrange had everything to offer as a desirable place of abode, except a house of worship. Therefore, Mrs. Gloster and her family determined to do all within their power to supply the community's greatest need!

Several accounts have been written descriptive of Mrs. Gloster's dramatic and inspiring service in behalf of the bringing of the Episcopal Church to the Western District. However, no research has revealed a more interesting, and it is felt more accurate, account than the following written by the late Miss Mae Anderson, a great-granddaughter of Mrs. Gloster.[8]

All of my life I have been told that the little church, Immanuel, a picture of which hangs on my wall, was Grandfather's church and that his negroes made the bricks from which it was built. He, Uncle George and Grandma and Grandma Gloster were so lonely for the church service and dear Mr. Green,[9] the first permanent rector in Warrenton and his good helpful sermons. They decided to have a church service at the Anderson home, asking those citizens who might like to join them. This they did and in a short time had a good congregation. Since Grandfather John Anderson always had prayer morning and evening in his home; I'm sure he read the service. This was the first service of the Episcopal Church held in the District of West Tennessee, then separate from the East.

In 1832, Grandma Gloster decided to go and see the Rev. Otey, her godson and Episcopal missionary in Tennessee. She rode on horseback with one of Grandfather John Anderson's good reliable old family negroes. The Rev. Otey, at once wrote to New York for a missionary, the Rev. Wright. Soon he organized Immanuel Church in LaGrange

---

[7] *Commercial Appeal,* Sunday, June 8, 1952.

[8] From a letter to Mr. Charles A. Tucker, Warrenton, North Carolina, from Miss Mae Anderson, El Paso, Texas, June 16, 1954, age 88 years.

[9] The Rev. William Mercer Green.

at a meeting of the citizens. For a while they used a small frame building provided by the family—Glosters and Andersons. Uncle George
died one year after the church was built and his executors had to give
bond for $100,000. This meant his estate equalled the bond, so I know
he contributed, to the church. He was twice a member of Warrentown
Vestry and Grandfather[10] was Senior Warden.

Since reading the History of the Church in Tennessee by the
Rev. Noll, I'm sure all the members contributed. I am sure Grandfather had most to do with it. It is right next to the land where the old
Anderson home stood—ten acres, and I'm sure Grandfather contributed
the land.

At the time Mrs. Gloster made the eventful ride to see Mr. Otey she
was fifty-two years of age. Family tradition has related that in one arm, as
she rode her horse, she held a grandchild, and that below her other arm,
tied to her side-saddle, was an earthen jug filled with peach brandy. Mrs.
Gloster's reasons were—the grandchild's presence would protect her from
any advances by males and the brandy would ward off chills and
fever! The stone jug remains today a prized possession of Mrs. Gloster's
descendants.[11]

No other woman has made a more significant journey in behalf of the
extension of the Episcopal Church in Tennessee than did dedicated, energetic, determined Mrs. Gloster. Her memorable horse-ride deserves to be
fully recorded in the annals of Church history as a selfless act wherein a
sincere Christian Lay-woman was busy about the business of her Heavenly
Father.

As enduring evidence of the religious fruitfulness of Mrs. Gloster's
journey and the far-reaching movement created by her effort, five churches
were organized in the Western District during the year 1832. St. Luke's,
Jackson, was organized by the Rev. Thomas Wright on July 23, 1832.[12]
Zion (Christ) Church, Brownsville, came into being on August 25, 1832 as
a result of the efforts of the Rev. Mr. Wright and the Rev. John Chilton.[13]
Immanuel Church, La Grange, was constituted under the guidance of Mr.
Wright and the Rev. Samuel George Litton.[14] Also organized by the Rev.
Mr. Wright was Calvary Church, Memphis, and St. Paul's at Randolph.
In reality, the founding of these churches became a record of the journey
of the pioneer missionary-organizer, the Rev. Thomas Wright, "through the
counties of Madison, Hardeman, Haywood, Fayette, Lauderdale, Tipton

---

[10] John Anderson.

[11] The jug is in the possession of the Rev. Charles M. Seymour, Jr., Rector,
Trinity Parish Episcopal Church, St. Augustine, Florida.

[12] Noll, p. 70.

[13] *History of Zion (Christ) Church*, Brownsville, Tennessee, p. 1.

[14] Noll, p. 70.

and Shelby."[15] Truly, the history of every parish and of every mission in West Tennessee is traceable to the consecrated determination of Mrs. Gloster, the influential vision of James Hervey Otey and the conscientious labors in the broad, challenging field by the Rev. Thomas Wright and his associates, the Rev. John Chilton and the Rev. Samuel George Litton.

To her—Mary Hayes Willis Gloster—must be accorded the title, "Mother of the Episcopal Church in West Tennessee." Resounding through one hundred and thirty-one years, her children in the faith and her children of the flesh rise up and call her "blessed."

> .   .   .   .   . happy he
> With such a mother! faith in womankind
> Beats with his blood, and trust in all
>   things high
> Comes easy to him, and though he trip
>   and fall
> He shall not blind his soul with clay.[16]

[15] *Ibid.*, p. 71.
[16] Author unknown.

CHAPTER VII

THE FIRST EPISCOPAL CHURCHES IN WEST TENNESSEE, 1832

Death of Bishop Otey, 1863
Dr. Quintard Elected Bishop, 1865

The five parishes organized in West Tennessee in 1832 had all credentials in order for admission to the Diocese at the fifth annual convention of the Episcopal Church held in Franklin, Tennessee, in 1833.[1]

Because of the founding significance of the five early churches in the Western District, which were admitted to diocesan fellowship in 1833, it seems appropriate that a brief sketch of the history of each of these be made a part of this account.

In the Masonic Hall in Jackson, where persons friendly to the Episcopal faith had gathered on July 23, 1832, the Rev. Thomas Wright of North Carolina presided over the organization meeting of the parish of *St. Luke.* Those who signed the Articles of Association were among the pioneers of Madison County.[2]

Until 1844, at which time a frame church was erected, places of meeting were the Madison County Court House, the Male Academy (now Union University) and the Methodist Church. It was in the Methodist Church that Bishop Otey held services in 1839.

Most significant was the occasion of Jefferson Davis' appearance in 1870 to address the congregation of St. Luke's Church, an opportunity shared by his many friends in Jackson. This was his first public speech following his release from prison. The crowd was so large that it overflowed the Church! This necessitated the moving of the meeting to a nearby grove in front of the splendid house of the late Samuel Jackson Hays, Mr. Davis' close friend for many years.

St. Luke's has been enlarged several times and the edifice today is one of the most beautiful to be found in this section. The exquisite pieces of religious art, the old bell dating back to 1853, the completely furnished

---

[1] Noll, p. 71.
[2] *Historic St. Luke's, Jackson, Tennessee,* by Lena Graham James (1962).

St. Luke's Church, Jackson, Tennessee

Christ Church, Brownsville, Tennessee

Immanuel Church, LaGrange, Tennessee

Calvary Church, Memphis, Tennessee

interior of black walnut, the stained glass windows and the numerous, meaningful memorials add great meaning and distinction to the historic, sacred setting.

The Rev. John Chilton was the first rector of St. Luke's and served from 1832-1834.

The Rev. John Chilton, the first minister ordained in the Diocese of Tennessee, was the first rector of *Zion Church*, Brownsville, in Haywood County. There were five communicants at the time of the organization of the parish on August 25, 1832.

In the report of the parish to the 1833 Diocesan Convention, Mr. Chilton stated, "The congregation worshipped in an upper room of the Court House, comfortably fitted up for the purpose," and he also spoke of "The pious zeal manifested for the cause of God." Bishop Otey in his message to the convention gave an account of his visitation to Zion Church on March 29, 1834.

Records show that during the succeeding years, prior to 1840, the Rev. Mr. Chilton preached at St. Andrew's in Fayette County, St. Gregory's Chapel and at Woodville. Mr. Chilton died at his father's home in Overton County in September 1840 and was buried there. During his ministry in West Tennessee he had made his home on a farm about two miles from Brownsville. In his will he left a burial plot on his farm known as Zion Cemetery and it was used by the members of Zion Church for interments.

Bishop Otey in his address to the 1841 Convention reported the death of the Rev. Mr. Chilton:

> From the date of his ordination to the time of his death he was in charge of parishes, at Jackson, Brownsville, and other places in West Tennessee. He was a very faithful priest and missionary and greatly beloved by his people and all who knew him.

In 1842 the Rev. Thomas West reported as minister in charge of the parish at Brownsville:

> This has been a year of considerable debility and hard labor to the missionary, yet, attended with many mercies and some encouragement. My field has been the counties of Haywood, Fayette, Tipton and Madison and my rides from twenty to fifty miles from place to place. My services have been two or three times a week in dwellings, school houses or some place of worship. The Lord gave me favor in the sight of the people, so that my poor labors have not been in vain in the Lord. My health is declining and like all my predecessors I must shortly submit to age and infirmities.

Among the rectors who served the church in later years were the Reverend Messrs. Louis Jansen, James M. Rogers, Cyrus Waters (from Maryland), J. A. Wheelock, Charles Francis Collins, R. A. Cobbs, J. J.

Ridley, Matthew Henry, Irenaeus Trout and Dr. Nevill Joyner. Prof. John P. Wendel came to Brownsville in 1856 and served as organist at Zion Church for nearly forty years.

Zion Church became Christ Church in 1898 following Bishop Gailor's canonical consent to change the name.[3]

The very small Episcopal Church built first in LaGrange now stands as the vestry of *Immanuel Church.* The Gloster-Anderson home was first used as a place of worship prior to the building of the small church. The present classical brick structure was erected and consecrated in 1843. Recent restoration has resulted most pleasantly in charting for many years to come the preservation of this venerable edifice.

During the Civil War, Immanuel Church, LaGrange, was a special target for vandals. Blinds and windows were broken, walls defaced, seats were removed and made into coffins for the dead of the Union Army! After the war the people of LaGrange made the necessary repairs.[4]

Since that day in 1832 when the Rev. Thomas Wright gathered with Mrs. Gloster, the Anderson family, and other citizens in LaGrange and organized a church of the Episcopal faith, which Mrs. Gloster called "Immanuel" for the church from whence they had come in Warrenton, North Carolina, the church has stood in the community ever a sentinel of faith, a harbinger of hope. Especially, it is a monument to the devotion of its founders.

A bronze tablet mounted on the wall of the vestibule of Immanuel Church commemorates Mrs. Gloster's contribution to her Church. The inscription follows:

To the Glory of God
and
in memory of
Mary Hayes Gloster
A.D. 1780 A.D. 1854
Beginning A.D. 1827
She was the leader in organizing
this church and erecting
this building.

....

This tablet was erected by the Rev. J. F. Plummer, minister, September 24, 1939. Among Mrs. Gloster's descendants present were James F. McNamee, Mrs. Lucy Wynn, C. E. Mason, Mrs. Bettie Prewitt, A. P. Rose and Mrs. Charles J. Wade.

---

[3] History of Zion Church, Brownsville, Tenn. (Early records compiled by The Rev. Charles Francis Collins. Unpublished).

[4] "Church at LaGrange," by Mrs. Margaret Letitia Wilkinson (written in her 91st year, a communicant), 1928 (an unpublished article).

A roadside marker to Immanuel Church stands in LaGrange at a nearby road intersection and gives the following record:

4 E 15

Immanuel Church

This Protestant Episcopal Church was first established as a mission in 1832 consecrated in 1843. Rev. Samuel George Litton was its missionary and first rector. It was established by the efforts of Mrs. Mary Hayes Gloster, a widow from Warrenton, N. C. Her slaves built it in exact copy of the church at her former home. Tennessee Historical Commission.

Of especial interest in the consideration of the sketches of history pertaining to the last two of the five churches organized in 1832 in the Western District, is the fact that Calvary in Memphis and St. Paul's at Randolph had beginnings in common.

Memphis — "It was but a prosperous village in 1832, a competitor for municipal importance upon nearly equal terms with the town of Randolph and of less consequence than LaGrange."[5]

It is entirely probable that a similar scene greeted the eager missionary-organizer, the Reverend Thomas Wright, as was experienced later[6] by Bishop Otey upon his arrival in Memphis, as recorded in the Bishop's Diary: "Rode to Memphis. The town was filled with Indians and the people too briskly engaged in traffic to think of their spiritual interest."[7]

Yet, there gathered on August 6, 1832[8] in a building on Second Street, between Adams and Washington, a group of faithful Christians interested in sharing the tenets of the Episcopal faith. There under the zealous leadership of the Rev. Mr. Wright, *Calvary* parish was chartered and in September, which followed, the church was organized with ten communicants.

Up the Mississippi River, a distance of thirty miles, Mr. Wright traveled to Randolph. From Randolph on August 11, 1832, he wrote a letter to his wife in which he related an account of his activities in Memphis and of his effort in Randolph. He gave this impression of the people of the Western District in the letter: "There is much more intelligence throughout the District than I had anticipated."[9]

The energetic Mr. Wright became Calvary's first rector and was also in charge of *St. Paul's*, Randolph. The pressing needs of the two churches bore heavily on the dedicated minister. Spurred by his awareness of the great cause to be served, Mr. Wright went to New Orleans in January, 1835. He

---

[5] Noll, p. 19.
[6] On December 19, 1834.
[7] Noll, p. 71; *Commercial Appeal*, Centennial Edition, Jan. 1, 1940.
[8] *History of St. Mary's Cathedral*, by John H. Davis, 1959, p. 12.
[9] *Ibid.*, p. 13.

went to solicit aid for the Church, "in order to enable the few Episcopalians in Memphis and Randolph to erect two small and plain church edifices."[10]

The founders of Calvary worshipped in the upper room of the Town Hall and in the little log school-house in Court Square, where Col. Eugene Magevney taught school. It was in 1838 that the first frame building was started. By 1844 a brick church had been erected at the corner of Adams and Second and was consecrated by the Rt. Rev. James H. Otey on May 12, of that year. There were one hundred fifteen communicants of Calvary Church at that time.[11]

Calvary was the only organized parish in Memphis in 1852, when Bishop Otey moved from Columbia to Memphis to make his home.[12] Between 1858 and 1859 Bishop Otey served as rector of Calvary parish.

At the twenty-sixth annual convention held in Knoxville in 1854, Charles Todd Quintard, M.D., was a delegate from St. Paul's Church, Randolph.[13] In Calvary Church on January 21, 1855, Dr. Quintard was ordained to the diaconate. In 1857 he became rector of Calvary Church.[14] And, it was in Calvary Church that the Right Reverend Charles Todd Quintard held, on November 28, 1865, his first service as Bishop of Tennessee.[15]

St. Paul's Church, Randolph, was burned during the Civil War.[16]

Calvary's communicants presently number one thousand five hundred nine, making her the largest parish in the Diocese of Tennessee. The Reverend Donald Henning, D.D., L.H.D., the present Rector, has faithfully served the Parish since 1949. The Rev. Anderson Orr is Associate Rector*; the Rev. Wyatt C. Hurst, Sr., Deacon and Dr. Adolph Steuterman is Organist and Choirmaster.

Today, in stately brick she stands—the Mother-Church Episcopal in down-town Memphis, hallowed by service and memories innumerable; a revered and beloved shrine—historic Calvary Church at Second Street and Adams Avenue![17]

That Tipton County, in West Tennessee, once vied with Maury County in the number of organized Episcopal Churches is worthy of mention. In Maury County there were St. Peter's, Columbia,[18] consecrated 1834; and

---

[10] Calvary Church Record, Memorandum of the Rev. Thomas Wright.
[11] *Ibid.*
[12] Noll, p. 110.
[13] *Ibid.*, p. 136.
[14] *Ibid.*, p. 137.
[15] *Ibid.*, p. 159.
[16] *Ibid.*, p. 146.
[17] The Hestyr Shortridge Chapter, Woman's Auxiliary, Calvary Church, is engaged in the project of writing a history of Calvary.
[18] Noll, p. 94.

St. Mark's,[19] Williamsport, and St. John's,[20] Ashwood, each consecrated in 1840. Tipton County had these churches: St. Paul's Church, Randolph, admitted to union with the Diocese in 1833; Ravenscroft Chapel, consecrated 1836; Trinity Church, Mason and St. Matthew's Church, Covington, organized in 1846.

The 1860 Diocesan Journal carried the proceedings of the Thirty-Second Annual Convention of the Protestant Episcopal Church in Tennessee. The meeting convened in St. Peter's Church, Columbia, on May 16-19. The list of the clergy of 1860, twenty-eight in number, as recorded in the Journal follows:

> The Rt. Rev. James H. Otey, D.D., L.L.D., Diocesan, Memphis;*
> The Rev. Charles F. Collins, Rector of Trinity Church, Tipton County;*
> The Rev. William Fagg, Rector of Immanuel Church, LaGrange;*
> The Rev. William C. Gray, Deacon-Missionary at Trenton, Dresden, Etc.;*
> The Rev. Wm. D. Harlow, Missionary at Edgefield;
> The Rev. John A. Harrison, Rector of St. Luke's Church, Jackson;*
> The Rev. George C. Harris, Rector of Church of Holy Trinity, Nashville;
> The Rev. Richard Hines, Rector of St. Mary's Church, Memphis;*
> The Rev. Thomas W. Humes, Rector of St. John's Church, Knoxville;
> The Rev. B. S. Judd, Deacon, Residing at Winchester;
> The Rev. Thomas B. Lawson, Missionary at Chattanooga, Cleveland, Etc.;
> The Rev. Henry T. Lee, Residing in Louisiana;
> The Rev. Edward McClure, Rector of Grace Church, Memphis;*
> The Rev. Thomas A. Morris, Missionary at Winchester;
> The Rev. Wm. Mowbray, Deacon, Missionary at Greeneville;
> The Rev. J. Thomas Pickett, Rector of St. James' Church, Bolivar;*
> The Rev. David Pise, D.D., Rector of St. Peter's Church, Columbia;
> The Rev. Charles T. Quintard, M.D., Rector of Church of the Advent, Nashville;
> The Rev. Joseph J. Ridley, D.D., Rector of Trinity Church, Clarksville;
> The Rev. James W. Rogers, Rector of St. Thomas Church, Somerville;*
> The Rev. Moses S. Royce, Residing near Franklin;
> The Rev. R. D. Shindler, Residing at Ripley;*
> The Rev. Leonidas L. Smith, Rector of Christ Church, Nashville;
> The Rev. Jonathan B. T. Smith, Missionary at Shelbyville;
> The Rev. Wm. E. Webb, Missionary at Murfreesborough;
> The Rev. George White, D.D., Rector of Calvary Church, Memphis;*
> The Rev. Bob Shepherd, Absent without leave;
> The Rev. Franklin G. Smith, Suspended. Not entitled to a seat in convention.

---

[19] *Ibid.,* p. 99.
[20] *Ibid.,* p. 100.
*Mr. Orr has entered the University of Virginia as a candidate for a Master's Degree. He hopes to enroll at Oxford in the Fall of 1964.
*In West Tennessee.

The death of Bishop James Hervey Otey on April 23, 1863, had left the Diocese of Tennessee without a bishop during the remaining years of the Civil War. It was on September 7, 1865, that Dr. Charles Todd Quintard was elected to the Episcopate of the State. On Wednesday, October 11, 1865,[21] Dr. Quintard was consecrated in St. Luke's Church, Philadelphia, at the first meeting of the General Convention following the Civil War.

That the hostilities of needless vicious warfare had ceased and that unity prevailed in the Church, gave cause for great thanksgiving by those who experienced the 1865 Convention. Neither personal nor sectional opinions and prejudices were permitted to be injected into the religious services of the Convention. The Churchmen present were dedicated to the preservation of the catholic precepts of the Protestant Episcopal Church in the United States. Entirely significant was the fact that even though several dioceses had united during the War to form the Episcopal Church of the Confederate States of America, they had never been dropped from the roll of the General Convention. "Though absent, the right of the Southern dioceses to be present was not denied! They were still regarded as members of the American National Church."[22] There were lay delegates from Tennessee, North Carolina and Texas at the 1865 Convention.

That Dr. Quintard's attitude toward the Federal government during the war had been made crystal clear by the official position in which he served, was never denied. Yet, when his name was presented to the House of Deputies as the Bishop-Elect of Tennessee and when the votes were cast, there was but one dissenting vote. By their approval, Dr. Quintard became the first Bishop of the Episcopal Church consecrated after the Civil War. "In Christ there is no North or South."[23]

The long, tedious years of Reconstruction confronted Bishop Quintard. Infinite courage and equanimity were needed if church-houses were to be rebuilt and bewildered, despairing congregations revitalized for vigorous worship. Attention to the many obvious depreciated needs of the Church was necessary. The program and power of the Church, the spreading of Church influence, benevolences and the field of missionary endeavor, each brought the need of analysis and of appropriate action.

Bishop Quintard, immediately after consecration, challenged by the gigantic commission which he had accepted, began to build firmly and soundly. His deep concern involved the gathering together of the people again; the repairing and rebuilding of church edifices; the enlistment of new ministers; the re-establishment of the University of the South; the urgency

---

[21] Noll, p. 158.
[22] *Ibid.*, p. 156.
[23] *So Great a Good* by Hodding and Betty W. Carter, 1955, p. 147.

of financial help and the adjustments to be made because of changed political and economic conditions.

As churches were restored or constructed throughout the diocese, each was of concern to Bishop Quintard. His keen sense of church architecture, coupled with his belief that beauty in structure and in appointments should characterize a house of worship, brought most acceptable rewards. Along the line of church architecture he elevated the taste of the people.

The Bishop's personal interest was expressed by gifts to many churches in the diocese. A number of churches have exquisite stained glass windows which were given by Bishop Quintard.

Representative of these priceless gifts is the Strahl-Marsh window in St. James Church, Bolivar, Tennessee. In Bishop Quintard's Memoirs of the Civil War is recorded:

> Just before moving toward Franklin, General Strahl came to me and said, "I want to make you a present" and presented me with a splendid horse, the Lady Polk. I used the horse through the remainder of the war and at its close sold her and with the money erected in St. James' Church, Bolivar, a memorial window to General Strahl and his inspector, Lieutenant John Marsh, both of them killed in the fearful battle of Franklin. Both of these men I had baptized but a few months previously and both were confirmed by Bishop Elliott."[24]

The memorial window bears this inscription, "In memory of Otho French Strahl and John Henry Marsh. Died November 30, 1864."[25]

Another church which received a beautiful gift from Bishop Quintard was historic St. Luke's, Jackson, Tennessee. While he was in England in attendance at the Lambeth Council in 1867, ". . . the Duchess of Tech presented him with a beautiful brass Altar Cross and Alms Basin, an exact duplicate of the one he admired in Westminster Abbey. She asked him to give them to one of his churches in America. They were studded with stones. Upon the Bishop's return, he gave them to St. Luke's in Jackson."[26] Both are still in use and are indeed beautiful.

St. Andrew's Church, Collierville, Tennessee, whose cornerstone was placed on November 30, 1890, with distinguished Bishop Quintard officiating, was the recipient of a very beautiful and enduring gift by the generous Bishop. All of the exquisite stained glass windows in the Church, except the altar window—a memorial, were the gift of Bishop Quintard and came from England. It is believed that Bishop Quintard selected the lovely windows for St. Andrew in 1888, when he attended the Lambeth Conference.

[24] Quoted from "A Brief History of St. James Church, Bolivar, Tennessee," by Miss Elizabeth Ingram.

[25] General Strahl was a native of Ohio and Lieut. Marsh was from Bolivar, Tenn.

[26] *Historic St. Luke's, Jackson, Tennessee,* by Lena Graham James, 1962, p. 9.

Through the years, the beautiful windows have been cherished and preserved, not only for their intrinsic value, but because they serve as an appropriate memorial to their beloved donor, Bishop Quintard. However, in the 1940's a definite calamity was experienced. A terrific hail-storm struck the town of Collierville and the window over the front door of the church was damaged. A striking feature of this window is a medallion centered by a design of the Holy Bible. The hail caused the heavily leaded medallion to fall from its position in the window.

The first person to discover the damage was Robert,[27] the veteran, faithful church sexton and a valued servant of three generations of the Mangum family in Collierville. Immediately, Robert shuffled off and to the old home place to tell Mrs. Helen Mangum Bedford what had happened. In his inimitable manner he shared his sad and startling discovery. "Ole Miss," said Robert, "De Bible done fell out o' de Church!" The beautiful window was successfully repaired and the medallion with the Holy Bible restored. The parishioners were pleased although the expense had exceeded two hundred dollars. Robert was especially happy that the Bible was again in the Church window!

Among the problems of great concern to the Southern dioceses after the Civil War was that of the Negro race. Early, Bishop Quintard and Bishop Dudley of Kentucky worked diligently toward aiding the spiritual life of the Negro throughout the South.

History records the interest and guidance exerted by the Churchmen of the pre-Civil War period in the spiritual needs of the Negroes for whom they were responsible. Records were kept of births, baptisms and confirmations, often in the family Bible of the Churchman-plantation owner, or in the local Parish-Register.

Early in Bishop Quintard's episcopacy he said, in speaking of the act of confirmation for all people, "Let him be confirmed according to the usage of the Church." And, Dr. Arthur Howard Noll wrote: "No one had dreamed that the simple performance of an ecclesiastical act altered in any way the social relations of the two races."[28]

Throughout the South a number of plantation churches of the Episcopal faith were built long before the Civil War. Each church was created with the thought of its being a place of worship for all the people of the plantation-family, the master's family members and the members of the slave families. All attended the same service, all heard the same sermon.

It was no unusual sight at a Sunday morning service in these churches, after all the white communicants had received, to see the

---

[27] Robert Parish. Story as related to the author by Mrs. Eldon C. Cooper.
[28] Noll, p. 184.

altar rail thronged with negroes, partaking with reverence of the soul-nourishing food of the Body and Blood of Christ.[29]

Not only Episcopal Churches of the ante-bellum period were built with a gallery or a balcony, but church-houses of other denominations, as well. Such arrangements were made that adequate seating might be provided for the Negro families. A balcony for this purpose was in the original historic Morning Sun Cumberland Presbyterian Church[30] in Shelby County, Tenn.

The winds of separation swept rapidly and certainly following the evil War. Fanned and aggravated by outside interference, political motives became more apparent, leaving the organization of separate churches the prevalently acceptable decision.

The Episcopal Church did no other, when the challenge came, than to assume her responsibility as did other Protestant denominations in the South. As speedily as theological training could be provided for Negro ministers they were placed in charge of the congregations of their people and given every possible assistance. Among these Episcopal Churches organized during the succeeding years were: Immanuel Church, Memphis; St. Stephen, Burlison; Holy Comforter, Columbia; St. Cyprian, Gallatin; St. Thomas, Jackson; St. Paul, Mason; St. Augustine and St. Paul, Nashville and St. Paul-on-the-Mountain, Sewanee.[31]

The effort by other denominations was vast and genuine. In 1866, the "Colored Baptists" organized. In Murfreesboro, in 1869, "The Cumberland Presbyterian Church, Colored" was organized and directed by the Cumberland Presbyterian Church, yet carried on by Negro ministers. "The Colored Methodist Church" was organized in 1870. Thus, the Negroes were given the responsibility of the leadership of their own churches to be attended by them. "To fix their own standards of faith, of worship, of morals, and of Christian requirements or discipline," all these comprised their opportunity.

Slavery as a practice was wrong in every way—morally, spiritually and economically. No man should be an object to be sold into human bondage! The system is still to be abhorred. Yet, no enlightened person of the twentieth century can be so naive as to believe that slavery was a sin peculiar only to the South in ante-bellum days. Though the scheme may differ, yet today, a century removed from the Civil War era, slavery continues in the world among several races of men. Therefore, it is to be intelligently recognized that slavery in America prior to 1861, which involved the races—Caucasian and Negro—and slavery of the twentieth century are dissimilar in that color

---

[29] *Ibid.,* p. 178.

[30] On Morning Sun Road, off the Old Stage Road (Hwy. 64) near Lenow. Address, Arlington R., Tennessee.

[31] Noll, p. 187.

lines are not the distinguishing features! In this space age, illuminated by scientific research, such atrocities, which are the by-products of greed, of power and of human indecencies, become nauseating to think upon! May the spirit of the Psalmist prevail, "O let the wickedness of the ungodly come to an end; but guide thou the just!"

The excellent groundwork in education established by Bishop Otey, the teaching-preacher, was built upon by Bishop Quintard. Church schools and schools with "churchly aims" were continued and others established in the grand divisions of Tennessee. All of these were open and engaged in the advancement of learning a short while after Bishop Quintard had succeeded as the diocesan: University of the South, Sewanee; Columbia Female Institute, Columbia; St. Mary's School, Memphis (by Sisters of St. Mary); Fairmount School, Monteagle; Beechcroft School, Spring Hill; St. Katherine's Hall (St. James' Hall), Bolivar; Parish School for Girls, Cleveland; Bedford University (Otey School for Boys), Mt. Pleasant; Parish School for Girls, Fayetteville; Arnold School, Rugby; a School at Cumberland Furnace and Chattanooga Female Institute, Chattanooga.[32]

Of importance in the history of the Church in West Tennessee was the creation of the Convocation of Memphis in 1887.[33] This provision was enacted by the convention on recommendation of a report of the Committee on Canons presented by the Reverend Thomas F. Gailor. The report prescribed Canon XII.

I—"The Bishop, Clergy and Laity, in Convention assembled, shall constitute the Board of Missions for the Diocese, and shall set apart one night during each annual session for the consideration of the Missionary work of the Church."

II—"For its missionary operations the Diocese shall be divided into three districts as follows:

All that part of the Diocese lying east of the Cumberland Mountains, commonly known as East Tennessee, to be known as the Convocation of Knoxville.

All that part of the Diocese lying between the Cumberland Mountains and the Tennessee River, commonly known as Middle Tennessee, to be known as the Convocation of Nashville. All that part of the Diocese lying west of the Tennessee River, commonly known as West Tennessee, to be known as the Convocation of Memphis.

---

[32] Chattanooga Female Institute was founded by Bishop Quintard, 1872.
[33] Diocesan Journal, 1887, pp. 14, 15.

CHAPTER VIII

MEN OF THE CROSS AND GOWN

The Bishops of the Diocese of Tennessee, 1834-1964

Faithfully identified with the history of the Protestant Episcopal Church in Tennessee are the names of the stalwart men-of-God who have served since 1834 as the consecrated Bishops of the Diocese. Broad is the record of Christian service carried forward by these dedicated prelates of the Church within the State.

Long ago, St. Paul recorded the ageless qualities of character, of which a man should be possessed, by which his worthiness might be denoted to be consecrated a bishop.

This is a true saying, If a man desire the office of a bishop, he desireth a good work.

A bishop then must be blameless, the husband of one wife, vigilant, sober, of good behavior, given to hospitality, apt to teach;

Not given to wine, no striker, not greedy of filthy lucre; but patient, not a brawler, not covetous;

One that ruleth well his own house, having his children in subjection with all gravity;

(For if a man know not how to rule his own house, how shall he take care of the church of God?)

Not a novice, lest being lifted up with pride he shall fall into the condemnation of the devil.[1]

And without controversy great is the mystery of godliness: God was manifest in the flesh, justified in the Spirit, seen of angels, preached unto the Gentiles, believed on in the world, received up into glory.[2]

An account of the names of the Bishops of Tennessee, their years, their earned academic degrees[3] and honorary degrees[4]—conferred because of intellectual achievement expressed in effective Churchmanship,—with their periods as diocesans, comprises a formidable record in the annals of church leadership:

---

[1] The Holy Bible, I Timothy 3:1-6.
[2] The Holy Bible, I Timothy 3:16.
[3] History of St. Mary's Cathedral, by John H. Davis, p. 239.
[4] Ibid.

James Hervey Otey, D.D., LL.D., b. Jan. 27, 1800, d. Apr. 23, 1863
    Jan. 14, 1834-Apr. 23, 1863

Charles Todd Quintard, M.D., D.D., LL.D., b. Dec. 22, 1824,
    d. Feb. 15, 1898
        Oct. 11, 1865-Feb. 15, 1898

Thomas Frank Gailor,[5] S.T.D., D.D., LL.D. (Oxon), b. Sept. 17, 1856,
    d. Oct. 3, 1935
        July 23, 1893-Feb. 15, 1898 Bishop Coadjutor
        Feb. 15, 1898-Oct. 3, 1935 Bishop

Troy Beatty, D.D., b. Nov. 12, 1866, d. Apr. 23, 1922
    Sept. 18, 1919-Apr. 23, 1922 Bishop Coadjutor

James Matthew Maxon, D.D., LL.D., b. Jan. 1, 1875, d. Nov. 8, 1948
    Oct. 18, 1922-Oct. 3, 1935 Bishop Coadjutor
    Oct. 3, 1935-Jan. 1, 1947 Bishop

Edmund Pendleton Dandridge, D.D., b. Sept. 5, 1881, d. Jan. 28, 1961
    Sept. 20, 1938-Jan. 1, 1947 Bishop Coadjutor
    Jan. 1, 1947-Sept. 20, 1953 Bishop

Theodore Nott Barth, D.D., b. July 11, 1898, d. Aug. 22, 1961
    Sept. 21, 1948-Sept. 20, 1953 Bishop Coadjutor
    Sept. 21, 1953-Aug. 22, 1961 Bishop

John Vander Horst, D.D., b. Jan. 10, 1912
    Mar. 2, 1955-Apr. 19, 1961 Suffragan Bishop
    Apr. 19, 1961-Aug. 22, 1961 Bishop Coadjutor
    Aug. 22, 1961 Bishop

William E. Sanders, D.D., b. Dec. 25, 1919
    Jan. 19, 1962 Bishop Coadjutor
    (consecrated Wednesday, April 4, 1962 and became the 586th
    in American Succession)

To give even a partial biographical sketch of any one of the devout men who has served as Bishop of the Protestant Episcopal Church in Tennessee, one should be possessed of the vocabulary of the scribe, the knowledge of a theologian, the solidarity of a realist, the business acumen of a capitalist, the imagination of a dramatist, the wisdom of a philosopher and the psychology of a diplomat! In so many, many ways these able men, the Episcopal Bishops of Tennessee, have distinguished themselves through the passing years. Their qualities of superior character and their accomplishments bear testimony of their ever-widening influence in the lives of the communicants of the Episcopal faith and of others with whom association has been experienced.

---

[5] Dr. Gailor was the first Assistant Bishop in Tennessee. The title was changed to Bishop Coadjutor at the General Convention of the Episcopal Church in 1895. (Noll, p. 220, n.)

James Hervey Otey

The Right Reverend James Hervey Otey
First Bishop of the Diocese of Tennessee

James Hervey Otey was a brilliant and astute scholar, a distinguished teacher and a noble preacher. Because of the magnitude of the qualities of character which he possessed and of his greatness in the professions which he had chosen, he was a leading citizen of his age. Although he became "the patron saint of Tennessee Episcopalians," because of his long, fruitful ministry to the Church, he continued ever in the hearts of the people as an educator, a position of esteem in which he was held throughout his life.

In an attempt to classify the vocations and professions in which mankind has engaged, someone has said, "Those who do, those who neither teach nor preach!" After full scrutiny of this thought, it is obvious that the spokesman was either dividing the "doers" from the intellectuals, or was attempting to imply that teachers and preachers actually "do" very little!

Those who have experienced, either actively or vicariously, the professions of the minister and of the teacher, know full well the tremendous effort required and expended in each endeavor when the end sought is that of conscientious, dedicated service. Particularly, such is true when the pursuit is devoted to the lifting of the hearts and minds and souls of men toward a keener awareness of the God-given potentialities of every individual.

The measure of preaching and the function of teaching have always involved the use of every fiber of mind, of muscle and of spirit. One who engages in either profession must be mentally alert, physically well, emotionally sound and stable, clean of mind and body, pleasing both in words and deeds, good to be with and good to look upon! To be happy and effective in effort there must be abundant feeding of the heart and soul from the wellspring on high, giving to the individual—minister, teacher, "doer"—the vision to see the hills and beyond, an ever present source of eternal light.

When divine inspiration has been experienced, the interpretation remains the task of those who seek to share knowledge. If by the great unconscious influence of example, desire and determination can be provoked and lived convincingly by another, a significant role has become effective. When the warp and woof of the lessons taught and of the sermons preached become the cherished ideals of Christianity, the genuine by-products can be no less than love of God, respect for all men of good will, devotion to home and loyalty to the traditions which have made America a nation great and wonderful.

It will be then, the people will know that preachers and teachers are truly busy in well-doing and their service is not only to be sought, to be appreciated, to be nurtured, but is exceedingly indispensable. In such manner, the youth, the man—the learner—shall have had created within him a desire to be full in faith and in function, busy in righteous thoughts and deeds, a child in grace, worthy of the loving protection of the Heavenly Father.

Many were the churches organized by Bishop Otey in Tennessee and they were the State's first of the Episcopal faith.

These schools which he established give evidence of his keen interest in the great needs of education within the borders of his beloved adopted state:

1821—Harpeth Academy (for boys) opened December 19, Franklin, Tennessee.

1837—Madison College, Madison County, Tennessee. Charter granted. Plans discarded because of financial conditions. (Prior to 1837 Bishop Otey was laying a foundation for an Episcopal University in the South.)

1838—Columbia Female Institute,[6] Columbia, Tennessee, founded by Bishop Otey and Bishop Leonidas Polk.

"Bishop Otey returned from a northern tour on which he solicited funds for Columbia Institute, a school for girls, which he and Leonidas Polk were sponsoring. He brought with him $3,000 in cash and $5,000 in promises. The school had about 130 girls enrolled and was 'very flourishing'." (1840)[7]

1844—Mercer Hall[8] (for boys), Columbia, Tennessee.

1847—Ashwood School (for girls) on Columbia-Mt. Pleasant Pike (nearly opposite Hamilton Place, residence of Lucius J. Polk).

1848—Ravenscroft Male Academy, Columbia-Mt. Pleasant, Tennessee.

1860—University of the South, Sewanee, Tennessee. Cornerstone laid on October 9, 1860, by Bishop Otey, Bishop Polk and others (cornerstone destroyed by Federal troops during Civil War. After War—only a charter and 10,000 acres of land remained!).

At "Mount Prospect," his father's farm home located at the foot of the Peaks of Otter in Bedford County, Virginia, James Hervey Otey was born on January 27, 1800, the seventh son of twelve children. His parents were of stout-hearted, good English stock who were independent thinkers with courage and convictions, spiritual and otherwise.

One very early ancestor, John Otey, had been one of the signers of the death warrant for Charles I. John Otey, the grandfather of James Hervey Otey, served as a Colonel in the Virginia Continental Line in the Revolutionary War.[9] Isaac Otey, the father, was descended through his mother

[6] Noll, p. 123.

[7] *General Leonidas Polk, C.S.A. (The Fighting Bishop)* by Joseph H. Parks, 1962, p. 90.

[8] *History of Maury County, Tennessee* by Wm. Bruce Turner, 1955, p. 138.

[9] *Historical Register of Virginians in the Revolution (1775-1783)* by John H. Gwathmey, 1938, p. 597.

"from Sir John Pettus, a member of the British House of Commons . . . one of the founders of the Virginia Colony and a benefactor of Norwich Cathedral."[10] Isaac Otey served for thirty years as a member of the Virginia Legislature. James Hervey Otey's mother was Elizabeth Mathews, a descendant of Tobias Mathews, Archbishop of York.

Because James Hervey Otey in early childhood showed signs of superior native intelligence, he was given the best scholastic advantages which the community offered and at fifteen years of age was enrolled as a student in the University of North Carolina. After graduation in 1820 with highest honors, he taught Greek and Latin at the University and was popular with both faculty and students.

In 1821 James Hervey Otey and Eliza D. Pannill (March 31, 1800-June 1, 1861), were married. The young couple journeyed to Tennessee and on to Franklin, where Mr. Otey taught school.

The full, vital years which lay ahead began to come into focus and the review of these years is indicative of a life of abundant activity and a great urge for faithful service. These are periods and achievements from among the many which comprised the years of Bishop Otey:

1823—Principal of Warrenton Male Academy, Warrenton, North Carolina.

1824—Confirmation, May 8.

1825—Ordained a Deacon, October 10.
Returned to Harpeth Academy, Franklin, Tennessee.

1827—St. Paul's Church, Franklin, organized (1827)
Christ Church, Nashville
Revisited Warrenton, N. C. Ordained a Priest of the Episcopal Church, June 7.

1828—St. Peter's Church, Columbia, organized.

1829—First Diocesan Convention, July 1 and 2, Nashville.
Visitation by Bishop John Stark Ravenscroft, N. C.

1830—Second Diocesan Convention, Nashville.
Visitation by Bishop William Meade, Va.

1832—Third Diocesan Convention.
Visitation by Bishop Levi Ives, N.C.

Mary Hayes Willis (Mrs. Thomas Benn) Gloster rode horse-back from LaGrange, Tennessee, to Franklin to interest the Rev. Mr. Otey in sending missionary ministers to the Western District.

Five churches were organized in the Western District.

1833—Fourth Diocesan Convention.
James Hervey Otey elected the first Bishop of Tennessee, June 27.

---

[10] *History of the Diocese of Tennessee,* by Arthur Howard Noll, 1900, p. 51.

Five churches admitted to diocese from the Western District:
St. Luke's, Jackson; Zion, Brownsville; Immanuel, LaGrange;
Calvary, Memphis; St. Paul's, Randolph.

Diocese consisted of five Priests, three deacons, one church
building and about one hundred communicants.[11]

1834—James Hervey Otey, consecrated as Bishop in Christ Church,
Philadelphia, January 14.

Appointed Missionary Bishop of the Southwest—his jurisdiction covered all territory lying south of Kentucky and Missouri and from the eastern coast of Florida (to the Pacific
Ocean) including Texas and Louisiana.

First visitation to the Western District: Bolivar, April 17;
Memphis, Dec. 19; Ravenscroft (confirmed Phillip W. Alston).

Purchased house in Columbia built in 1820 by Dr. Wm.
Leacock,[12] once owned by James K. Polk (never lived there).
Later named house "Mercer Hall."

1836—Consecrated Ravenscroft Chapel, October 23.

1838—Columbia Female Institute established.

Bishop Leonidas Polk relieved Bishop Otey of all missionary
duties (in Southwest) except in Mississippi.

1844—Relieved of missionary charge of Mississippi.

Established "Mercer Hall" (named for friend and benefactor,
Dr. Wm. Newton Mercer of New Orleans.)

1850—To North Carolina, persuaded the Rev. Richard Hines to take
charge of St. Mary's Chapel, Memphis.

1852—Moved to Memphis from Columbia, November 12.

1859—Bishop Otey and Dr. Hines, two clerical delegates from Tennessee to General Convention, Richmond, Virginia.

1861—Last Diocesan Convention held until 1865.

In Tennessee there were twenty-six parishes, five missions
and thirty-four ministers.

War clouds everywhere! Bishop Otey did everything within
his power to prevent the Civil War.

Bishop Otey wrote two prayers: "Time of War and
Tumult"; "For Those in Service" and recommended their use
with Litany. Accepted recommendation that "Confederate
States" be substituted for "United States" in prayer for President.

By 1860: Bishop Otey had organized the Diocese of
Mississippi; had laid foundation for dioceses of Alabama,
Louisiana, Texas, Florida, Arkansas and had blazed a trail
through Indian territory for other missionaries to follow.

1862—Memphis fell to Federal gunboats. Bishop Otey returned from a
visit to his son, ill in Mobile.[13]

1863—Bishop Otey died in Memphis, April 23.

[11] *St. Mary's Cathedral,* by John H. Davis, 1958, p. 11.
[12] "Historic Homes of Tennessee D.A.R." by Ellen Davies-Rodgers, *N.S.,D.A.R.
Magazine,* August 1957.
[13] Davis, p. 37.

"He ascended at Easter-time." Funeral service was held at Calvary Church. His body was placed in a receiving vault at Elmwood Cemetery and after the Civil War was removed to St. John's Ashwood, Maury County, Tennessee, for interment.

1865—Sunday, September 10, Interment in St. John's Churchyard.

About Bishop Otey there was a singular dignity of character which set him apart from others of his time. By his zeal, piety and learning he was distinguished among the bishops of the United States. That he was among the first pulpit orators and that he won wide approbation from dignitaries of the church for his statesmanlike direction of church affairs has long been a matter of record.

The teachings of Bishop Otey were based upon his belief which was founded on broad study, honest, resolute convictions, and definite Christian fortitude. He taught and preached, as he believed, that the Episcopal Church was catholic—universal, ecumenic, heaven-wide, world-wide. He believed the Church offered the Apostles' Creed as the test of Christian fellowship through and as an expression of faith:

> I believe in God the Father Almighty, Maker of heaven and earth; And in Jesus Christ his only Son our Lord: . . . I believe in the Holy Ghost: the holy catholic church; the communion of saints; the forgiveness of sins; the resurrection of the body—and the Life everlasting.[14]

In like manner, Bishop Otey taught and preached, as he believed, that the prayers of the Episcopal Church offered breadth in brotherhood:

> O God, the Creator and Preserver of all mankind, we humbly beseech thee for all sorts and conditions of men; that thou wouldest be pleased to make thy ways known unto them, thy saving health unto all nations. More especially we pray for thy holy church universal; that it may be so guided and governed by thy good spirit, that all who profess and call themselves Christians may be led into the way of truth, and hold the faith in unity of spirit, in the bond of peace, and in righteousness of life. . . .[15]

Bishop Otey's simple avowal of truth as he believed it, was not always understood by all Protestants nor by those of the Roman Catholic Church. Invariably, his answer to criticism was: " 'Tis truth and I must tell it; 'tis gospel and I must preach it. Far safer to bear anger from men than woe from God!"

A glimpse of the very appreciative, friendly and humble nature of Bishop Otey is revealed in his address to the Diocesan Convention of 1848. The death of his dear, good friend, John Anderson, had occurred in

---

[14] Book of Common Prayer. "The Apostles' Creed," p. 15.
[15] *Ibid. "A Prayer for all Conditions of Men,"* p. 18.

LaGrange, Tennessee, on May 4, 1847.[16] In his address he said of Mr. Anderson:

> He was in Christ before me and to his meek, but instructive conversation, to his exemplary deportment witnessed twenty-five years ago, do I now feel that I am greatly indebted under God's blessing, in being turned away from the love of the world and to seek Christ and the peace He alone can give.

As was said in the beginning is repeated in conclusion, James Hervey Otey, Tennessee's first Bishop of the Episcopal Church, was throughout his strenuous and rewarding life, both a teacher and a preacher. That he was a doer, in the full sense of the word, has been fully verified in the documentary evidence of his life's history. Though, through all the vicissitudes which he experienced—in travel, in dangers to life and limb, in discouragement which came, due to the slow growth in education and in religion—he was sustained by dedicated faith, unquenchable hope and abundant charity for all.

The years might have lasted longer for the beloved first Bishop had there been convenience in travel and more healthful conditions available, where physical exhaustion would have been lessened.

At the close of the day when Bishop Otey recorded his activities in his diary, at many, many times he wrote:

Weary, weary, weary!

The Right Reverend Charles Todd Quintard
Second Bishop of the Diocese of Tennessee

The lineage of Charles Todd Quintard began with Isaac Quintard, born in Lusignan in the province of Poitou, France. Unknown is the date of birth of this progenitor of the family, whose position of distinction and influence was sustained in its native province until the family members left for religious reasons. Marie has been given as the name of the wife of Isaac Quintard. He was a "Sargettier," a manufacturer of the Sergette, which was a fine-twilled cloth, commonly known as serge. Soon after the revocation of the Edict of Nantes, 1685, Isaac Quintard, his wife and their only child of record, Isaac Quintard II, emigrated from France to Bristol, England.[17]

[16] Gloster, Anderson, Plummer Family Records. Also Noll, p. 133. Other references consulted about Bishop Otey: *History of Memphis*, by J. M. Keating, Vol. 2; *Memoir of James Hervey Otey*, by William Mercer Green; *History of Maury County, Tennessee*, by William Bruce Turner; *So Great a Good*, by Hodding Carter and Betty W. Carter; *The Commercial Appeal*, Centennial Edition, Jan. 1, 1940; *James Hervey Otey of Tennessee* (a pamphlet) by Frank M. McClain.

[17] (a) The Genealogy of John Lindsley (1845-1909) and his wife, Virginia Thayer Payne (1856-1941) of Boston, Massachusetts, by Herbert Armstrong Poole. 1950.

Charles Todd Quintard

The family name of Quintard has been spelled variously as it has appeared in Norman-French Rolls and Records. In 1415, Jehan Quiennart was the Captain General of the Chatteau of Pierrepout; the Councillor of the King of Poitou in 1519 was Sire Charles Quynart and in 1686, Sire Francois Quintard was a Consul. Thus began the spelling of the name, as it has come down through seven generations of the family in England and in America to the generation of Charles Todd Quintard, the subject of this sketch.

Isaac Quintard II was born in Lusignan, province of Poitou, France, in 1670. Preserved in Somerset House, London, in the Bristol French Church Register is recorded:

November 26, 1693—Isaac Quintard from Lusignan, Poitou, France was married in the Chapel of the Gaunt, to Jeanne Fume.[18]

In 1697 Isaac II sailed with his wife and two young children from Bristol, England, to New York City. They became members of the French Church on Wall Street. He entered the mercantile business.

The four children of Isaac II and Jeanne Fume Quintard were: Marie Anne Quintard, born Jan. 5, 1695, Bristol, England, married Samuel Morin; Isaac Quintard III, born Dec. 12, 1696, Bristol, England; Abraham Quintard, born New York City, 1698, died young; and Pierre (Peter) Quintard, born Jan. 14, 1670.

On October 1, 1708, Isaac Quintard II, purchased land in Stamford, Connecticut from Robert Embree. Of interest is the fact that among the lots which were the boundaries of the land acquired, there was the home lot of Samuel Hait (Hoyt). At the death of Isaac II, in 1714 in Stamford, Isaac III inherited much of the property in Stamford, while Pierre (Peter), the other son, came into ownership (by his mother) of his father's property in New York City. In such manner these two brothers became the progenitors of the branches of the Quintard family in the respective cities— Isaac in Stamford and Peter in New York and nearby Norwalk. All of the Quintards in the United States are descended from one or the other of these two brothers.

Isaac Quintard III, b. Dec. 12, 1696, d. Stamford Feb. 28, 1738, md. Stamford, July 16, 1716 to Hannah Knapp,[19] b. Stamford March 10, 1699, d. 1790. He was a staunch Episcopalian, as a majority of his descendants have been. Their children were: twin sons, b. Apr. 3, 1721, died young;

(b) Quintard Family Records, in possession of Charles Quintard Wiggins, New Orleans, Louisiana, a great-grandson of Charles Todd Quintard.

[18] The parents of Jeanne were David (Daniel) and Esther Herault Fume, Poitou, France. The family came to New York in 1698.

[19] Hannah Knapp was the daughter of John Knapp (b. July 25, 1664, d. Apr. 5, 1749), who was married June 10, 1692, to Hannah Ferris (Knapp).

Mary Quintard, b. Oct. 21, 1722, md. Nathaniel Hubbard; Hannah Quintard, b. June 28, 1724, md. Jonathan Ketchum; Isaac Quintard, b. Dec. 29, 1727, md. Oct. 10, 1754 to Lucretia Burroughs; and Peter Quintard, b. Oct. 29, 1730, d. 1817, md. Sept. 14, 1761 to Elizabeth DeMille, b. July 29, 1742, d. Apr. 2, 1837.

After three generations of "Isaacs" the line descended through Peter Quintard (b. 1730) and his wife, Elizabeth DeMille.[20] Their five children were: Mary (Polly) Quintard, b. Sept. 3, 1762, md. Stephen White of Rome, New York; Isaac Quintard, b. at Stamford Apr. 28, 1764, d. Stamford Nov. 4, 1855, md. Mar. 20, 1786 in Stamford to Hannah Palmer, b. Sept. 22, 1770, d. May 12, 1811; Fanny Quintard, b. May 11, 1766, md. John R. Hennessey of Rye, New York; Peter Quintard, b. July 25, 1768, unmarried; Abraham Quintard, b. Mar. 29, 1772.

In the Revolutionary War, Peter Quintard fought in Captain Seymour's Company of Connecticut Volunteers with the rank of Sergeant.

Isaac Quintard (b. 1764), son of Peter and Elizabeth DeMille, and his wife, Hannah Palmer[21] were born in Stamford and died there. He lived in the house occupied by his father in 1780. The elopement of Isaac, twenty-two years of age, and Hannah, sixteen, was one of the earliest romances of Stamford. His first enterprise was the grocery business. Isaac Quintard served in the Revolutionary War, as did his father, Peter, and he was a pensioner in 1832. From 1793 to 1806 the Union Masonic Lodge met in a room furnished by Isaac Quintard.

The seven children of Isaac and Hannah Palmer Quintard were: Deborah Quintard, b. Aug. 26, 1787, d. Feb. 11, 1792; William Seth Quintard, b. Dec. 27, 1789, d. July 14, 1820, md. Marie Ferris; Seth Palmer Quintard, b. Sept. 18, 1792, d. Apr. 19, 1878, md. Susan Letitia Ferris; Isaac Quintard, b. May 15, 1794, d. Mar. 17, 1833, md. Sept. 6, 1821, Clarissa Hoyt[22] (Shaw), b. Mar. 17, 1793, d. Mar. 6, 1871; Peter DeMille Quintard, b. Oct. 31, 1795, d. Sept. 15, 1866, md. Lucy Ford; Robert Palmer Quintard, b. Jan. 15, 1799, d. Mar. 29, 1873, md. Sarah Peck (a cousin); and Hannah Elizabeth Quintard, b. July 3, 1802, d. Mar. 2, 1900, md. Peter Smith.

[20] Elizabeth DeMille was the daughter of Peter DeMille (b. about 1700, d. between 1774 and 1781) and Abigail Banks (b. Jan. 23, 1707, d. August, 1774) who married in 1730. Joseph and Hannah Purdy Banks were the parents of Abigail Banks.

[21] The parents of Hannah Palmer were Seth Palmer and Deborah Peck, who md. May 14, 1746; Seth, b. 1741, d. Jan. 26, 1831; Deborah, b. May 14, 1746, d. July 18, 1837. Seth Palmer was the son of Messenger Palmer (1718-1792), a member of the Committee of Safety and Inspection, Greenwich, Conn., 1766.

[22] Clarissa Hoyt was the seventh of the eight daughters of Joseph and Hannah Seeley Hoyt, md. June 11, 1771. She married William Shaw, had four daughters; he died March, 1821.

Isaac Quintard (b. 1794) was a wealthy and highly respected citizen of Stamford. Like his father, he owned a grocery. Seth Palmer, his maternal grandfather, left Isaac a few houses, and lots in Stamford which seemed of little value at the time the bequest was made.. However, by 1843 Isaac had built a block of two brick stores, the property became very valuable, as it was around this area—Quintard Block—the city of Stamford grew.

As a lifelong resident of Stamford, he had lived in the same house for eighty-nine years. He was a man of sound business, just and firm in his convictions. His funeral service was held in St. John's Episcopal Church, Stamford.

It has been said that the children sent by Isaac and Clarissa Hoyt Quintard into the world were truly representative of the family "whose careers have illustrated the native energy and ability of the Quintard stock!" Their children (the brothers and sisters of Bishop Quintard) were: (1) George W. Quintard,[23] b. Stamford, Apr. 22, 1822, d. New York, Apr. 2, 1913 (buried in Greenwood Cemetery, Brooklyn), md. Feb. 15, 1844, Frances Elizabeth Morgan; (2) CHARLES TODD QUINTARD, b. Stamford, Dec. 22, 1824, d. Darien, Georgia, Feb. 15, 1898 (buried in Sewanee Cemetery, Sewanee, Tennessee), md. at Roswell, Georgia, Oct. 19, 1848, Eliza Catherine Hand,[24] of Marietta, Georgia, b. Feb. 2, 1826, d. 1904; (3) Edward Augustus Quintard,[25] b. Stamford, Dec. 27, 1826, d. New York City, June 26, 1899 (buried in Kensico Cemetery, New York), md. (a) Mary Matilda Gillespie, (b) Mary Skiddy; (4) Mary Clarissa Quintard, b. Stamford, Mar. 16, 1828, d. Stamford Mar. 30, 1912 (buried Woodland Cemetery, Stamford), md. Rufus Hoyt, Esq. (a first cousin); and (5) Anna Virginia Quintard, b. Stamford, June 1, 1831, d. Stamford June 30, 1907 (buried Woodland Cemetery, Stamford), md. Augustus Wellington Payne, Esq.

Bishop Charles Todd Quintard and his wife, Eliza Catherine Hand Quintard were the parents of five children:

Bayard Quintard, b. Roswell, Georgia, Aug. 25, 1849, d. young.

Clara Eliza Quintard, b. Roswell, Georgia, Oct. 20, 1851, baptized in St. John's Church, Stamford, Connecticut, June 27, 1852, d. young.

---

[23] George W. Quintard was an eminent New York millionaire. His wife, Frances Morgan, daughter of Charles Morgan of Morgan Steamship Line. He was president of the Charleston Steamship Company. Among his bequests was—"to Mrs. Charles Todd Quintard, sister-in-law, $10,000."

[24] Eliza Catherine Hand was the daughter of Bayard E. and Eliza Barrington King Hand and granddaughter of Roswell King of St. Simon's Island, Georgia.

[25] Edward Augustus Quintard served a year in the Union Army during the Civil War. He was Capt. 71st New York State Militia on staff of Col. A. S. McHugh, whose regiment left New York, Apr. 21, 1861, 950 strong and won high praise in the bloody Battle of Manassas. He was a vestryman for many years at the Church of the Transfiguration (Little Church Around the Corner), New York City.

George William Quintard, b. Rome, Georgia, Aug. 1, 1856, d. New York City in September 1908. Md. in New York City on Dec. 11, 1888 to Jean Safford. Their children were: Charles Todd Quintard, Daniel Safford Bigelow Quintard, Helen Todd Quintard, Elise Katherine Quintard and Adele Quintard. He was an architect, educated in France.

Edward Augustus Quintard, b. Nashville, Tennessee, June 12, 1860, d. Apr. 21, 1903, in Washington, D. C. Graduated University of the South, 1882. Md. Oct. 22, 1885, to Mary Young Shephard. Their children: Mary Katherine Quintard, Edward Alexander Quintard, Alexander Shepherd Quintard, Dorothy Quintard and Alexina Shepherd Quintard.

Clara Eliza Quintard, b. Roswell, Georgia, Oct. 20, 1861, d. Feb. 14, 1915, in Ferguson, South Carolina. Md. in St. Augustine Chapel, Sewanee, Tennessee, on June 20, 1886, to Professor Benjamin Lawton Wiggins, b. Sand Ridge, South Carolina, on Sept. 11, 1861, d. June 4, 1909, in Sewanee. Professor Wiggins graduated in 1880 from the University of the South and became Professor of Ancient Languages—later Vice Chancellor of the University. Their three children were: (1) Katherine Quintard Wiggins, b. Sewanee, Feb. 7, 1887, d. Chattanooga Feb. 13, 1916, md. Jan. 23, 1911, to Guy Turner Ward, no children; (2) Charles Todd Quintard Wiggins, b. Trenton, Georgia, Jan. 13, 1890, d. Oct. 2, 1944, in Hot Springs, Arkansas, md. in Rossville, Georgia, on Nov. 1, 1914, Amelia Dolly Wallace. One child—Charles Todd Quintard Wiggins, Jr., b. Sept. 17, 1915, in Chattanooga, graduate of Vanderbilt University in electrical engineering, md. in Dalton, Georgia, June 14, 1935, Margaret Lawson Low (b. Hebron, North Dakota, daughter of Dugald McKinnon Low and Mary Watson Ferguson Low). They had one child—Charles Todd Quintard Wiggins III, b. Chattanooga, Dec. 25, 1936, presently associated with the Memphis Publishing Company in department of research and promotion, also editor of *Memphis Market News*. He is a great great grandson of Bishop Charles Todd Quintard. (3) Elizabeth Barrington Wiggins, b. Sewanee, June 25, 1893, md. (a) at Sewanee, Jan. 23, 1911, Aubrey Falls Lanier, b. Feb. 18, 1888, d. Apr. 25, 1936. They had one child, Barbara Barrington Lanier, b. Aug. 3, 1912 (md. Shreveport, La., Oct. 2, 1935, Raymond Stewart Allison, one child, Elizabeth Louise Allison, b. Oct. 19, 1936); md. (b) Shreveport, Louisiana, Oct. 19, 1939, Dr. Thomas P. Lloyd, b. Grand Junction, Tennessee, Sept. 6, 1871.

That we may know better the great and noble Charles Todd Quintard —doctor, minister, chaplain-soldier, bishop—let us look upon him through the record which he wrought by deeds of a whole heart invested and maintained in marvelous works.

1824—December 22. Charles Todd Quintard was born in Stamford, Connecticut. Educated at Trinity College, New York.

1846—M.D. degree, University of the City of New York, Medical College. He studied under eminent professors—Dr. James Wood and Dr. Valentine Mott, a great surgeon of his time. Interned at Bellevue Hospital and New York Dispensary. Wrote extensively for medical journals.

1848—To Georgia to practice medicine—Athens, Rome, Met and married Miss Eliza Catherine Hand of Roswell, Georgia.

1851-1855—Professor of Physiology and Pathological Anatomy, Tennessee Medical College, Memphis, Tennessee. Dr. Quintard and Dr. A. P. Merrill were editors of "The Medical Recorder," a bi-monthly periodical, established by Memphis Medical College.[26]

1852—A friendship was begun with Bishop Otey. Dr. Quintard "made up his mind that a man's soul was worth more than his body."

1853—M.A., Columbia University.

1854—January, admitted as a candidate for Holy Orders.

1855—January 21, Ordained Deacon at Calvary Church, Memphis, Tennessee. Served diaconate on the Alston Plantation at Ravenscroft Chapel and St. Paul's, Randolph. Later St. Matthew's, Covington, was added to this group and the area was named "Quintard Parish."

1856—January 6, Ordained a Priest.

1857—Rector, Calvary Church, Memphis, Tennessee.

1858—January, Rector, Church of the Advent, also served Church of the Holy Spirit and St. Ann's, Nashville, Tennessee. Diocesan Book Society organized by Dr. Quintard, led to establishment of Episcopal book-shops.

1859—Organized Rock City Guard, a militia company composed largely of young men of Nashville. Dr. Quintard was Chaplain. Afterwards company merged into First Tennessee Regiment, Dr. Quintard continued as Chaplain of the Regiment in Civil War, 1861.

1860—October 9, cornerstone laid, University of the South, Sewanee, Tennessee.

1861-1865—Chaplain of the Confederate Army during Civil War.

1865—October 11, Consecrated, Second Bishop of the Protestant Episcopal Church, Diocese of Tennessee. Service of consecration held in St. Luke's Church, Philadelphia, Pennsylvania.
Tennessee Trustee, University of the South, 1865-1898. Between November 28 and March 22, 1866, traveled over major part of Diocese—confirmed 314 persons. Viewed devastation of churches, homes and properties wrought by Civil War.

---

[26] *History of Memphis,* by J. M. Keating, Vol. 2, p. 120.

1866—February, began revival of the University of the South; on March 22 elected first Chancellor of the University, served six years. First Diocesan Convention held since consecration of Bishop Quintard, held at St. James, Bolivar. (1,498 communicants in Tennessee.) S.T.D., Columbia University, New York.

1867—LL.D., Cambridge University, England. Recorded in 1867 Journal recommendations for improved church architecture. Communicants in Tennessee, 1,998.
In England—attended first Lambeth Conference. He was Chaplain of the Order of the Hospital of the Knights of St. John in Jerusalem, of which the Prince of Wales was the Grand Pryor.

1868—September 8, official re-opening of the University of the South, Sewanee, Tennessee.[27]

1871—January 1, Vestry of St. Mary's Church, Memphis, tendered St. Mary's to the Bishop for a Cathedral Church.[28]

1876—The "Bishop's House," by St. Mary's Cathedral, first occupied by Bishop Otey, had become the property of the Diocese as a permanent Episcopal residence.

1877—March, School of Theology opened, University of the South.[29]

1878—D.D., University of the South, Sewanee, Tennessee.
The aid of the Sisters of St. Mary was secured. The Sisters served during the yellow fever epidemic (several lost their lives); started St. Mary's School for Girls; aided Church Home.

1885—In Diocese there were 47 ministers; 4,150 communicants; 32 parishes, several missions.

1887—May, Bishop Quintard reported to Convention of progress made. "Many of the churches have been improved and beautified. There is an evident growth in churchly and religious life. . . . We are gradually getting to a better style of ecclesiastical music. In the six or eight parishes in which surpliced choirs have been introduced, they have given great satisfaction to the worshippers."[30]

1888—Attended Lambeth Conference.

1890—Made a trip East to raise money for work in the interest of Negroes.

1891—Hoffman Hall[31] established at Fisk University,[32] Nashville, Tennessee, for the training of Negro clergymen.

1895—April 20, Diocesan Convention voted to elect an Assistant Bishop for the Diocese. The Rev. Thomas F. Gailor was unanimously elected the first Assistant Bishop (Bishop Coadjutor).

---

[27] Sewanee Alumni News, Centennial Directory, Edited by Helen Adams Petry and Elizabeth Nickinson Chitty, 1957.
[28] St. Mary's Cathedral, by John H. Davis, 1958, p. 51.
[29] Sewanee Alumni News, 1957.
[30] Diocesan Journal, 1887.
[31] Named for Dr. Charles F. Hoffman, New York, a generous donor. Hoffman Hall was sold in 1910 and funds were used to build Industrial School (Hoffman-St. Mary's) for Negroes, later known as Gailor Industrial School near Mason, Tennessee.
[32] Fisk opened March, 1890.

1897—May, Diocesan Convention (65th) held at Sewanee, the last
attended by Bishop Quintard.
In summer, attended Lambeth Conference and was the only
bishop present who had taken part in the first conference in 1867.
1898—Over 5,274 communicants in Diocese of Tennessee. More than
230 ministers on roster of clergy during the years of Bishop
Quintard.
Bishop Quintard died Tuesday morning, February 15, at Darien,
Georgia, while he and his wife were visiting old friends. Buried
February 19, in family plot in University Cemetery, Sewanee,
Tennessee.

The steadfast friendship of Bishop James Hervey Otey and Dr. Charles
Todd Quintard was of significance in the history of the Episcopal Church.
In 1852, when their friendship began, Bishop Otey was fifty-two years of
age and Dr. Quintard was twenty-eight. Doubtless, at the outset, each must
have in some degree realized the impelling force of their association. Surely,
they must have felt certain forebodings that a friendship such as theirs was
destined to impressive achievement!

To this happy meeting of mind and spirit, Bishop Otey brought a
knowledge of the abundant power and the benevolences of God, an affection
for the classics and an enviable background in purposeful pedagogy. Dr.
Quintard brought his genuine faith in a Heavenly Father, an insatiable
desire for knowledge through scientific medical research and a clean-carved
positive individuality.

Throughout history few men have united and assimilated such gifts of
mind and heart in the cause of God's kingdom as did Bishop Otey and Dr.
Quintard. The story has been well written often; yet, in its worthiness must
be told and retold that all may read!

Dr. Quintard, inspired by the example of his religious adviser and warm
friend, became eager to study for the ministry. At the time, he was professor of Physiology and Pathological Anatomy at the Tennessee Medical
College in Memphis, Tennessee. By day Dr. Quintard taught and practiced
medicine; by night he studied theology and the canons of the Episcopal
Church. And when his period of preparation had been concluded, he
"abandoned a lucrative medical practice to adorn the ministry of the
Church in Tennessee."[33]

In rapid sequence the events created by Dr. Quintard's choice were
actuated. First, a candidate for Holy Orders 1854, ordained a deacon 1855
and advanced to the Priesthood in 1856.

Dr. Quintard's organization in 1859, of the Rock City Guard, a militia
company composed largely of young men of Nashville, afterwards became

---

[33] Noll, p. 91.

an integral part of the First Tennessee Regiment. Dr. Quintard had been the chaplain of the group, so it was natural that these men would want him as chaplain for the whole Regiment when the Civil War came in 1861. Through four harrowing years he served as priest and as physician to soul-torn, physically maimed, courageous soldiers. Paramount was the unselfish devotion and Christian fortitude which he portrayed.

Dr. Quintard's faithfulness and efficiency won for him great favor among his fellow chaplains. Happily, in 1863, Dr. Quintard was specially assigned by General Braxton Bragg to have general charge of all the hospitals of the corps of General Leonidas Polk, "with the privilege of oversight and ministration for the care of the sick and wounded."[34] The Bishop-General Polk was in charge of the First Division of the Army of Tennessee.

A distinguished visitor who came to the headquarters of General Polk in Shelbyville, Tennessee, during the Civil War was Lieutenant Colonel Arthur Fremantle of England, a member of the Coldstream Guards. The Colonel kept a detailed diary of his visit. Among his notations were sketches of several officers whom he admired. He wrote of General Polk:

He had more of the appearance of a soldier than of a clergyman. He is much beloved by the soldiers on account of his great courage and agreeable manner. Fifty-seven, tall and erect - - - .

The Reverend Charles Todd Quintard conducted prayers both morning and evening—there was singing. General Polk joined with much zeal.[35]

Colonel Fremantle also observed that many of the soldiers were Methodist, Baptist, Presbyterian and so on, but that most of the officers were Episcopalians.[36]

It was known that as far as the Church and the Civil War were concerned General Polk and Chaplain Quintard shared a common problem. Most certainly each had done all within his power to prevent war when the smoldering began. Full well they knew that should they survive the dangers of the terrific struggle they would return to their pulpits and continue their unquenchable urge to preach the Gospel of Jesus Christ to spiritually hungry humanity! Yet, war was in progress and it was not of their making! They were in the position of one who "finding his house on fire would use every means in his power to extinguish the flame, and would then resume his ordinary pursuits."[37]

---

[34] *Ibid.,* p. 145.

[35] *General Leonidas Polk, C.S.A. (The Fighting Bishop)* by Joseph H. Parks, 1962, p. 305.

[36] *Ibid.,* p. 307.

[37] *Ibid.,* p. 305 (from Col. Fremantle's Diary).

Chaplain Quintard had prepared a small book for use by the soldiers of the War, which he entitled "Confederate Soldier's Pocket Manual of Devotions." This small book was widely distributed among the men of the Confederate ranks. Its content was read and shared and cherished during the trying hours before and after battle.

On the morning of June 14, 1864, General Polk went forward atop Pine Mountain near Etowah, Georgia, to inspect the troops in action under his command. In the breast-pocket of his coat he carried three copies of Dr. Quintard's small volume of Devotions. Each was inscribed: one to General John Bell Hood, another to General Joseph E. Johnston and the third to General William J. Hardee. On that fatal morning an enemy cannon ball entered General Polk's breast and death came instantly. The blood-stained Soldier's Pocket Manuals were removed from his pocket and given to the three Generals whom he had designated "each of whom he had baptized."[38]

Truly, it may be said of General Polk and Chaplain Quintard, that they were noble Churchmen wherever found—in the pulpit or on the field of battle.

These excerpts taken from the War Diary[39] of Chaplain Quintard reveal glimpses of the horror and pathos of the days which he spent during the Civil War:

> 1864—November 23—Wed. Got breakfast by daylight and started off by myself, determined to overtake the Army . . . came up with my friend, General Strahl . . . met my dear friend John Marsh . . . I rode on to Strahl's ambulance train . . . to spend the night . . . I was very tired.
>
> November 24, Thurs.—Prayers at headquarters before sunrise. Command moved at daylight on the road to Waynesboro . . . we marched toward Mt. Pleasant . . . in all 22 miles today. . . . It is very delightful to mark each stage of our progress by prayer to God for his blessing.
>
> November 25, Fri.—Up and had prayers and breakfast long before day. Troops in motion at earliest dawn . . . to Gen. Hood's hdqrs., . . . a most cordial welcome. Met Gen'l Pillow . . . I concluded to go on to Gen'l Lucius Polk's three and a half miles toward Columbia. I, therefore, rode forward with Gen'l Pillow. Such a greeting! How I thank God for the friends he has given me . . . Gen'l Cheatham and staff were guests of Gen'l Polk. Met Gen'l Forrest and Gov'r Harris . . . I find . . . that the enemy have destroyed a vast amount of property in Rome, Ga., among other things the Quintard Iron Works! Had prayers with the family . . . Oh! for the peace which floweth like a river, making

---

[38] *So Great a Good,* by Hodding Carter and Betty W. Carter, 1955, p. 130.

[39] *History of Maury County* by William Bruce Turner, 1955, pp. 216-222. Original manuscript of Chaplain Quintard's War Diary is preserved, University of the South, Sewanee.

life's desert places bloom and smile! Oh! for the faith to grasp Heaven's bright "forever," amid the shadows of earth's little while!

November 26, Sat.—This has been indeed a day of real enjoyment. I have not moved out of the house—just rested and realized that I was once more in Tennessee! . . . All day . . . a stream of visitors to the family . . . Gen'l Hood, Gov. Harris, Gen'ls Brown, Bates, Gibson, Walthall . . . that this was the residence of a brother of the late Gen'l Polk one replied, 'Yes, we looked on him as the father of all Louisianians.'

November 27, Advent Sunday—Had full morning prayer at the residence of General Lucius J. Polk . . . after service I started for hdqts . . . found Gen. Hood at residence of Mrs. Warfield on Pulaski Pike . . . he detailed to me his plan of taking Nashville . . . Had evening prayers at which the ladies of the family were present, with the ladies of the Hon. James H. (Houston) Thomas family, who have been obliged to leave their home as it is in our line of skirmishers.

November 28, Monday—Enemy left Columbia at 6 P.M., last evening and our forces entered the town at night. I rode in about 7 A.M., after prayers. . . . Gen'l Beauregard telegraphed Gen'l Hood that Sherman is making his way to the Atlantic Coast and urges him to press forward so as to relieve Gen'l Lee.

November 30, Wednesday—Walked in town with Pise[40] . . . called to see a young man . . . belonging to Forrest's Cavalry, who was shot through the lungs. I had sent him morphine the evening before, which had a very beneficial effect. Had prayers with him. . . .

December 2, Fri.—This has indeed been a day of darkness and distress to me. At 12 noon, I officiated at the funerals of Brg. Gen'l Strahl, Captain James Johnston and my very dear friend Lieut. John H. Marsh. At 3 P.M., I buried from the residence of Mrs. D. Polk, Maj. Gen'l Cleburne, Brig. Gen'l Granbury and Col. Young. . . . A military escort was furnished . . . every token of respect was shown to the memory of the glorious dead. Brig. Gen'l John Adams of Pulaski, Tennessee, whom I had dined with at Hon. James H. Thomas' the day before he left Columbia, fell most gallantly. I wrote letters to Mrs. Marsh and Mrs. Johnston informing them of the deaths of their sons. It will be a crushing blow to them both. . . . Rode out with Gen'l Lucius Polk to Hamilton Place to spend the night.

An attempt to give a summation of the character and achievement of Bishop Quintard cannot be easily accomplished. That he was one of the most colorful personages among the bishops of the State cannot be questioned. Possessed was he with a strong physical nature; he was ever alert, an immense force wherever he appeared, he was the kind of person to be remembered forever. He was generous, dynamic and a man of striking personality.

With boundless energy Bishop Quintard pursued his course with dedicated missionary zeal, fortified by a sympathetic heart, a faith strong and

[40] The Rev. David Pise, D.D., rector St. Peter's Church, Columbia, Tennessee.

complete, a culture wide and varied and with bouyant humor. Daily he worked for the cause of the kingdom of God. He constantly sought to make his energy contagious, that those about him might also lose themselves in service to others. He was a very outspoken, positive person who had no tolerance for those who suffered from chronic indifference! Someone has said of him, "He was a prince of hospitality."

> He ministered his professional medical healing to master and servant alike; he preached the unsearchable riches of Christ, not only from chancel and pulpit on the Lord's Day, but as he went to the bedside of sick men, women and little children; he administered the sacrament of baptism to the newborn infant, white and black, whose advent into the world's arena he had assisted professionally; and when he had done all that medical science could do for the fatally ill, he fed with the Bread of Life and the Cup of Salvation those whose inner eyes would soon look upon the Lamb on His throne in light and join in the heavenly pean of the redeemed.[41]

It is in the typical American tradition that people and places are often given the names of persons of influence of the period. Appropriately, the name of Bishop Quintard has been often memoralized. These are among the known which bear his name: C. Quintard Wiggins, II, a great grandson and C. Quintard Wiggins, III, a great, great grandson; Quintard Joyner, the son of Dr. Nevill Joyner, a faithful minister, once at the Church of The Holy Innocents; Quintard House, Medical College, University of Tennessee, Memphis; Quintard Parish in Tipton County, Tennessee and Quintard Street, Arlington, Tennessee.

In Memphis, Tennessee, at eight-thirty o'clock on the evening of February 15, 1898, Bishop Thomas F. Gailor wrote in his Diary:

> I received a telegram announcing the death of my dear Bishop and father in God, Charles Todd Quintard, at Darien, Georgia. It was a great shock to me, for while I knew that he was not well, I had received letters so regularly that I could not believe him to be in any immediate danger of death.
>
> He was my oldest friend; and every important event in my life was connected with him. He confirmed me, admitted me as a candidate for the ministry, ordained me to the Diaconate and the Priesthood, married me, and consecrated me Bishop. For twenty-five years I enjoyed the privilege of his intimate friendship, and was blessed with love and confidence of his great heart, which was rich beyond the measure of ordinary men, in generosity and power, giving forth with abounding unselfishness, and ever graceful and gracious with the love of the Lord Jesus Christ.[42]

[41] *The Commercial Appeal*, Memphis, Tennessee. Centennial Edition, Jan. 1, 1940. Article by Bishop Maxon, pp. 3 and 17.
[42] *Some Memoirs*, by Thomas F. Gailor, 1937, p. 160.

Thomas Frank Gailor

The Right Reverend Thomas Frank Gailor
Third Bishop of the Diocese of Tennessee

Statesman of the Church, Honored by Oxford University, and friend to humanity was the Rt. Rev. Thomas Frank Gailor, third Bishop of Tennessee, protege of Bishop Quintard after Bishop Gailor's father, one time editor of the *Commercial Appeal*, died at the Civil War battle of Perryville, Ky. Regarded for years as Tennessee's first citizen . . . .[43]

Thomas Frank Gailor, son of Frank M. and Charlotte Moffett Gailor, was born September 17, 1856, in Jackson, Mississippi. Frank M. Gailor, the father, was born in 1832. He was the son of Amize Hazen Gailor and Lucinda Mallory (Gailor) and a grandson of Col. Caleb Hazen of the Revolutionary War.[44] Frank M. Gailor was a descendant of a Huguenot family which migrated from France to the County of Somerset, England. About 1630, Walter Gailor (Gailord) came to America and settled in Dorchester, Massachusetts.

In 1850, Frank M. Gailor moved to Jackson, Mississippi, where he became the editor and eventual proprietor of a local newspaper, "The True Witness."

Charlotte Moffett (Gailor) was the daughter of James Moffett and Charlotte Langston (Moffett), and was a native of Castlebar, Ireland. She was born in 1834. Charlotte Langston was the daughter of General John Langston. Charlotte Langston Moffett, with her four children, came to America in 1853 and went to Cincinnati to make her home. Mrs. Moffett was a devout member of the Church of England.

Soon after Mrs. Moffett came to Cincinnati she began to open her house every Sunday morning and invited persons interested to attend the Episcopal services held there. These meetings ultimately led to the founding of the Church of the Advent on Walnut Hills. Significant indeed is the fact that "in 1925 a Memorial Chapel of that church was dedicated to her memory."[45]

Charlotte Moffett visited friends in Jackson, Mississippi, in 1854. It was there that she met Frank M. Gailor. They were married in St. Andrew's Church, Jackson, during the following year.

At the beginning of the Civil War, Frank M. Gailor volunteered. Following the Battle of Shiloh he was promoted to the rank of Major. He was killed in the battle of Perryville, Kentucky.

---

[43] *The Commercial Appeal,* Centennial Edition, Jan. 1, 1940 (copy of by-line under picture of Bishop Gailor, p. 3).
[44] *Some Memoirs,* Thomas Frank Gailor, 1937, pp. 1 and 2.
[45] *Ibid.,* p. 3.

The early years of Thomas Frank Gailor were lived closely with his mother, whose great strength of character and devotion gave him courage and abundant inspiration. Coupled with the able guidance given by his mother was the great interest and affection of Bishop Quintard. Early, he took the boy under his protecting care and held him in close association for many years. Bishop Quintard saw in young Thomas Frank Gailor the characteristics of the man whom he believed the boy to be capable of becoming. Bishop Quintard was ever gratified by the achievements of his beloved son-in-faith.

The Reverend Richard Hines, D.D., brought to Memphis by Bishop Otey and placed in charge of St. Mary's Church on Poplar, was also a great influence in the life of young Thomas F. Gailor. In a building on the church grounds, Dr. Hines conducted a school which was attended by the growing boy. There he learned Latin grammar and "began to understand what the Church meant."[46] Later studies under the tutelage of Capt. T. C. Anderson, Principal of the High School[47] in Memphis, led to graduation at the age of fifteen years and nine months. He was the first boy graduate of this institution. During the year 1872, he was employed by a Queensware Company.

After recovery from yellow fever in 1873, Thomas F. Gailor went by boat with his mother to his grandmother's in Cincinnati. In September of that year he entered Racine College, having saved enough of his salary to pay the fees for the first year.

I was graduated at Racine in June 1876, with the "Centennial" Class. It was my fortune to make the valedictory oration at commencement and to get the Greek Prize of fifty dollars which helped me to pay my way to New York to enter the General Theological Seminary.[48]

Ordered a deacon May 15, 1879, by Bishop Charles Todd Quintard and ordained a priest, September 17, 1880, Thomas F. Gailor began his ministry in the Episcopal Church.

Friday, September 17, 1880—On this my 24th birthday the Bishop is with me, and Dr. Harris, Beckett, Fitts, Harrison and Davenport. I was ordained to the priesthood at 11 A.M. Delightful service— Davenport preached an admirable sermon. Tonight the Bishop confirmed 5 persons—I am very happy and hopeful—Oh! the future! What shall I make of it?[49]

The distinguished clergyman—in embryonic stage—had written in his diary a note of happiness, of hopefulness, yet, with a question of the future, "What shall I make of it?" The remainder of this sketch will be

---

[46] *Ibid.*, p. 18.
[47] Presently called "Central High School."
[48] *Memoirs*, Gailor, p. 21.
[49] *Ibid.*, p. 67.

devoted to the answering of this poignant question asked by the minister of himself!

In his own words is this account of his first sermon:

> My first sermon was on the evening of Ascension Day. I read the service to a good congregation and just when I had announced the text of my sermon, the fire-bell rang and the entire congregation left the church to see where the fire was. I waited until they returned and then went on with my sermon.[50]

The record of magnanimous service diligently rendered to all mankind by so princely a person cannot be fully written. His question of his future— "What shall I make of it?" These milestones[51] give evidence in part of the manner in which the effort of his lifetime answered his question: Rector, Church of the Messiah, Pulaski, Tennessee, 1879-1882; Professor of English and Literature, Lecturer on Theology, University of the South, Sewanee, 1882-1886 and University Chaplain, 1883-1893.

In 1885, Chaplain Gailor married Miss Ellen Douglas Cunningham and took her to "The Mountain" to make their home.

He was elected Vice Chancellor of the University of the South, 1890-1893; consecrated Bishop Coadjutor, July 25, 1893 and Bishop of Tennessee, February 15, 1898. He was elected Chancellor of the University of the South in 1908, a position in which he served until his death.

Bishop Gailor became the first President of the National Council of the Episcopal Church in America in 1919 and served until 1925.

January 19, 1926 marked the completion of St. Mary's Cathedral, Memphis and Gailor Memorial was added to the name. Hoffman-St. Mary's School for Negroes, near Mason, was changed to Gailor Industrial School about that time. The end of forty years of service as Bishop was celebrated appropriately at Sewanee, July 25, 1933.

Bishop Gailor was the recipient of three degrees, D.D., one conferred by each of these colleges: Trinity College, Hartford, Connecticut, 1892; University of the South, Sewanee, Tennessee, 1893, and Oxford University, England, 1920. Oglethorpe University and the University of Georgia in 1923 conferred the LL.D.

On Bishop Gailor were bestowed the highest honors of the Protestant Episcopal Church in his beloved Tennessee, in America and in England. He preached several times in Westminster Abbey at the invitation of King Edward VII and King George V.

Great acclaim came to Bishop Gailor by his service as preacher, teacher, administrator, bishop. Through all and to all he was a scholar, a spiritual

---

[50] *Ibid.*, p. 57.
[51] *Sewanee Alumni News,* Centennial Directory, p. 346.

counsellor, an esteemed public citizen, an author, a distinguished ecclesiastic and a loyal friend.

Outstanding in its simplicity was this advice often spoken by him to one grown faint in well-being: "Don't be afraid, only believe." This thought permeated many of the scholarly addresses made by the Bishop on numerous occasions before many types of organizations, religious meetings, and on college[52] and high school[53] commencement programs.

The Bishop's House in Memphis as well as the Gailor summer home in Sewanee, was ever a mecca for persons from all walks of life.

Any account of Bishop Gailor's life would be sadly incomplete without naming the children of whom he and Mrs. Gailor were the grateful parents. Their oldest child, Nancy, married Robert Daniel and had a son, Dr. Robert Daniel, professor at Kenyon College. Charlotte was the second child. Miss Gailor makes her home in Sewanee, Tennessee. Frank Hoyt married Mary Louise Pennell. They were the parents of three daughters: Mary Ann Gailor, married Roy M. Scott, Jr.; Ellen Douglas Gailor, married Shephard Kenworthy; Nancy Pennell Gailor, married J. R. Cortner. The fourth and last child of Bishop and Mrs. Gailor was Ellen Douglas; she married Richard Folsom Cleveland and had the following children: The Rev. Thomas Grover Cleveland (presently serving St. James Mission, Tanana, Alaska); Ann Cleveland, married T. Bolling Robertson, and Charlotte Cleveland married David Look.

The life of Bishop Gailor was filled with varied experiences of pathos, great joy and of humor.

Vivid always were his memories of his mother's grief caused by the untimely death of his father during the Civil War. Mrs. Gailor had made great effort to learn the location of her husband's grave. On her second journey (1863) to learn what she could, she took her young son, a Mrs. Dudley and a driver for the wagon. Many in Memphis had learned of her going and had prevailed on her to take their letters to husbands, sweethearts, fathers. As such letters were "contraband" they had to be hidden.

---

[52] Commencement preacher University of the South, 1886, 1897 and 1923; orator 1932.

[53] Typical of the many high school graduating classes addressed by Bishop Gailor was the class of Bolton College, Agricultural High School, Shelby County, Arlington, Tennessee, on Tuesday morning, May 5, 1914. The graduates were: Ruby Clarice Blakey (Mrs. J. B. Griffin, Brunswick, Tennessee); Ora Pearl Fortner (Mrs. Philip S. Day, Winter Park, Florida); Warren Howell (Memphis); Mabel Marshall (Mrs. E. H. Hadley, deceased); Fannie Mai Ricketts (Mrs. E. Warren Jetton, Memphis); Robert B. Stewart (deceased 1962); Casey Smith (Methodist Minister, Denver, Colo.); Uldine Shelton (Memphis); Clara Timbs (Mrs. Dennie Norris, West Point, Miss.); Paul Taylor (Memphis); Connie Williams (D.D.S., Memphis); Bettie Williams (Mrs. Thomas Osborn, Bolton, Tenn.).

"The most important of them were sewn in the lining of my jacket, which was buttoned up to my throat, and I remember that I felt like a mummy, hardly able to move. . . . I remember the officer coming . . . looking at me as I sat there . . . in my stiff jacket, and he called me 'Buddy,' to my indignation!"[54]

Later, Mrs. Gailor made another attempt to contact officers who had been friends of her husband, that she might learn the facts concerning her husband's death. She took the train to Chattanooga. Thomas F. Gailor, then six and a half years of age, went with her.

The train was crowded with Confederate soldiers, some were eating raw sweet potatoes, and boy-like I was glad to eat with them, in spite of my mother's remonstrance.

Major Martin Walt, a friend of ours, was on the train, and just as we were approaching the tunnel, near Sewanee, he brought a satchel to my mother, saying: "We are about to enter a long tunnel and there are no lights. This satchel is full of money for the soldiers, who are to be paid in Chattanooga. There are rough people on the train who may attack me in the tunnel. Please keep the satchel and hold it tight until we get out of the darkness." . . . When we moved into the dark tunnel Mother said to me: "Tom, quick, someone is trying to take this satchel away from me."

I reached over and felt a hand pulling at the satchel and I bit into it with all the might of my strong young teeth! The hand was hurriedly withdrawn. When we emerged from the tunnel we saw a woman in the seat in front of us nursing her hand![55]

The story is told of an occasion, during an evangelistic service conducted by the famous preacher, Billy Sunday, which was attended by Bishop Gailor. The sermon had been long and vibrant. When concluded, the Rev. Mr. Sunday gave an invitation to those present to come forward and make their profession of faith. No one came. In desperation he called out: "Everybody who wants to be saved, stand up!" Everyone in the congregation stood except Bishop Gailor. Billy Sunday, of course, knew Bishop Gailor well. He singled him out by saying: "Bishop Gailor, I see that you are not standing. Do you not want to be saved?" To this, the distinguished Episcopal Bishop stood and in full voice replied: "Not today, Mr. Sunday! Not today!"[56]

Once Bishop Gailor had gone to a small town in Mississippi to preach on a very hot August day. His vestments, because of the extreme heat, became wet with perspiration, wrinkled, and in bad condition. Following the service he was invited to a home in the town for the noon-day meal. His hostess knew the condition of the Bishop's vestments and gave them to her cook to wash and iron. While at the table eating the meal, the cook

---

[54] *Some Memoirs,* Gailor, p. 10.
[55] *Ibid.,* p. 14.
[56] As told to the writer by the Rev. Paul Shields Walker, Rector, Holy Trinity, Memphis, Tennessee.

stuck her head inside the door and said: "Miss Jane." "Yes, Sally, what is it?" Said Sally, "I wonder if de arch-angel wants starch in hes shimmy, or no!"[57]

Mrs. Gailor was ever a tower of strength to her great and beloved husband. Her inestimable qualities of character, staunch convictions, thoughtfulness, and gentleness of manner made her a devoted, gracious companion throughout their forty-six years of married life.

When St. Mary's Cathedral had been completed and a large celebration had been held in commemoration of the occasion—at which time it was named Gailor Memorial—a dinner was given at the Gayoso Hotel in honor of Bishop Gailor. In reporting the meaningfulness of the day the local press had noted:

> It was an expression of the joy of his people in welcoming him back home, in pledging their loyalty, their devotion, their love.

The Bishop sat and listened intently to words of praise and affection as he was lauded, probably as no other living Memphian had been. When the time came for his response he did so in characteristic fashion. Whatever measure of success he had attained, he said, he owed to God, his sincere belief in the efficacy of prayer, his mother and Mrs. Gailor.[58]

Totally expressive of Bishop Gailor's numerous experiences abroad, where he was ever associated with the great of Church and State, is this account written by him of June 25, 1930:

> Wore my robes and was in the procession at the great service at the reopening of St. Paul's Cathedral. It was a great occasion. Their Majesties the King and Queen were present, and many thousands of people, including the great ones of the land; but the most interesting thing to me was the procession of carpenters, bricklayers and stonemasons, who had worked on the building and were given special seats.[59]

Ellen Douglas Cunningham Gailor died on October 8, 1931. Bishop Gailor, in his accustomed Christian faith bore his grief and great loss. Of her passing he said, "Thank God, I am a Christian. I know I shall see Nellie again."[60]

On October 3, 1935, Bishop Gailor died at Sewanee, after a short illness.

On the day of his funeral at Sewanee, as on the day of his fortieth anniversary, the Mountain was thronged with those who came to pay their last tribute, and from far and wide came messages of love and sympathy. The funeral service in All Saint's Chapel, was conducted by Bishops who had been especially near to him: Bishop Maxon, Bishop

---

[57] *Ibid.*
[58] *St. Mary's Cathedral,* Davis, p. 154. Quoted from *Commercial Appeal,* January, 1926.
[59] *Memoirs,* Bishop Gailor, p. 296.
[60] *Ibid.* (Conclusion by the Rt. Rev. Henry J. Mikell, D.D., Bishop of Atlanta), p. 339.

Bratton of Mississippi, Bishop Mikell of Atlanta, Bishop Juhan of Florida and Bishop Morris of Louisiana.

Mingled with the sorrow of those who gathered at the Mountain Cemetery at Sewanee, was a great pride in a great life of service and thankfulness to God who had for so long given us so great a leader.[61]

Fifty-five years as a priest and forty-two years the Bishop of the Protestant Episcopal Church in Tennessee! His fame was not only Tennessee's, but the nation's. He was an international figure. Six years as President of the National Council of the Episcopal Church! Twenty-five years as Chancellor of the University of the South! An unexcelled record of rewarding service to God and to his fellowman.

Truly, it may be said of Bishop Gailor: "A great man and the friend of the great, he never lost his simple kindliness."[62]

> The grand old Church is marching
> Into the far flung battle line,
> Where the voice of God is calling us;
> And the task is yours and mine.
>
> And Tennessee must answer well
> With Hearts both brave and true;
> Our Southland dear, with vision clear,
> Must learn to think and do.
>
> The short, short days are winding
> Into the long, eternal years;
> Our lives are only training times
> With labor, hopes and fears.
>
> Let us bless our work with service
> In the Kingdom, far and nigh,
> And save our souls with peace that rolls
> Serene from Him on high.[63]

The Right Reverend Troy Beatty
Bishop Coadjutor of the Diocese of Tennessee

The devoted pastoral qualities of Troy Beatty endeared him to churchman and neighbor alike. The remarkable character of his youth lasted through manhood. Total integrity, abundant energy and fervent religious

---

[61] *Ibid.*

[62] *St. Paul's Episcopal Church, Chattanooga,* by Edwin S. Lindsey, 1953, p. 86.

[63] A Hymn, *Forward,* written by Bishop Gailor and printed on the program—"Fortieth Anniversary of the Consecration to the Episcopate of The Rt. Rev. Thomas F. Gailor and the 25th Anniversary as Chancellor of the University of the South, Sewanee, Tennessee." (Tune—"There's a Long, Long Trail.")

Author's Note: Bishop Gailor confirmed me at Calvary Church. Miss Ellen Douglas Gailor, the Bishop's daughter, taught English at St. Mary's Episcopal School

Troy Beatty

sentiment combined to make him a splendid gentleman and a consecrated, beloved minister.

In recounting the achievement of the blessed, dedicated men who served as bishops of the Diocese of Tennessee, during the early years, these phrases have been used to delineate their individuality:

> Bishop Otey, The Educator
> Bishop Quintard, The Churchman
> Bishop Gailor, The Statesman
> Bishop Beatty, The Pastor.[64]

Daniel Troy Beatty was born November 12, 1866 in Tuscaloosa, Alabama. He was the eleventh of the twelve children of William Henry and Rebecca Troy Beatty. When he was three years of age the family moved to Mobile, Alabama.

> The large family . . . the aftermath of the Civil War, yellow fever epidemics combined to make life anything but easy, and he started to work before he was in his teens. His first job was in a cotton warehouse and he soon developed into a competent classer. His younger sister remembers one evening, when he was only fourteen, his father proudly telling him that a gentleman had introduced himself to him on the street that afternoon, and told him that he was his son's employer and that the boy was one of whom a father should be very proud.[65]

Business opportunities were thought to be better in Chattanooga, Tennessee, than in Mobile. Troy Beatty was sixteen when the family moved to Chattanooga. Soon thereafter, he began a profitable and satisfactory association with the *Chattanooga Times*. Throughout his life, he held in grateful memory the interesting and varied newspaper experiences which he had in this connection.

Young Troy Beatty became a choir boy at St. Paul's Episcopal Church in Chattanooga. The Reverend George William Dumbell, D.D., Rector of St. Paul's (1885-1892), took much interest in the splendid lad and under Dr. Dumbell's influence he became a Lay Reader. Bishop Charles Todd Quintard and Dr. Dumbell encouraged him to enter the ministry. Thereafter, the young man bent all of his efforts toward working and saving the money which he earned with which to further his education.

At the time of the family's move to Birmingham, Alabama, Troy Beatty secured employment with the *Birmingham Age Herald*. He left this position when he matriculated on March 29, 1887, at the University of the South,

(by the Cathedral on Poplar). I was her student. Miss Mary Louise Pennell, who married Frank Hoyt Gailor, the Bishop's son, was my college classmate.

[64] *Commercial Appeal*, Centennial Edition.

[65] *Beatty, A Family History* by Troy Beatty, Jr., 1952, p. 64.

Sewanee, Tennessee. Full and vital were the years which followed as verified by this chronology of activities and events:[66]

1889—Entered School of Theology, University of the South, Sewanee.
1891—Ordained a Deacon by Bishop Gregg of Texas and spent nearly a year in Texas assisting the Bishop.
1892—May 18—In Calvary Church, Memphis, ordained to the Priesthood by Bishop Charles Todd Quintard.
November 24, married at Sewanee, Tennessee, Miss Frederika Priest Mayhew.
1893—(-1897) Rector, St. Andrew's Church, Darien, Georgia.
1897—(-1916) Rector, Emmanuel Church, Athens, Georgia. Served on the State Diocesan Council.
1901—Elected Diocesan Deputy to General Convention of the Church.
1908—Delegate to Pan Anglican Congress (all churches in world affiliated with Church of England), London.
1916—(-1919) Rector, Grace Church, Memphis, Tennessee.
1917—D.D., University of Georgia.
1919—May 7—Elected Bishop Coadjutor, Diocese of Tennessee.
Sept. 18—Consecrated Bishop Coadjutor in Grace Church, Memphis; Presiding Bishop Daniel Sylvester Tuttle, Chief Consecrator.
1919—(-1922) Tennessee Trustee, University of the South.
1920—D.D., Honorary degree awarded by University of the South.
1922—April 23—Death came in Nashville, Tennessee.
Funeral service was held in Grace Church, Memphis, Tennessee.

The five children of Troy Beatty and Frederika Mayhew Beatty were: (1) Troy Beatty, Jr., born February 5, 1895, in Darien, Georgia; graduated from the University of the South in 1916, B.A. degree; employed by Union Planters National Bank, Memphis; served in Air Force, World War I and was commissioned Second Lieutenant; in 1922 he graduated with an LL.B. degree from Memphis Law School and was admitted to the Bar; since 1926 he has held positions of rank with the First National Bank, Memphis; he has served on the Vestry of Grace-St. Luke's Episcopal Church, Memphis; he is a Kiwanian. On December 21, 1938, he married in Auburn, Alabama, Miss Ernestine Patterson Hill, born May 14, 1913; their children are Troy Beatty, III, Ernestine Hill Beatty and Anita Mayhew Beatty; 2) Frederika Beatty, born March 3, 1897, in Darien, Georgia; graduated from Bryn Mawr, 1919, B.A.; Columbia University, M.A., in 1922 and Ph.D. in 1939; for many years a member of English Faculty, Hunter College, New York; 3) Georgiana Mayhew Beatty, born Atlanta, Georgia, February 12, 1899; graduated from Peabody College, Nashville, B.S., 1922, Miss Lucy Gage,

---

[66] (a) *Sewanee Alumni News*, Centennial Directory, 1957. (b) *Beatty, A Family History*, by Troy Beatty, Jr., 1952. (c) *St. Paul's Episcopal Church, Centennial History, Chattanooga*, by Edwin S. Lindsey, 1953. (d) *St. Mary's Cathedral, Memphis, Centennial History*, by John H. Davis, 1958.

as major professor; taught in Chattanooga and at Memphis State University as professor of Early Elementary Education;[67] married October 14, 1925 in Grace Church, Memphis, Arthur Gates Merriman, born August 15, 1896. Their children are: Elizabeth Ann Merriman, Arthur Gates Merriman, Jr., and Frederika Beatty Merriman; 4) Mary Beatty, born in Athens, Georgia, August 13, 1900; died there on May 3, 1901; 5) Charles Henry Mayhew Beatty, born Athens, Georgia, January 2, 1902; B.S., Georgia School of Technology, Atlanta; married, Nashville, June 17, 1931, Miss Mary Dickey. Their children: Charles Henry Mayhew Beatty, Jr., Mary Baird Beatty. He was a Lieut. Col. in World War II; killed February 4, 1948.

The families of Beatty, Troy, Mayhew, Day, Gibbs, Barksdale and Pearson combined to create a lineage of distinction for Bishop Troy Beatty.[68]

The Beatty family was originally from Scotland and went to Ireland between 1603 and 1625. Samuel Beatty of Dublin, Ireland, was the first of the family to come to America. In 1767, he married Bridgett Day (born 1748), in Ireland, daughter of Sir Cately Day, who also had two sons—John and Bunberry Day. Samuel Beatty and his brother-in-law, Capt. John Day, owned sailing vessels.[69]

It is recorded that a few months after his marriage, Samuel Beatty "set sail for San Domingo in the West Indies, leaving his wife with her mother in Dublin. From San Domingo he journeyed to North Carolina, and made a prospecting trip up the Cape Fear River. Going as far as he dared, he anchored the ship near the mouth of Black River, and with a few of his men pushed on in small boats up the river to the place now known as Beatty's Bridge, some forty miles above Wilmington. Here he was taken ill with fever, and when Capt. John Day, stopping at Wilmington on his way to San Domingo, heard of his illness he immediately made a trip up the river . . . . He found his brother-in-law too ill to be moved. Capt. Day hastened to Wilmington and sent a message by a ship's captain, to his sister in Dublin advising her of her husband's serious illness."[70]

In time the letter was received by Bridgett Day Beatty in Dublin. A son, William Henry Beatty, born December 15, 1768, then six months old, was

---

[67] Author's Note: Miss Mayhew Beatty, daughter of Bishop Beatty, was Professor of Early Elementary Education for several years at Memphis State University. I was her student. More than once she said to me, "Ellen, after you get your Master's degree you will be back here as head of this department, as I am now!" A few years passed. Miss Beatty had married. I had received an M.A., from Columbia University. The late beloved educator, Dr. John Willard Brister, College President, appointed me to the position which I held for ten years. Troy Beatty, Jr., witnessed the will of my late uncle, Dr. Wm. Little Davies, a brother of Dr. Julius Augusta Davies.

[68] *Beatty, A Family History,* by Troy Beatty, Jr.

[69] *Ibid.*

[70] *Ibid.,* p. 9.

left with her mother as she sailed for Wilmington on the next available vessel. Upon arrival, she learned that her husband, Samuel Beatty, had died.

Evidently, her personal charm and innate qualities contributed much toward the acceptance of the young widow by the five families of the neighborhood. "Traditions of her winsomeness and popularity still linger, and she was apparently of the type well able to take care of herself under any circumstances. An expression: 'That's a Biddy Day for you', is said to be still in vogue in the neighborhood a century and a half later."[71]

About a year after Mrs. Samuel Beatty came to America she married James White of Bladen County, North Carolina. Soon thereafter, she arranged for her two year old son to be brought from Ireland by her brother, Capt. John Day, on his sailing vessel.

William Henry Beatty grew to manhood in America and became the progenitor of this branch of the Beatty family in this country. On January 13, 1792 in New Bern, North Carolina, he married Sophia Gibbs, born February 5, 1773, a daughter of Sir George Gibbs and Margaretta Barksdale. Sophia Gibbs was a niece of Lord John Gibbs, who served as King's Councilor at New Bern. About three miles from Beatty's Bridge, on the road to Fayetteville, North Carolina, William Henry and Sophia Gibbs Beatty built "Pleasant Retreat," a beautiful house which was the seat of the Beatty family until it was destroyed by fire about 1927. "How tragic it is that this so happily christened cradle of the family in America could not have been preserved for posterity's pilgrimages."[72] William Henry Beatty was a substantial farmer, a landowner, a civic-minded citizen who served as Chairman of the Board of Magistrates of Bladen County and as a Ruling Elder of Black River Presbyterian Chapel. His portrait is a prized possession of Troy Beatty, Jr., Memphis, Tennessee.

The genealogy continues—William Henry Beatty, b. Dec. 15, 1768, d. June 13, 1853, md. Jan. 13, 1792, Sophia Gibbs, b. Feb. 5, 1773, d. Apr. 3, 1827. Children: Eliza Margaret, b. Dec. 10, 1792, d. young; William Gibbs, b. Nov. 3, 1794, d. Sept. 28, 1832; Sophia Sarah; John Day, Margaret Ann; George Samuel; Henry Bunberry; Caroline Bridgett; Anabelle and Hays White Beatty.

William Gibbs Beatty, born at "Pleasant Retreat," Beatty's Bridge, Bladen County, North Carolina, son of William Henry and Sophia Gibbs Beatty, md. Feb. 17, 1822, Eliza M. Pearson. He was a vestryman of St. James Episcopal Church, Wilmington, and a member of the House of Commons from Bladen County in the State Assembly of 1818. Their five children were: William Henry Beatty, b. Wilmington, North Carolina, June

---

[71] *Ibid.*, p. 10.
[72] *Ibid.*, p. 15.

17, 1823, d. Nov. 11, 1896; Richmond Pearson, b. 1825, d. 1826; Richmond Pearson, b. 1827, d. 1832; Charles and Douglas Pearson Beatty.

Dr. William Henry Beatty, son of William Gibbs Beatty and Eliza Pearson Beatty, married Jan. 5, 1848, Rebecca Troy, b. Mar. 10, 1829, d. May 8, 1912. Their twelve children were: William Gibbs, b. Beatty's Bridge, North Carolina, Jan. 9, 1849, d. Whistler, Alabama, Sept. 14, 1889; Fannie Troy, b. Aug. 13, 1850, d. Grenada, Mississippi, May 30, 1890, md. Sidney B. Smith; Isaac Croom, b. Oct. 21, 1852, d. Oct. 5, 1926; twins, a son died in infancy and Eliza Pearson, b. June 10, 1854, d. June 10, 1880, md. Pleasant Madison Morris; Rachel Landon, b. Mar. 23, 1856, d. Nov. 4, 1910 (she was known as Sister Mary Rachel in an Episcopal Sisterhood); Alexander James, b. Mar. 15, 1858, d. Sept. 28, 1959; Sarah Sabine, b. Nov. 18, 1859, d. Sept. 18, 1863; Nicholas Cobbs, b. Jan. 19, 1862, d. Nov. 27, 1869; Douglas Pearson, b. Oct. 13, 1864, d. Mar. 3, 1915; DANIEL TROY BEATTY (more presently); and Mary Ann Beatty, b. May 12, 1868, md. the Rev. Richard Warner Lewis Anderson, an Episcopal clergyman of Albemarle County, Virginia.

Dr. William Henry Beatty, the father of Bishop Troy Beatty, was a graduate of the University of North Carolina, the New York Medical College and the Medical College of the University of Pennsylvania. He practiced medicine first at Beatty's Bridge, North Carolina. In 1858, Dr. Beatty moved with his family to Tuscaloosa, Alabama. He was a Major in the Confederate Army in the Civil War and was stationed at the Camp of Instruction, Tuscaloosa. In 1863 he was Chief Surgeon on the Staff of Brigadier General J. R. Chalmers. On November 3, 1863, Dr. Beatty was captured by Yankee soldiers at Collierville, Tennessee, and was held a prisoner in Memphis until December of that year. On account of ill health he was honorably discharged by President Jefferson Davis on June 26, 1864. During subsequent years Dr. Beatty and his growing family made their home in Mobile, Alabama, Grenada, Mississippi, Chattanooga, Tennessee and Birmingham, Alabama, where he died in 1896.

Rebecca Troy,[73] the mother of Bishop Beatty, was the daughter of Alexander Troy, born Salisbury, North Carolina, June 20, 1787, died Wadesboro, North Carolina, April 30, 1841. Alexander Troy was a prominent lawyer of his day. He married in Whiteville, North Carolina, Frances Eleanor Shipman. The parents of Alexander Troy were Michael Troy and Rachel Potts Troy.

At the time Dr. Beatty was consecrated Bishop Coadjutor of the Diocese of Tennessee, Bishop Gailor had been very recently elected president of the

---

[73] *Ibid.,* p. 185.

National Council of the Episcopal Church. Truly, Bishop Gailor needed help, the type of assistance which Dr. Beatty was thoroughly able to provide. To this new official task, Bishop Beatty brought a record of devoted service to the Episcopal Church in both Georgia and in Tennessee.

On April 25, 1922, Bishop Thomas F. Gailor wrote in his diary:

Met funeral party at seven A.M. Ten-thirty officiated at Bishop Beatty's funeral. Bishop Woodcock, Green and Denby present. His service in the Episcopate was brief—only two and a half years—but he had won the love and admiration of the people of his diocese. The simplicity and earnestness of his character endeared him to all who knew him—and in my absence he administered the affairs of the diocese with marked ability.[74]

"His life was an inspiration, one to make any son feel very proud and very humble," wrote Troy Beatty, Jr., in concluding an excellent account of the life history of his distinguished father, Bishop Troy Beatty.

It is felt that to end this sketch of the life of a man so greatly beloved with the words, in part, from the hymn which was his favorite is most appropriate.

The strife is o'er the battle done,
The victory of life is won;
The song of triumph has begun.
Alleluia!

. . . . .

Lord! by the stripes which wounded thee,
From death's dread sting thy servants free,
That we may live and sing to thee.
Alleluia![75]

The Right Reverend James M. Maxon
Fourth Bishop of the Diocese of Tennessee

Entered in his diary by Bishop Thomas F. Gailor was this notation:

Nashville, October 18, 1922—Christ Church, St. Luke's Day. I acted as consecrator for consecration of James M. Maxon as Bishop Coadjutor. Woodcock preached sermon. Burton presented. Great service.[76]

Dr. Maxon became Bishop Coadjutor of the Diocese of Tennessee at a time when his service was fully needed by the Church. Immediately, he began his duties by giving faithful assistance to the inimitable, overworked Bishop Gailor. The Diocese had grown greatly during the many years under Bishop Gailor's guidance. The third Bishop had built soundly upon the

---

[74] *Some Memoirs,* by Thomas F. Gailor, p. 241.
[75] The Hymnal. Easter, Hymn 91.
[76] *Memoirs,* Gailor.

James Matthew Maxon

organization of Bishop Otey and upon the stabilizing reorganization by Bishop Quintard. On September 21, 1922, Bishop Gailor had been reelected President of the National Council of the Episcopal Church, an election over his protest. Thirteen full years lay ahead to be shared by the distinguished Bishop and the able Dr. Maxon, who had been chosen as Coadjutor.

James Matthew Maxon was born on January 1, 1875, in Bay City, Michigan. In 1906 he completed his studies for the ministry at the General Theological Seminary. His ordinations in 1907 were as a deacon and as a priest. He was rector of Grace Church, Galesburg, Illinois, and between 1910-1917 was rector of St. John, Versailles, Kentucky. From 1920 until 1922 he was rector of Christ Church, Nashville, immediately prior to his consecration as Bishop Coadjutor of the Diocese.

Dr. Maxon's association with the University of the South, Sewanee, Tennessee, was in several capacities: 1919-1920, Dr. Maxon was a Kentucky Trustee; 1922-1948, a Tennessee Trustee; 1938-1944, Regent; and between 1942 and 1944 he served as the eleventh Chancellor of the institution.

He was the worthy recipient of three honorary degrees: from Knox College, M.A., 1910; from the University of the South, Sewanee, D.D., 1921; and in 1941 Southwestern University, Memphis, conferred the LL.D.[77]

Dr. Maxon married Miss Blanche Morris of Bay City, Michigan, the place of his birth. They were the parents of two sons—James Matthew Maxon II and John Burton Maxon.

During his time of rectorship at Christ Church, Nashville, Dr. Maxon was extremely active in vital community service. Among his accomplishments in this field were the organization of a club for paper-boys and an extensive, valuable program of rehabilitation for ex-convicts. He helped to organize the Community Fund in Nashville. In behalf of the program of the Church, he improved the Sunday School and organized mid-week Bible Classes. He was largely responsible for having started Camp Gailor-Maxon in 1929.[78]

In succeeding the beloved Bishop Troy Beatty as Coadjutor, Dr. Maxon found his program of duties well organized and in need only of his pursuing the well advanced steps created by his eminent predecessor. An interesting example of the thoroughness of the type of help which he gave to minister and layman when called upon was in this situation. Bishop Maxon had been contacted by members of the vestry of St. Paul's Church, Chattanooga, and his advice sought concerning the finding of a new rector, to succeed upon the resignation of Dr. Loaring-Clark. The interesting concise comments written by the Bishop were:

---

[77] *Sewanee Alumni News*, Centennial Directory, by Petry and Chitty, 1957, p. 353.
[78] *St. Mary's Cathedral*, Davis, p. 172.

St. Paul's is a very important parish. It occupies a strategic position. It is a cornerstone of the Diocese. It can best express its life by helping the Diocese to grow. It needs an outstanding man for its rector . . . a sound Churchman convinced of the importance of the church's organization and its mission to save souls; a preacher able to interpret the Gospel according to the needs of the times; an administrator capable of holding together the varied elements of a big parish, a pastor who would keep in close touch with his flock, an educator, and a civic leader.[79]

In his being personally possessed of all of the characteristics of a minister so carefully outlined for St. Paul's needs made Bishop Maxon fully capable of making these complete recommendations!

A very beautiful facet of the character of Bishop Maxon was that of appreciation, a social grace, at some time forgotten or ignored by busy people. Acts of thoughtfulness which may have seemed unimportant to others were always grasped as reasons for his expression of sincere gratefulness. Neither his rank nor his clerical demeanor ever caused Bishop Maxon to feel that an act of kindness bestowed was less personal than had he been a usual citizen. If such were in part due to his position, he felt doubly the duty of the acknowledgment of the deed.

These activities as recorded by Bishop Maxon in his diary[80] give especial glimpses of his work and express his steadfast devotion to two Bishops of the Diocese, whose memory he held in reverence:

April 8—At Sewanee . . .

Two P.M., addressed the faculty and students of the Theological Department of the University. Went to Winchester . . . "In the afternoon at Sewanee I visited the grave of that devoted soul, Bishop Quintard, Second Bishop of Tennessee."

April 20. Easter Day.

Ten-thirty A.M., in St. Paul's Franklin . . . Proceeded to Columbia . . . Proceeded to Mt. Pleasant. "At six P.M., (sunset), I stopped on my way at St. John's, Ashwood, to visit the grave of Bishop Otey. Placed a flower on the grave of this heroic First Bishop of Tennessee and offered a prayer. 7:30 P.M. in Holy Cross Church, Mt. Pleasant, the Rev. H. K. Douglass read Evening Prayer and I preached, confirmed three persons and addressed them. Motored to Nashville."

In 1926 Bishop Maxon decided to make his home in Chattanooga and to serve the Diocese from that vantage point. It is needless to say that the people of the area were delighted by his choice. A Bishop's Residence was purchased. Bishop Maxon, Mrs. Maxon and their sons moved to Chattanooga in April.[81]

---

[79] *St. Paul's Episcopal Church (1853-1953)* by Edwin S. Lindsey, 1953, pp. 57, 58.
[80] Diary of Bishop Maxon, Diocesan Journal, 1925, p. 83.
[81] *St. Paul's Episcopal Church,* by Edwin S. Lindsey, 1953, p. 68.

The Bishop Coadjutor exerted full effort toward the completion of St. Mary's Cathedral and was in charge of arrangements for the opening of the completed church on January 19, 1926.[82]

In the passing of Bishop Thomas F. Gailor on October 3, 1935, James Matthew Maxon, Bishop Coadjutor, became the Fourth Bishop of the Protestant Episcopal Church in the Diocese of Tennessee. The first official installation in the history of St. Mary's Cathedral was that of Bishop Maxon. Because of the historical significance of this installation a copy of the Order of Service is included:

Order of Service
for
The Installation of
The Right Reverend James Matthew Maxon
D.D.
Fourth Bishop of Tennessee

St. Mary's (Gailor Memorial) Cathedral
Memphis, Tennessee

7:30 P.M., Sunday, November 3, 1935

The Order of Service

The Procession of Laity, Clergy, and the Bishop shall enter the Cathedral singing the
Processional Hymn, "God of the Prophets!"....................451

Then shall be said Psalms 122 and 46, and the Creed, the Bishop standing in the midst of the choir, and the others in their accustomed places.

The Creed ended, the Bishop shall kneel before the entrance to the sanctuary, all others standing; and the Dean shall say:

Good People, we are here met in the sight of God, to receive, and install in his office, him who has been elected and consecrated to the office and dignity of Bishop of this Diocese. We ask you to give reverent heed to that which we do, and to offer your earnest prayers that the grace of God may be with us in our undertaking, and may rest upon him now to be installed as our Bishop.

Let the Letters of Consecration now be read.

The Chancellor of the Diocese shall then read the Letters of Consecration.

The Senior Priest, addressing the Bishop shall then say:

You, the Right Reverend James Matthew Maxon, have been duly elected according to the Will of God and the Canons of this Church, and duly consecrated to the office and dignity of Bishop of the Diocese of Tennessee.

---

[82] *St. Mary's Cathedral,* Davis, p. 151.

We, representing the Clergy and People of this Diocese, do ask of you, in the Name of God, your intention and purpose in respect thereof.

The Bishop shall answer:

I, James Matthew Maxon, by the grace of God Bishop of this Diocese of Tennessee, do promise and declare that it is my intention and purpose, well and faithfully to rule and govern the Church in this Diocese; that I will firmly observe the rights and privileges of both Clergy and People, and the laws of the State; I will observe all the statutes and ordinances of this Cathedral Church; and, as much as in me lies, will take care that they are observed by others; and I will also endeavor to promote the welfare and honour of the Diocese and of this Cathedral Church. So help me God. Amen.

Minister. The Law was given by Moses;

People. But Grace and Truth came by Jesus Christ:

Minister and People. Who is God over all, blessed for evermore. Amen.

Minister. The Lord be with you.

Answer. And with thy spirit.

Minister. Let us pray.

Most gracious Father, the giver of all good and perfect gifts, Who of Thy wise Providence has appointed divers Orders in Thy Church; Give Thy Grace, we beseech Thee, to Thy servant, to whom the charge of this Diocese is now committed; and so replenish him with the truth of Thy doctrine, and endue him with innocency of life, that he may faithfully serve before Thee, to the glory of Thy great Name, and the benefit of Thy Holy Church; through Jesus Christ our only Mediator and Redeemer. Amen.

Then, all standing, shall be sung

Hymn, "Come, Holy Ghost, our souls inspire"..................455

After which, the Dean and Chancellor shall conduct the Bishop to the EPISCOPAL CHAIR, and shall place him therein, saying:

We, the Very Reverend Israel Harding Noe, Dean of this Cathedral Church of Saint Mary, and Samuel Bartow Strang, Chancellor of the Diocese of Tennessee, do hereby Induct and Install you, the Right Reverend James Matthew Maxon, into the real, actual and corporal possession of the Bishopric, and Cathedral Church of Saint Mary, of the Diocese of Tennessee, and do place you in the Episcopal Chair, In the Name of the Father, and of the Son, and of the Holy Ghost; promising for ourselves and the Diocese all honour and obedience to your person and office as to our Father in God. The Lord preserve thy going out and thy coming in, henceforth and for evermore. Amen.

Then shall be sung

"Te Deum Laudamus"...................................Lloyd
and then shall follow

The Bishop's Address

after which an Offering shall be taken.

Offertory Anthem: "How Beautiful upon the Mountains".....Harker
Then shall follow

A LITANY OF THE DISCIPLES' WAY

Vers. We are disciples of Christ and called by His Name. Let us draw near unto Him, Who is the Living Way.

Resp. Help us, O Master, to walk in Thy Way.

Vers. For our weakness and failures, grant us true repentance; and that we may TURN from self to Thee.

Resp. Help us, O Master, to walk in Thy Way.

Vers. Through each day's plans and choices, grant us vision and courage to FOLLOW Thee.

Resp. Help us, O Master, to walk in Thy Way.

Vers. Grant us growing minds, that by eager study we may LEARN ever more of Thee and Thy truth.

Resp. Help us, O Master, to walk in Thy Way.

Vers. In joy and in sorrow, in victory or defeat, in all times and occasions, be Thou our confidence and strength as we PRAY in Thy Name.

Resp. Help us, O Master, to walk in Thy Way.

Vers. Stir us to go forth and SERVE Thee, Thou Who art one with all sufferers, the perplexed, and all who need.

Resp. Help us, O Master, to walk in Thy Way.

Vers. In Thy House and at Thine Altar, in fellowship with Thy People, grant us through WORSHIP new power to do Thy Will.

Resp. Help us, O Master, to walk in Thy Way.

Vers. By Thy gift on the Cross, by Thine eternal self-giving, make us ready to SHARE with all who will receive.

Resp. Help us, O Master, to walk in Thy Way.

Our Father, Who art in heaven, Hallowed be Thy Name. Thy Kingdom come, Thy Will be done, On earth as it is in heaven. Give us this day our daily bread. And forgive us our trespasses, As we forgive those who trespass against us. And lead us not into temptation, But deliver us from evil. For Thine is the kingdom, and the power, and the glory, for ever and ever. Amen.

Then shall the Bishop let them depart with his Blessing.

Recessional Hymn, "Christ for the World we Sing"..............486

* * *

Immediately following this Service, the People are invited to tarry and greet the Bishop, who will be in the Chapel of St. Mary, next door to the Cathedral.

* * *

COMMITTEE ON ARRANGEMENTS

The Rev. Charles F. Blaisdell, D.D.
Dean of the Convocation of Memphis.

The Very Rev. Israel H. Noe
Dean of St. Mary's (Gailor Memorial) Cathedral.

Mr. I. N. Chambers
Organist and Musical Director:

Mr. Lawrence Meteyarde, A.R.C.M.
Organ Preludes:

Mr. Adolph Steuterman, F.A.G.O.

Bishop Maxon immediately grasped his duties as he saw them and as he understood the needs of the thriving diocese. One important item which received his attention was the need of reorganization of practices concerning St. Mary's Cathedral. He stated the Cathedral should be "a great Mother Church in which every communicant in the diocese will have a real sense of proprietorship. I do not intend to come to the Cathedral and shine awhile and then go elsewhere . . . A Cathedral is not a place to exalt the ego, to win a front seat in heaven. It must be a great spiritual center reaching out with vision, to the people everywhere."[83]

To stress the evangelism of music, through Evensong of all Memphis parishes every Sunday at the Cathedral; to have the Dean visit other churches and to have other ministers fill the Cathedral pulpit at times; to make the Cathedral a center of missionary work, religious education, and social service and to work toward a better understanding of the "Cathedral Idea" on the part of the clergy and laymen alike, all these were among the objectives of Bishop Maxon.

In June 1937, Bishop Maxon and his family moved to Memphis and occupied the new Episcopal Residence. He had felt the Bishop's House on Poplar was too large for his family's needs. Also, it was a part of his plan that the Bishop's House, by the Cathedral, should become the Diocesan House, and therefore, serve as a location for the various offices of the diocese. All this was accomplished.

The Rev. Edmund P. Dandridge of Christ Church, Nashville, was elected Bishop Coadjutor in 1938.

The highly publicized clerical situation created by Dean Israel H. Noe, as a result of his mental and physical health at the time, caused stirring comment. It was required of the Bishop to state his position in the matter. This he did in kindness and in firmness by a letter to Dean Noe in which he removed the Dean from his position at St. Mary's Cathedral. In concluding his letter to Dean Noe he wrote:

I am taking this occasion also to urge and beseech you to discontinue the fast you are now undergoing, and under medical advice to take the nourishment which you should have.

Bishop Maxon met all vicissitudes with definite Christian courage and diplomacy cushioned in kindness.

The coming of William Evan Sanders to the Cathedral, appointed by Bishop Maxon first as an assistant on the Cathedral staff and later, in 1946, as Acting Dean, was a beacon light in the Bishop's last years as diocesan.[84]

---

[83] *Press-Scimitar,* Dec. 9, 1935. Quoted from *St. Mary's Cathedral,* by Davis, p. 173.
[84] Acting Dean Sanders began on December 23, 1947, as Dean of St. Mary's Cathedral, appointed by Bishop Dandridge.

Bishop Maxon resigned on January 1, 1947, the leadership of the diocese.

Death came to the beloved Bishop on November 8, 1948. He sleeps in the churchyard cemetery of St. John's, Ashwood, a glorious, sacred setting created by the Bishop-General (The Fighting Bishop) Leonidas Polk,[85] and his family, a setting hallowed through the years by the passing of great men who were noble Christians.

The Right Reverend Edmund Pendleton Dandridge
Fifth Bishop of the Diocese of Tennessee

Edmund Pendleton Dandridge, the son of Lemuel Purnell and Isabelle Lawrence Dandridge, was born on September 5, 1881, in Flushing, New York. His brothers and sisters were Florence; Martha, who married Lewis B. Franklin, and Lawrence Dandridge, never married.

Edmund Pendleton Dandridge was descended both maternally and paternally from families of distinguished American lineage. The father, Lemuel Purnell Dandridge, was the son of Adam Stephen Dandridge, who married Serena Pendleton; the grandson of Adam S. Dandridge, who married Martha Pendleton; the great grandson of Alexander Spotswood Dandridge and his wife, Ann Stephen Dandridge; the great grandson of Nathaniel West Dandridge and Dorothea Spotswood Dandridge, and the great-great grandson of William Dandridge, of Elsing Green, and his wife, Unity West.

The mother, Isabelle Lawrence, was the daughter of John W. Lawrence, who married Mary K. Bowne, whose parents were Walter Bowne and Elizabeth Southgate Bowne. Walter Bowne's lineage goes back paternally through James Bowne, Samuel Bowne to John Bowne, for whom the Bowne House in Flushing, New York, was named.

John W. Lawrence was the son of Effingham Lawrence, who married Elizabeth Watson, and back through John Lawrence; Richard Lawrence, who married Hannah Bowne; Joseph Lawrence, who married Mary Townley (daughter of Sir Richard Townley) the line goes to William Lawrence.

On October 6, 1909, Edmund Pendleton Dandridge married in Alexandria, Virginia, Miss Mary Robertson Lloyd. She was the daughter of the Right Reverend Arthur Seldon Lloyd, Suffragan Bishop of the Diocese of New York and Elizabeth Robertson Blackford Lloyd.

The Reverend and Mrs. Dandridge were the parents of two children. A son, Edmund Pendleton Dandridge, Jr., was born February 5, 1912, and

---

[85] *General Leonidas Polk, C.S.A., "The Fighting Bishop,"* by Joseph H. Parks, 1962.

Edmund Pendleton Dandridge

married on April 30, 1938, Ann Davis of Lynchburg, Virginia. Their children are: Ann Davis Dandridge, Sarah Pendleton Dandridge, and Edmund Pendleton Dandridge, III. A daughter, Elizabeth Robertson Dandridge, was born November 23, 1914, and married Angus William McDonald. Their children are: Angus William McDonald, Jr., Edmund Dandridge McDonald, Mary Lloyd McDonald, and Edward Leavell McDonald.

Edmund Pendleton Dandridge, Jr., is a prominent attorney of Baltimore, Maryland. Elizabeth Robertson Dandridge (Mrs. Angus W.) McDonald lives in Lexington, Kentucky.

Edward Pendleton Dandridge studied at Woodbury Forest School. From the University of Virginia he received a B.A. degree in 1902, and in 1903, a Master of Arts degree. In 1906, he earned a B.D. from the Virginia Theological Seminary, and in 1921, the Seminary conferred the honorary degree D.D. He received from Oxford University, England, a B.A. degree in Theology in 1908. The University of the South also conferred upon Dr. Dandridge the honorary degree, Doctor of Divinity, in 1938.

Following his ordination as a deacon in June 1906, and as a priest in December 1908, he began his first ministry in Greenbrier Parish, Virginia, where he served from 1908 until 1911. During World War I, he was in France as an Army Chaplain. Between 1911 and 1923, Dr. Dandridge was rector of St. Paul's Church, Petersburgh, Virginia. He became rector of Christ Church, Nashville, Tennessee, in 1923.

"The Bower," the ancestral home near Martinsburg, West Virginia, was retained by Dr. and Mrs. Dandridge and was enjoyed by them and their growing children as a pleasant summer home.

At a special convention called by Bishop Maxon on April 20, 1938, Dr. Dandridge was elected Bishop Coadjutor of the Diocese of Tennessee. He was consecrated in Christ Church, Nashville, on September 20, 1938. He continued to make his home in Nashville.

Upon the retirement of Bishop James M. Maxon on December 31, 1946, Dr. Dandridge became the fifth bishop of the Protestant Episcopal Church in Tennessee.

On January 1, 1947, in traditional, solemn ceremony in St. Mary's Cathedral, Memphis, the Right Reverend Edmund Pendleton Dandridge was formally installed as the bishop of the one hundred eighteen year old diocese. The Cathedral was filled by the more than two thousand persons who came from over the state to witness the impressive service.

The installation was conducted by Dr. Prentice Pugh, rector of the Church of the Advent, Nashville, senior priest in Tennessee, and S. Bartow Strang of Chattanooga, diocesan chancellor.

The colorful ceremony began at five o'clock in the afternoon with a procession of the choristers, ministers, and lay leaders led by a crucifer, the trumpeters, the candle-bearers and followed by the flags of the nations in the church. Among the lay leaders in the procession were these local men of the field of education—Dr. O. W. Hyman, dean, University of Tennessee College of Medicine; Dr. Charles E. Diehl, president, Southwestern University, and Dr. J. Millard Smith, president, Memphis State University. Walter Chandler, former mayor of Memphis, was master of the procession.

Upon completion of the prescribed ceremony of installation, official greetings from The Honorable Jim Nance McCord, Governor of Tennessee, were expressed at the altar by Dudley Gale, prominent Episcopal layman of Nashville. Dr. George P. Myers extended the affectionate greetings and loyalty of the University of the South, Sewanee.

Bishop Dandridge delivered a sermon from the high brass-railed Cathedral pulpit. He appealed to lay members and to the clergy "to meet the difficulties that lie ahead in these soul-testing times." He urged increased cooperation among all denominations.

Bishop Dandridge worked diligently during his time toward the accomplishment of a number of objectives. Significant among these were: the establishment of a closer relationship between parishes within the Diocese; a closer relationship of each parish with the Cathedral parish; planned a graduate training center for religious education; created a greatly needed vault in the Cathedral crypt for the storage of the important records of the Diocese; organized a planning committee for Shelby County and in other urban areas through the state; started a Summer Music Conference at Sewanee and earnestly sought to interest young men to become ministers, to relieve the shortage of clergymen in Tennessee.

Bishop Dandridge experienced the great satisfaction during his regime of the consecration of St. Mary's Cathedral, in 1951.

The positions of national scope in which Dr. Dandridge so worthily served, caused him to become one of the most influential bishops of the Episcopal Church. He was a member of the Episcopal National Council from 1940-1946; a member of the Forward Movement Commission in 1940. He served as chairman of the very important Budget and Program Committee of the General Council. Five times he served as a deputy to the General Convention.

The beloved wife of Bishop Dandridge—Mary Robertson Lloyd Dandridge—died of a cerebral hemorrhage on December 11, 1951, in Nashville, Tennessee, where they made their home in the Elliston Apartments. She was taken to Martinsburg, West Virginia, where she was interred in the family graveyard.

At his retirement as Bishop of the Diocese of Tennessee, Dr. Dandridge, the Virginia gentleman who had served the ministry of the Episcopal Church for forty-seven years, was saluted as a "Great, Good Man." At a very elaborate testimonial banquet given in his honor early in 1953 at the Richland Country Club, Nashville, and attended by more than three hundred-fifty persons, the beloved minister was paid abundant and deserved tribute. To the homage which came to him, the ever-modest Bishop replied, "These tributes are your accomplishments and I return them to you!"

Among the several published testimonials, which gave notice of the Bishop's decision to be relieved of the duties of leadership of the Diocese, was this timely editorial entitled "Retirement of Bishop Dandridge:"[85a]

The Rt. Rev. Edmund P. Dandridge's announcement of his impending retirement from his post as Bishop of the Episcopal Diocese of Tennessee will not, we are certain, mean his retirement from public life. For this eminent churchman will regard the extra time at his disposal simply as an added opportunity for him to serve his fellow man in some new way.

The good works and worthwhile achievements of Bishop Dandridge are past any full recounting. In all manner of civic, church and humanitarian enterprises, he occupies himself with a zeal and a devotion which make their beneficial influences and effect felt throughout his spiritual domains, his community, his state and his region.

He is a man of dignity yet a man of humility. He is a scholarly thinker with a keen mind, yet an intensely human person with a warm personality. His convictions and his courage and faith in following those convictions cannot help but impart to others a knowledge of what may be needed in themselves to find the greater contentment which is so necessary to complete living in this or any other age . . .

He is a man who believes in and who exemplifies the good life. and he has made that good life shine in the eyes and hearts of all who have had the privilege of knowing him and associating with him.

He has been and is a lofty and living ideal in action, a never-failing example of the supremacy of service among the values which mankind has established for its standards. He has been and will continue to be an inspiration for strengthening and renewing man's devotion to the more enduring purposes and values of life. . . ."

Brief, indeed, was the retirement of this vital, vigorous man of faith and earnest devotion to the advancement of God's Kingdom among men. On February 6, 1953, Bishop Dandridge was chosen as Dean of the School of Theology, the University of the South, Sewanee, Tennessee, to succeed

---

[85a] *The Nashville Banner*, Nashville, Tenn., Thursday, Jan. 22, 1953.

Dean F. Craighill Brown, resigned. Of the appointment, Vice-Chancellor Edward McCrady said:

The University is happy to announce that Bishop Dandridge will assume the post of the Dean of the Seminary. There is no need to attempt to define for the friends of the University and for the Church the high standing that Bishop Dandridge holds in the ecclesiastical world. We are happy, too, that we are able at this time to assure the students and the bishops and clergy of the twenty-two dioceses owning the University of the assembling of a faculty of sound learning and experience in teaching . . .

I am convinced that the training of Negro clergy is more than ever before, a matter of crucial concern; also that the issues involved cannot be resolved in a vacuum. I assume, therefore, that I would be expected to exercise whatever Christian conviction I possess in deciding the issues of concrete cases—namely, the application of a qualified Negro candidate for admission to the Theological Seminary. I hope that the trustees of the University can clarify this issue for the sake of the future educational effectiveness of the Theological Seminary and the conscience of everyone involved."

Bishop Dandridge served for three years as Dean of Theology at Sewanee. At the conclusion of this service to the University of the South, this resolution by the Board of Trustees expressed the gratitude and affectionate esteem of its members to Bishop Dandridge:

Called from a well-earned period of retirement to aid the University of the South in its all important School of Theology, he responded with characteristic alacrity and from a well developed sense of obligation.

His term as Dean of St. Luke's couched between painful controversy and a disastrous fire, he proceeded to rebuild the School of Theology into the likeness of its great days—an undertaking appropriately symbolized in the present expansion of the fabric of St. Luke's.

To this vital task of healing and reconstruction he brought God-given talent for administration, and Spirit-given personal attributes so essential to its successful prosecution. He humored some; others he commanded. Some he drove; others he led—as the Lord's work required. All he respected and encouraged. Rare is the combination of scholarship, pastoral wisdom and administrative gifts that adorn him.

He moves to retirement belatedly, but with the gratitude of a Church happily more enlightened concerning her responsibilities for theological education. He turns over to another remarkably qualified person—as Dean—an institution which, once more, can proudly face its peers.

Significantly and with distinction, the East Window of St. Luke's Chapel, Sewanee, was dedicated in honor of Bishop Dandridge on June 6, 1957. The order of the service of dedication follows:

Order for the Dedication of the East Window

OF

St. Luke's Chapel

The School of Theology, The University of the South

SEWANEE, TENNESSEE

EVENSONG, THURSDAY, JUNE 6, 1957, AT 5:30 P.M.

*After the Hymn following the Collects, the Chancellor shall say:
  V. The Lord be with you.
  R. And with thy spirit.
  V. Let us pray.

The University Prayer

ALMIGHTY GOD, the Father of our Lord Jesus Christ, we, Thy servants, implore Thy blessing upon this University. Give the Spirit of Wisdom to all those to whom Thou hast given the authority of teaching and of government. Let the students grow in grace day by day; enlighten their minds, purify their hearts, and sanctify their wills. Bless all who have contributed to this Institution; and raise up to the University, we humbly pray Thee, a never-failing succession of benefactors, through our Lord and Saviour, Jesus Christ. *Amen.*

The Prayers for The School of Theology

O ETERNAL GOD, inspirer of the prophets and priests of old, look down from heaven, we humbly beseech Thee, and inspire those who go forth from this place to preach the Gospel of Thy blessed Son. Open their eyes that they may see the wondrous things of Thy law; deepen their faith that they may believe in the coming of Thy kingdom; so that, seeing and believing, they may bring many to Jesus Christ our Lord. *Amen.*

O GOD, whose blessed Son Jesus sat humbly in the midst of the doctors, both hearing them and asking them questions; grant us, Thy servants, both aptness to teach and willingness to learn; that we may daily increase in wisdom and humility and be made obedient followers of Thy Son, our Saviour, Jesus Christ. *Amen.*

Antiphon. I will make thy windows of agates, and all thy borders of pleasant stones.
  V. Look upon the rainbow, and praise him that made it;
  R. Very beautiful it is in the brightness thereof.
  V. Let us pray.

O GOD, who hast filled the world with the radiance of Thy glory; Bless, we beseech Thee, this Window, which we dedicate to Thee, in honour of Thy faithful servant Edmund Pendleton Dandridge, that as the light shines through it in many colors, so our lives may show forth the beauty of Thy manifold gifts of grace; through Jesus Christ our Lord. *Amen.*

*Then shall the Chancellor pronounce the Benediction.

Death came to Bishop Dandridge on January 28, 1961, in his seventy-ninth year. He suffered a fatal heart attack at the home of his daughter, Mrs. Angus W. McDonald and Mr. McDonald, in Lexington, Kentucky, where he had resided since his final retirement in 1956.

Energetic, scholarly, beloved, Edmund Pendleton Dandridge—a man of grace, full in faith, a man of good deeds, the fifth Bishop of the Episcopal Diocese of Tennessee was called "The Missionary."

The Right Reverend Theodore Nott Barth
Sixth Bishop of the Diocese of Tennessee

He was a choir boy when he was seven, a bishop at fifty years of age. "I practically grew up in the Church," Bishop Barth once said. His parents, George Godfrey Barth and Mary Elizabeth Markel Barth, were active communicants of St. George's Episcopal Church in Mount Savage, Maryland.

It was in Mount Savage that Theodore Nott Barth was born, July 11, 1898. German, Swiss and Dutch progenitors contributed to his ancestry.

At an early age, the precocious boy showed a distinct talent in music. He studied piano and violin under private instructors in nearby Cumberland, Maryland and became proficient in the art. For quite a while young Theodore Barth was a member of a string quartette. In manhood, he continued to play both violin and piano, an accomplishment which provided for him great personal enjoyment.

After graduation from High School, Cumberland, Maryland, college years and ordinations followed:

1918—B.A., University of Virginia; Phi Beta Kappa.
1921—Dec. 17. Ordained to Diaconate in Bishop's Chapel, Baltimore, Maryland.
1922—B.D., Virginia Theological Seminary.
1922—Oct. 18. Ordained, Priest in St. George's Chapel, Mt. Savage, Maryland.
1922-1924—Rector, Deer Creek Parish, Harford County, Darlington, Maryland.
1924-1928—Rector, All Saints Church, Reisterstown, Maryland.
1928-1940—Rector, St. Bartholomew, Baltimore, Maryland.
1940—Mar. 10-1948, Sept. 21. Rector, Calvary Church, Memphis, Tennessee.
1943—D.D. Honorary Degree awarded by Southwestern, Memphis, Tennessee.
1948—April 21. Elected Bishop Coadjutor, Diocese of Tennessee.
1948—Sept. 21. Consecrated Bishop Coadjutor in Calvary Church, Memphis. Tuesday morning at ten o'clock, St. Matthew's Day— the Apostle and the Evangelist.

Theodore Nott Barth

1953—Sept. 21. Installed as Bishop of the Diocese, in St. Mary's Cathedral, Monday morning at ten o'clock.

On June 4, 1923, Theodore Nott Barth and Elizabeth Pike Ellicott were married by the Rt. Rev. John Gardner Murray in a beautiful garden setting in Baltimore. Elizabeth Pike Ellicott was the daughter of Charles Lewis Ellicott and Elizabeth Wetherill Thompson Ellicott. Through her great grandmother, Mary Ann Thomas, Mrs. Barth was descended from Phillip Thomas of Maryland. Bishop Barth once said this of his wife:

> She has more than been my helpmate through the years—she is always there to rejoice with me in glad tidings and encourage me in times of stress.

A son and a daughter were their children. Theodore Nott Barth, Jr., married Mary Bayless of Athens, Tennessee. They have one daughter, Melissa Bayless Barth, born August 13, 1961. They make their home in Maryville, Tennessee. Sarah White Barth married Aubrey Tomlin. They have one daughter, Elizabeth Barth Tomlin, born August 8, 1951. They reside in Metairie, Louisiana.

Beginning with the very first sermon preached in March 1940, at Calvary Church, by the new rector, the Rev. Theodore Nott Barth, copious words of praise prevailed. The rectorate of his predecessor, the late Dr. Charles F. Blaisdell, had lasted for twenty wonderful years. To succeed a man so beloved as was Dr. Blaisdell was indeed a challenge. Abundant energy of mind and spirit were evident as the Rev. Mr. Barth began the task of ministering to Calvary's appreciative flock.

Only a man full of faith, diligent in leadership and capable of distinguishing himself by forceful sermons and dedicated service, could have won the approbation of the communicants of the historic parish. Dr. Barth possessed all of these qualities and during his rectorate of eight years won the sincere and lasting affection of the people of Calvary. These years are recorded among the brightest and most fruitful in the church's history.

Most certainly it may be said that as Bishop Otey preached through his teaching, Bishop Barth taught through his preaching! Fervent in prayer, he sought with perseverance to share with all men the joy which he had found through prayer. The schools of prayer and the retreats conducted by Bishop Barth are recalled as memorable experiences, rich in the abundance of God's grace and in glorious closeness to the Master!

Early in his episcopacy, Bishop Barth became interested in making the Diocesan House a more efficient and comfortable environment for the administration of the affairs of the Diocese. Therefore, a program of renovation was initiated and necessary improvements were made both to the interior and exterior of the large stone building. Concerning the project he had remarked before the 1953 Convention:

> It is a lovely old house. . . . I hope to gather around me there the various offices and officers who ought to be near at hand. . . . I have asked for enough (money) to keep it in good repair . . . I am going to spend my working hours there. But in a very real sense it is your house. . . . We want to look our best when company comes.

The plan of record-keeping started by Bishop Dandridge was earnestly continued by Bishop Barth. The vault in the crypt of St. Mary's Cathedral was completed. At the 1955 Convention the Bishop urged each Parish to assemble its records and to use the vault as a depository for the historical documents of the church. He felt keenly the great need of preserving all kinds of church records. He said that numerous irreplaceable items of church history had been either lost or destroyed during past years. That he foresaw this important step as just a beginning would seem plausible. He must have foreseen the future inadequacy of the arrangement which he encouraged. That to meet the future needs of the Diocese a larger room might be required—certainly fire proof, accessible, comfortable during all seasons, where the records and objects of church history might be preserved, observed and consulted.[86]

Canon James R. Sharp moved the diocesan records to the vault. In 1956, M. C. Nichols of Chattanooga was appointed to serve as Administrative Assistant to Bishop Barth. He also performed many duties previously carried forward by Canon Sharp.

Far reaching indeed were the objectives and the accomplishments during the days of Bishop Barth. The purchase and renovation of property on which was created the Du Bose Conference Center at Monteagle, Tennessee, was an effort of gigantic proportions and great reward. On eight college campuses in Tennessee new student centers were established, thereby providing representation of the Episcopal Church on every college campus within the State. The organization of All Saints' Mission, Memphis; the creation of a fund with which to aid in the building of church-houses; the rebuilding of Emmanuel Church, Memphis; participation in a Diocesan Survey sponsored by National Council, and the decided increase in membership during Bishop Barth's constructive years, all were evidences of marked achievement of the Church in Tennessee.

In commemoration of ten years of growth and progress in the diocese since Bishop Barth's consecration as bishop, special services were held at St. Mary's Cathedral, on Sunday, September 21, 1958. The Festal Evensong,

---

[86] The Archives Room of the Episcopal Church, Diocese of Tennessee, an appropriate name.

in honor of Bishop Barth, was planned by Tennessee Episcopal clergy. More than eighty clergymen were present. The assembly comprised of laymen, diocesan staff members and friends, totalled more than two hundred fifty persons. Among the groups whose representatives brought tributes to Bishop Barth were the Episcopal Churchmen of Tennessee, the Woman's Auxiliary and the House of Young Churchmen. Bishop Nobel C. Powell, of Maryland, long a warm friend of Bishop Barth was present and spoke. He said of Bishop Barth:

> He is a custodian of the Christian faith, an humble man, who despite his great responsibility, has never forgotten he is a brother to all mankind and friend to all who knew him.

A beautiful reception which honored Bishop and Mrs. Barth was held in St. Mary's Parish House following the service. At seven-thirty that evening a splendid dinner by the Episcopal clergymen of Tennessee honored Bishop Barth. On this delightful occasion the Rt. Rev. John Vander Horst, Suffragan Bishop, presented a new crozier, or bishop's staff, to Bishop Barth. To this the Bishop said:

> I look back over the past ten years of my work as bishop with a feeling of great joy and thankfulness. This period takes in five years of my own administration as diocesan, as well as the five I spent as Bishop Dandridge's Coadjutor.

Bishop Barth's reply to the many eulogies spoken was in part:

> It is the Lord's work. Whatever has been done has been of His ordering and in His sight. We shall endeavor to continue to do His will to His glory and advancement of His church and kingdom among us.

The well-rounded, versatile personality of Bishop Barth made him popular as an evangelist in the pulpit and as a guest in the home! He was a gifted and pleasing conversationalist. His love of music, his keen appreciation of sculpture and painting; his fondness for travel—all these were among his cultural interests.

He was an enthusiastic sportsman. Fishing was a favorite diversion and he was a baseball enthusiast. He found great pleasure in being at the helm of a sailing yacht! Annually, he made a trip with friends who sailed in Chesapeake Bay. He was a Rotarian.

Although prevented by illness from presiding at the one hundred twenty-ninth Diocesan Convention held at the Church of the Holy Communion, Memphis, Tennessee, in January, 1961, Bishop and Mrs. Barth were present for a while at a session of the Convention. Bishop John Vander Horst, Suffragan Bishop, was elected by the Convention to preside. The Bishop's Message was read by Dean William E. Sanders. A part of his message follows:

The Kingdom of God is His Kingdom and He alone can build it. It is not given to us, as it is sometimes thought, to build it for Him. Our part is simply to yield ourselves to Him in faith and trust and obedience so that He might use us as living stones for the structure. Our first task is to be men of God as St. Paul wrote to the Ephesians—"fellow citizens with the Saints!"

Death came to distinguished and beloved Bishop Barth on August 22, 1961, Tuesday night, at nine forty-five, in the Baptist Hospital, Memphis, Tennessee. His illness had been long and arduous. From February until August, while he was hospitalized, he welcomed his friends and remained remarkably active under the circumstances of declining health.

During those months, gifts of food and flowers, of books, a flask or so of his favorite brandy, and many other items of a material nature were carried to his hospital room by friends innumerable. And, not one person came away empty-handed! To each person who called, he gave in his own inimitable manner, not only his greeting but his blessing. A smile of hope, a word of courage, an eager interest in the world outside, — in which he was aware he could never move again as a cherished, happy participant, — all these manifestations of faith, he shared with friends and family during his last days.

Of the many words of praise which have been so well written, descriptive of the life and work of Bishop Barth, no account has been found which better expresses, than does the following, the fullness of spirit and the abundant goodness which were typical of this dedicated disciple:

Peace, which is held so tenuously by the multitude, was magnified in the lifework of the Rt. Rev. Theodore N. Barth and attained in his death.[87]

The sixth bishop of the Episcopal Diocese of Tennessee was a true disciple of Christianity, leaving its mark of grace on whatever he touched.

Resplendent in the robes of his office, he remained an humble man, a servant happy in the work to which he was dedicated. In the pulpit, he had a mighty ringing voice which he could soften to a dramatic whisper, drawing the minds of his listeners down the paths of his teachings.

In his gentle eyes, one felt he saw and knew the future, and indeed he was a man reaching out to eternity. No man felt more strongly the burden of man's sin and weakness, and no man carried the burden more easily in the knowledge that spiritual life supersedes physical life.

No more significant burial day could have occurred for Bishop Barth. Today is St. Bartholomew's Day in the Anglican Church, and it

---

[87] *Commercial Appeal,* Memphis, Tennessee, August 24, 1961, an Editorial,, "Bishop Theodore Barth."

was this apostle whom the bishop had taken to be his patron saint. He often recalled those words Jesus spoke of Bartholomew (Nathanael):
"Behold an Israelite indeed, in whom is no guile"
The words were an appropriate epitaph for Bishop Barth.
Those close to him always felt the peace that walked beside him.
In his death, he simply draped himself in the mantle of "the peace of God which passeth all understanding."

On Thursday, August 24, 1961, less than an hour before five o'clock, the appointed time for the graveside service and interment of Bishop Barth, a shower of rain fell at St. John's and over the surrounding countryside. It was not in reality a wetting rain but one gentle, soft and refreshing. Falling as it did at that time, on a late summer afternoon, it was happily received and was indeed lovely. From all over the Diocese ministers, churchmen, churchwomen and friends had come bearing their grief, each in his own way, in the loss of so great a man of God.

Only a moment before the pallbearers, bearing the red-bronze mahogany casket, approached the open grave, the clouds dispersed, the sun came through and shone across the church grounds and the verdant green hills beyond. On leaves and flowers all about, raindrops were illuminated in varied hues and the entire setting seemed the result of some special, kindly dispensation.

So there at St. John's, Ashwood, in Maury County, the Sixth Bishop of Tennessee was committed to the earth by his successor, the Right Reverend John Vander Horst, D.D., Bishop Coadjutor, and the Very Reverend William E. Sanders, Dean of St. Mary's Cathedral. And, there was a new grave only a few feet removed, to the north, from the grave of Bishop Otey, the First Bishop of the Diocese of Tennessee.

At the 75th Annual Meeting of the Churchwomen of the Diocese, held at St. John's in Memphis, May 1-3, 1962, an oil tinted photographic portrait of Bishop Barth was unveiled. It was a gift of the past and present diocesan Churchwomen's Board Members. The portrait was given to be hung over the mantel in the "Bishop Barth Common Room" at Du Bose. More than three hundred were present and adopted the following resolution of presentation by standing in silence while the resolution was being read:

> Whereas our beloved bishop, Theodore Nott Barth, departed this life in sure and certain hope of the Resurrection to eternal life through our Lord Jesus Christ; therefore we, the Episcopal Churchwomen of the Diocese of Tennessee, in convention assembled, do resolve to joyfully remember the countless wonders God worked through him while he sojourned with us, and do pray that what was so nobly begun on earth may have its perfect consummation in the Church Triumphant.

John Vander Horst

The Right Reverend John Vander Horst
Seventh Bishop of the Diocese of Tennessee

"Let us all have thankful hearts and be gay," he said, after he had spoken with fervent distinction the invocation. Guests had assembled for a beautifully appointed luncheon[88] which honored clergymen, invited laymen and ladies and followed a service of ordination[89] in Trinity Church, Mason, Tennessee.

The spacious rooms of the Diocesan House rang with musical tones created by one lustily whistling (interspersed by song), and seemingly unaware of having an audience. "Who is that who whistles so joyously," a visitor asked. The pleasant, alert secretary replied, "Oh that is our new Bishop of the Diocese whose office is upstairs—our happy, 'Whistling Bishop'!"

And those cherished words, of admonition concerning thankful hearts and being gay, had been spoken by the dedicated, dignified, magnetic "Whistling Bishop"—the Right Reverend John Vander Horst, D.D., Tennessee's seventh bishop of the Episcopal Church.

To be possessed of those qualities of character which embody dedication of total personality in deeds of duty and devotion to God; a dignity appropriate to every need in administering the ecclesiastical rites of the Church; a magnetism by which people are fortified in faith and are drawn together in worship, most assuredly denote "the mystery of godliness," concerning which St. Paul[90] wrote. And, when coupled with all these, the heart of the man is found to be grateful and gay, the true qualities of a steward have been achieved.

Faithfully written by Bishop Vander Horst in his journal in August 1961, were the following records, significant in church history:

8/22—"Call from Mrs. O'Kane[91] at home telling me of the death of the Rt. Rev. Theodore Nott Barth, D.D., Father-in-God and Friend of the Diocese of Tennessee. . . ."

8/24—"St. Bartholomew's Day—8:30 A.M., celebrated a memorial service of the Holy Eucharist to the Glory of God and for the repose of the soul of Theodore Nott Barth, Sixth Bishop of Tennessee. 10 A.M., assisted by Dean Sanders and the Rev. Thorne Sparkman, D.D., rector of the Church of the Redeemer, Bryn Mawr, Pennsylvania, read the Burial Office for the bishop. 5 P.M., St. John's Ashwood, the Dean and I read the interment service together. . . ."

---

[88] In the home of Mr. and Mrs. J. N. M. Taylor, Mason Tennessee.
[89] The Rev. Ben H. Shawhan, Jr.
[90] I Timothy, 3:16.
[91] Mrs. Barney (Bernice Wolcott) O'Kane, secretary to Bishop Barth, June 1951-August 1961 and continues as secretary to Bishop Vander Horst.

More than a thousand persons crowded St. Mary's (Gailor Memorial) Cathedral on the morning of October 12, 1961. Each had come to witness the solemn, colorful service of installation of the Right Reverend John Vander Horst, seventh bishop of the Protestant Episcopal Church in Tennessee.

At ten-thirty o'clock "Bishop Vander Horst rapped soundly on the massive West Door of the Cathedral and requested admission for installation. . . ."[92] Thus began the service of induction, investiture and installation. The Bishop's knock on the door was answered by the Standing Committee of the Diocese and the Cathedral Chapter of St. Mary.

At the foot of the chancel steps the Bishop knelt and there received the blessing of Bishop Louttit.[93] He received at the altar the crozier, a symbol of his office. He was escorted by the Canons[94] of the Cathedral to be seated in the Cathedra, the bishop's chair. Following the service of the Holy Eucharist, Bishop Vander Horst addressed the large assembly.

The magnificent music was a splendid contribution to the memorable service. Truly, the choir, the organ, the trumpets, the drums blended to enhance the solemn beauty and great religious dignity of the historic rites.

On the day of Bishop Vander Horst's installation, a special session[95] of the 129th Convention was held and unanimous approval was obtained of his request that a Bishop Coadjutor be elected. After such action had been taken, he announced the election would be held on January 19, 1962, during the Diocesan Convention. Bishop Vander Horst also authorized a "Prayer for the Bishop Coadjutor" to be used throughout the Diocese:

> Almighty God, the giver of all good gifts, who of thy divine providence hast appointed divers Orders in thy Church; Grant, we beseech thee, that the Convention of the Church in this Diocese may have grace and wisdom to choose a godly and well-learned man to be ordained and consecrated Coadjutor Bishop, who may evermore be ready to spread abroad thy Gospel, the glad tidings of reconciliation with thee, and use the authority given him not to destruction, but to salvation, not to hurt but to help; so that, as a wise and faithful servant, giving to thy family their portion in due season, he may at last be received into everlasting joy; through Jesus Christ Our Lord. Amen.

---

[92] Forward in Tennessee, November-December, 1961.

[93] The Right Rev. Henry I. Louttit, Bishop of South Florida and president of the Fourth Province of the Church.

[94] The Rev. M. C. Nichols and the Rev. Wm. A. Dimmick.

[95] Called on Sept. 11, 1961 by Bishop Vander Horst to meet following his installation on Oct. 12, 1961.

John Vander Horst was born in Orange, New Jersey, on January 10, 1912, the son of Elias and Ella Virginia Cole Vander Horst. He attended the Gilman School, Baltimore, Maryland. At Stephen's House, Oxford, England, and the Virginia Theological Seminary he pursued the study of Theology.

Ordained a deacon in June 1938, a priest in 1939, he began his first rectorate at St. John's Church, Ellicott City, Maryland, where he was the rector until 1942. Other churches which he served were: St. Paul's Church, Macon, Georgia, 1942-1945; Church of the Good Shepherd, Philadelphia, Pennsylvania, 1945-1951, and St. Paul's Church, Chattanooga, Tennessee, 1951-1955.

Obviously destined to serve his Church in positions of rank, the Reverend Mr. Vander Horst was elected on March 2, 1955, Suffragan Bishop. On April 19, 1961, he was chosen Bishop Coadjutor and on August 22, 1961, became Bishop of Tennessee. In such manner, Bishop Vander Horst became the first to have served the Diocese as Suffragan, Bishop Coadjutor and as Bishop.

Bishop Vander Horst has been the recipient of two honorary degrees, D.D. Both degrees were conferred in 1955, by the Virginia Theological Seminary and the University of the South, respectively.

Gathered around "the shepherd of the flock" in Tennessee, in the sizeable "Bishop's House"[96]—in front of which an expanse of green lawn greets a passerby—is a most enthusiastic and attractive family. It is there, Helen Lawrence Vander Horst presides as the capable, gracious wife of the Bishop and the mother of their four attractive children: Helen (married the Reverend Peter Gaines Keese); John, Jr., Ella and Allston Vander Horst.

During the two years which have passed since Dr. Vander Horst became the Bishop of Tennessee, a formidable program of effort has been organized and is in progress. Of course, continued in full measure, are the pace-setting accomplishments of former diocesans. One of the great objectives of Bishop Vander Horst and his associates, has been that of expansion. This program includes the forward look of purchasing land for church sites in and around the metropolitan areas and in smaller counties, as well, while land is available and no higher in price. Strengthening the student center units, Barth House and Quintard House, Memphis, and others over the state, is recognized as a very important need. The task of giving essential guidance to the work of the Diocese, comprised of one hundred sixteen Parishes and Missions and one hundred forty-eight Priests and Deacons, is unquestionably a broad, magnificent challenge.

---

[96] *Bishopstead,* 3460 Central Ave., Memphis, Tennessee.

All these and more, constitute the duties in stewardship of the present Bishop of Tennessee. It is he, this stalwart man-of-God, who, with grace and great joy, carries forward the business of his Heavenly Father.

> I bind unto myself today
> The power of God to hold and lead,
> His eye to watch, his might to stay,
> His ear to hearken to my need;
> The wisdom of my God to teach,
> His hand to guide, his shield to ward;
> The word of God to give me speech,
> His heavenly host to be my guard.[97]

The Right Reverend William Evan Sanders
Bishop Coadjutor, Diocese of Tennessee

On appointment by the Right Reverend James M. Maxon a well qualified and thoroughly likeable young priest began to serve as Acting Dean of St. Mary's Cathedral. The date was December 23, 1946. And, of this young man, the Reverend William Evan Sanders, whom he had appointed, Bishop Maxon wrote:

He is a cherished son in the Gospel upon whom I lean in my declining years. . . . He has ability, in my judgment, equal to that of any Priest in the Diocese.

And, one year later on the very same day, the Acting Dean was appointed Dean, by the Right Reverend Edmund Pendleton Dandridge. Dean Sanders was popular, from the beginning, with the people, both young and old. It was a predecessor, Dean Harold Brown Hoag, who said of him that he would carry forward "the greatest period in Cathedral history." And, most likely he did!

Dean Sanders' period as Dean of the Cathedral stands unsurpassed in scope. This is verified by the fact that he served as Acting Dean or as Dean under four Bishops of the Diocese: Bishop Maxon, Bishop Dandridge, Bishop Barth and Bishop Vander Horst.

William Evan Sanders was born on Christmas Day, 1919, in Natchez, Mississippi. His parents were Walter R. and Agnes Jones Sanders.

After graduation from high school, in Nashville, he entered Vanderbilt University, where he received a B.A. degree in 1942. Enrollment in the University of the South followed and in 1945, he earned a B.D. degree. In 1946, the S.T.M. (Master of Sacred Theology) was earned in Union Theological Seminary, New York. The University of the South conferred an honorary degree, D.D., in 1959. His ordinations were as a Deacon in February 1945 and as a Priest in June 1946.

---
[97] The Hymnal. Hymn 268.

William Evan Sanders

Interesting indeed is a brief account of the time served by Deacon Sanders as Curate to the Reverend Thorne Sparkman at St. Paul's Church, Chattanooga, Tennessee. The Rev. Mr. Sparkman, a Rhodes scholar, a brilliant preacher, easily won the admiration of intelligent young men of the Church. He was recognized by his "ecclesiastical superiors" as being most capable of instructing young deacons in pastoral duties and in procedure. Therefore among the seven young men who served their apprenticeships under Mr. Sparkman were: Eric Sutcliffe Greenwood,[98] 1944-; William Evan Sanders, 1945, and James O. Bodley,[99] 1947-1949. All did well and continue to serve the Episcopal Church with diligence and with dedication.

In a very beautiful service at St. Mary's Cathedral, Dean Sanders married on June 25, 1951, Kathryn Cowan Shaffer. They are the parents of three daughters: Elizabeth, Kathryn and Laura Sanders.

Dr. Sanders was elected on January 19, 1962, to serve as Bishop Coadjutor of Tennessee. By his consecration, on Wednesday, April 4, 1962, he became the five hundred eighty sixth in the American Succession.

In conclusion, may we summarize the meaningful and appropriate titles which have been given through the passing years to the Bishops of the Diocese:

Bishop Otey — The Educator;

Bishop Quintard — The Churchman;

Bishop Gailor — The Statesman;

Bishop Beatty — The Pastor;

Bishop Maxon — The Administrator;

Bishop Dandridge — The Missionary;

Bishop Barth — The Evangelist;

Bishop Vander Horst — The Steward.

Truly, it is believed that whatever titles may be bestowed, by choice or by achievement, on the present, popular Bishop Coadjutor, not one can excel in meaning—nor in affection—his time honored title—"The Dean!"

---

[98] Rector, Church of the Holy Communion, Memphis, Tennessee.

[99] Rector, St. John's Church, Decatur, Alabama. Son of the late Dr. Bodley and Mrs. James W. Bodley of Memphis.

Foremost and distinctly the Bishops of Tennessee, above all others, have carried the torch of faith and service by which the pathway of the Church's romance has been brilliantly and eternally lighted. Whatever words may be chosen, through which testimony is expressed the admirable selflessness of these great churchmen, it must be said that the Bishops have worked and continue in full effort as servants of the servants of God! Church history records the lives of these just, good men and bespeaks their enduring faithfulness. The full story, however, can be told only as lived by them and transcribed as noble deeds in The Book of the Master.

Their names
Are as a song heard far in the future; and
Their examples reach a hand
Through all the years to meet
And kindle generous purpose;
And to mold it into acts
As pure as theirs.[100]

---

[100] Author unknown.

CHAPTER IX

CHART OF CHURCHES IN WEST TENNESSEE
1832-1964

A chart of the Episcopal Churches, established in the Western District of Tennessee since 1832, has been compiled. The headings are self explanatory. No attempt has been made to give the history in full of each church. When compared to the far-reaching, rich life of each church, the notations are nothing more than thumb-nail sketches.

However, it is a fond hope that this account of the beginnings of the Episcopal Church in West Tennessee may give aid to an abundant harvest of full achievement, duly recorded during the years to come.

THE PROTESTANT EPISCOPAL CHURCH

in

THE WESTERN DISTRICT
(West Tennessee)

TENNESSEE

1832-1964

The most enduring and spiritual of the material monuments of men which have survived the passage of time, are the temples which men have created from age to age to their God.

THOMAS NELSON PAGE

NAME OF CHURCH	LOCATION	DATE ORGANIZED	DATE ADMITTED TO DIOCESE	DATE OF FIRST CHURCH-HOUSE	FIRST RECTOR (DATE)	PRESENT RECTOR (SINCE, DATE)
All Saints	Memphis Shelby County	9/4/1956	1/20/1960	4/18/1957	The Rev. Robertson Eppes, Jr. (Priest-in-charge) Aug. 1956-1/20/1960	The Rev. Robertson Eppes, Jr. 1/1/1960

First service as a mission was held Aug. 12, 1956. Present communicants number 306.

Calvary	Memphis (Second at Adams) Shelby County	Sept., 1832	1833	1838 Present Church 1844	The Rev. Thomas Wright	The Rev. Donald Henning, D.D. 1949

Organized by the Rev. Thomas Wright. Memphis' first Episcopal Church.

Christ Church	Brownsville Haywood County	8/25/1832	1833	1846	The Rev. John Chilton 1832-1840	The Rev. Robert Rickard 1962 The Rev. Wayne Kinyon Jan., 1963

Organized by the Rev. Thomas Wright. Name changed from Zion to Christ Church, 1898.

NAME OF CHURCH	LOCATION	DATE ORGANIZED	DATE ADMITTED TO DIOCESE	DATE OF FIRST CHURCH-HOUSE	FIRST RECTOR (DATE)	PRESENT RECTOR (SINCE, DATE)
Christ Church	Whitehaven Shelby County	5/25/1947	6/10/1947 (as a mission)	1949 1962	The Rev. George Bladgett Stuart Hale 1947- 6/1/1951	The Rev. Francis W. Klephart, Jr. 5/1/1961

Land for first church given in memory of Hestyr Shortridge Palmer by her sons, Robert and John Palmer and by their half-brother, Marvin Holder Palmer. A mission of Grace-St. Luke's. Ground broken for church-house 11/11/1948. First service held in church, Easter 1949. Church consecrated on second Sunday after Easter by Bishop Barth. Church began with 35 communicants; present number comprises 250 families.

NAME OF CHURCH	LOCATION	DATE ORGANIZED	DATE ADMITTED TO DIOCESE	DATE OF FIRST CHURCH-HOUSE	FIRST RECTOR (DATE)	PRESENT RECTOR (SINCE, DATE)
Church of The Holy Innocents	Arlington (Haysville, Wythe Depot) Shelby County	1856	1880 (Date of first Diocesan Assessment)	1882	The Rev. Charles Francis Collins 1872 (first minister-in-charge)	

The original church organ was given to the author of this volume and was placed with appropriate ceremony of rededication (1960) in the parlor of Davies Manor, Brunswick, Tennessee. Inspired by the gift of the organ, a volume *The Church of The Holy Innocents* has been written about this church, the town of Arlington and many of the early families of Shelby County. The church house was torn down in 1929. (No longer in existence.)

NAME OF CHURCH	LOCATION	DATE ORGANIZED	DATE ADMITTED TO DIOCESE	DATE OF FIRST CHURCH-HOUSE	FIRST RECTOR (DATE)	PRESENT RECTOR (SINCE, DATE)
Emmanuel	Memphis Shelby County	(Started in 1860's) 1874	Church had 127 communicants in 1898	Feb. 1884	Deacon George H. Jackson The Rev. Isaac Black	The Rev. S. D. Rudder The Rev. Cecil Marshall 1963

Old church on Third at Court and Jefferson sold (1908), new church erected and consecrated before March 13, 1910; church rebuilt in 1956.

NAME OF CHURCH	LOCATION	DATE ORGANIZED	DATE ADMITTED TO DIOCESE	DATE OF FIRST CHURCH-HOUSE	FIRST RECTOR (DATE)	PRESENT RECTOR (SINCE, DATE)
Grace Church	Paris Henry County	Started 1832	1888	1895 Consecrated 11/10/1895 By Bishop Gailor		The Rev. W. Harold Pauley 2/15/1959 The Rev. Franklin Ferguson 1963

Present number of communicants 40. Through a bequest of a former member the church was completely renovated in 1939.

NAME OF CHURCH	LOCATION	DATE ORGANIZED	DATE ADMITTED TO DIOCESE	DATE OF FIRST CHURCH-HOUSE	FIRST RECTOR (DATE)	PRESENT RECTOR (SINCE, DATE)
Grace-	Memphis Shelby County	Started 1850 3/28/1853 1856 reorganized 1894	1858	1867	The Rev. George Weller 1850-	The Rev. C. Brinkley Morton 6/1/1962.
St. Luke	Memphis Shelby County		1898	Started 1895 Consecrated 2/22/1903	The Rev. E. Bazett Jones	

Grace Church started as a mission of Calvary Church.
Prior to 1891 Dr. E. Spruille Burford, Rector, Calvary Church, held services on Idlewild. Later Bishop Gailor and Dr. F. P. Davenport, of Calvary, chose original site for St. Luke at corner of Idlewild and Union.
Grace and St. Luke merged Nov. 28, 1940 and became Grace-St. Luke Church.

NAME OF CHURCH	LOCATION	DATE ORGANIZED	DATE ADMITTED TO DIOCESE	DATE OF FIRST CHURCH-HOUSE	FIRST RECTOR (DATE)	PRESENT RECTOR (SINCE, DATE)
Good Shepherd	Memphis Shelby County	1865 (on Good Shepherd Day)	1872	1866 (at Mill and 4th St.)	The Rev. James Junius Vaulx 1865-1870 The Rev. Charles Carroll Parson 1870	The Rev. Homer C. Carrier Jan. 1955
	Congregation organized by the Rev. James Junius Vaulx, 1865, Church property sold in 1943 and present church was built at University and Jackson Avenue.					
Holy Communion	Memphis (Walnut Grove Rd. and Perkins) Shelby County	1938 First service and consecration of first chapel (on Poplar at Perkins) 1/1/1939 by Bishop Maxon organized by Dr. Charles F. Blaisdell.	1/24/1951	First chapel 1938 Present church-ground broken 10/24/1948 First service and dedication 1/1/1950 by Bishop Dandridge	Dr. Charles F. Blaisdell, Rector, Calvary Church, conducted the first services at the chapel. The Rev. Eric Greenwood Vicar 3/1948-1/19/1951 (a mission of Calvary Church)	The Rev. Eric Greenwood 1/24/1951

(Continued, p. 180)

Mrs. Emma Denie Voorhies gave $10,000 to Dr. Charles F. Blaisdell, Rector of Calvary Church to use as he saw fit. Immediately he said, "There's my chapel!" With the money he bought the land, built the chapel, furnished and equipped it. Dr. Blaisdell named the chapel "Holy Communion" for a former Parish which he served in St. Louis, Mo. Later the small chapel and land were sold and the present acreage purchased. 1,364 communicants, Jan. 1963. Calvary gave land and $200,000.

NAME OF CHURCH	LOCATION	DATE ORGANIZED	DATE ADMITTED TO DIOCESE	DATE OF FIRST CHURCH-HOUSE	FIRST RECTOR (DATE)	PRESENT RECTOR (SINCE, DATE)
Holy Innocents	Trenton Gibson County	In 1853 The Rev. Charles Francis Collins held services in Trenton (Dioc. Jl. 1887) 2/12/1878 Mission revived 1930		Rectory completed 1883 Church consecrated 1886	The Rev. Joseph R. Gray 1878 The 2nd Rector was the Rev. Charles Francis Collins 1883-1889	The Rev. Armand T. Eyler

Lot for church acquired by gift 5/4/1872. Brick church torn down in 1925. A new Parish House was built in 1959. chapel dates from June 1930. Present

NAME OF CHURCH	LOCATION	DATE ORGANIZED	DATE ADMITTED TO DIOCESE	DATE OF FIRST CHURCH-HOUSE	FIRST RECTOR (DATE)	PRESENT RECTOR (SINCE, DATE)
Holy Trinity-in-the-Fields (Old Trinity)	(near) Mason Tipton County	1/25/1846	1846	8/1/1847 Church consecrated by Bishop Otey 12/11/1853	The Rev. James W. Rogers The Rev. J. A. Wheelock The Rev. Charles F. Collins	

→

Major William Taylor gave an acre of land near his residence. A small church was erected and named Holy Trinity. A tablet on the wall inside the church bears this inscription: "George Tarry Taylor and his wife Mary Goodloe Somervell built this church in 1847." An annual pilgrimage is held.

NAME OF CHURCH	LOCATION	DATE ORGANIZED	DATE ADMITTED TO DIOCESE	DATE OF FIRST CHURCH-HOUSE	FIRST RECTOR (DATE)	PRESENT RECTOR (SINCE, DATE)
Holy Trinity	Memphis Shelby County	3/21/1902	1909	Built 1902 (at Cummings and McLemore) Consecrated 4/4/1904. Present church at 3749 Kimball	The Rev. Peter Wager 1902-1905 The Rev. Prentice Pugh Oct. 1905-	The Rev. Paul Shields Walker 4/1/1962-

In choosing the site of the original church, Bishop Gailor remarked: "Thank Heaven, we have found a piece of property where I will not be disturbed by the clanging of the street cars when I am preaching during a visitation!" Holy Trinity church was sold. The congregation moved to site of St. Edward's mission on Kimball Ave. (1959) The present church of Holy Trinity was built from funds derived from the sale of the old church and of St. Edward's. The land of the present church was a part of the original Greer Plantation. The Parish house dates from 1848.

NAME OF CHURCH	LOCATION	DATE ORGANIZED	DATE ADMITTED TO DIOCESE	DATE OF FIRST CHURCH-HOUSE	FIRST RECTOR (DATE)	PRESENT RECTOR (SINCE, DATE)
Immanuel	LaGrange Fayette County	1832	1833	1843 (consecrated)	The Rev. Samuel George Litton 1832-1846	The Rev. W. Joe Moore 1961-

Organized by the Rev. Thomas Wright. Mary Hayes Willis (Mrs. Thomas Benn) Gloster, was the founder of Immanuel Church. John and George Anderson aided in the organization of the church.

NAME OF CHURCH	LOCATION	DATE ORGANIZED	DATE ADMITTED TO DIOCESE	DATE OF FIRST CHURCH-HOUSE	FIRST RECTOR (DATE)	PRESENT RECTOR (SINCE, DATE)
Immanuel	Ripley Lauderdale County	1850	Prior to 1860	1858 Addition to present chapel in 1961	The Rev. Charles Francis Collins	The Rev. Wayne Kinyon Jan., 1963-

Dr. Samuel Oldham gave the land for the church. Building cost $1,500.00. Church consecrated by Bishop Quintard "Third Sunday after Easter 1874." Present communicants, 21.

NAME OF CHURCH	LOCATION	DATE ORGANIZED	DATE ADMITTED TO DIOCESE	DATE OF FIRST CHURCH-HOUSE	FIRST RECTOR (DATE)	PRESENT RECTOR (SINCE, DATE)
Otey Memorial Chapel	Oakville-Whitehaven (corner of Raines and Tchulahoma Roads) Shelby County	1865 1866 Reorganized as a mission Nov. 1961	First account of chapel in Diocesan Journal of 1866.	1866 Chapel razed about 1892	The Rev. John Miller Schwrar 1866-	The Rev. Gordon Bernard (Priest in charge) 1961-1962

NAME OF CHURCH	LOCATION	DATE ORGANIZED	DATE ADMITTED TO DIOCESE	DATE OF FIRST CHURCH-HOUSE	FIRST RECTOR (DATE)	PRESENT RECTOR (SINCE, DATE)
Ravenscroft Chapel	5 miles east of Randolph (Formerly on Ravenscroft Plantation) Present Address: Brighton Tipton County	1834		Consecrated by Bishop Otey	10/23/1836 George H. Batchelor, Lay Reader for thirty years.	The Rev. H. Sheldon Davis

The first Episcopal Church built in West Tennessee. Built by J. J. Alston, a brother of the Rev. Phillip Alston. Chapel badly damaged during Civil War.

Edmund Dozier Bray (9/29/1811-1/14/1880), early vestryman of Calvary Church, Memphis, gave 10 acres of land to Diocese in 1866 for a church. He, largely, built the first chapel. Present building used as chapel for the Episcopal Church Home located nearby.

Presently a parochial mission of St. John, Memphis, admitted 3/28/1962

Present chapel dedicated by Bishop Vander Horst 5/27/1962.

The Rev. John Paschall Davis, Jr. Vicar July, 1962

NAME OF CHURCH	LOCATION	DATE ORGANIZED	DATE ADMITTED TO DIOCESE	DATE OF FIRST CHURCH-HOUSE	FIRST RECTOR (DATE)	PRESENT RECTOR (SINCE, DATE)
St. Alban's Mission	Memphis (Florida Street) Shelby County	1903		1905	The Rev. G. R. Cadman	

A Mission of St. Mary's; Dean James Craik Morris, organizer. Property sold in 1946 and proceeds given to the Church of the Good Shepherd. (No longer in existence.)

NAME OF CHURCH	LOCATION	DATE ORGANIZED	DATE ADMITTED TO DIOCESE	DATE OF FIRST CHURCH-HOUSE	FIRST RECTOR (DATE)	PRESENT RECTOR (SINCE, DATE)
St. Andrew	Near corner of 3 counties—Haywood, Tipton, Fayette.	March, 1834	1837	1836	The Rev. John Chilton 1834- / The Rev. John H. Drummond 1837- / The Rev. Wm. Steel 1839-	

The church burned in March, 1845. (From Trinity Parish Register, Mason, Tenn.) Old Trinity was an outgrowth of this parish. (No longer in existence.)

NAME OF CHURCH	LOCATION	DATE ORGANIZED	DATE ADMITTED TO DIOCESE	DATE OF FIRST CHURCH-HOUSE	FIRST RECTOR (DATE)	PRESENT RECTOR (SINCE, DATE)
St. Andrew	Collierville Shelby County	1881	4/22/1890		The Rev. W. A. Gray 1881-1889	The Rev. Carson Fraser 7/1/1961

In 1875 Miss Anna Holden attended a Diocesan Convention in Memphis. There she met Dr. W. C. Gray of St. James Church, Bolivar, and enlisted his interest in coming to Collierville to conduct services.

Dr. George White of Calvary held services in the home of Mrs. J. H. Mangum and in the Christian Church.

The cornerstone was laid 11/30/1890 by Bishop Quintard and Dr. Burford of Calvary. Dr. Arthur Howard Noll was resident minister, 1895-1897.

NAME OF CHURCH	LOCATION	DATE ORGANIZED	DATE ADMITTED TO DIOCESE	DATE OF FIRST CHURCH-HOUSE	FIRST RECTOR (DATE)	PRESENT RECTOR (SINCE, DATE)
St. Andrew's Chapel	Memphis Memphis Boys' Town (4067 Summer Avenue) Shelby County	4/15/1942	A mission (building to be used as a chapel by Memphis Boys' Town)	10/12/1946 (Date of dedication)	The Rev. Vernon Lane, (in charge) Rector, Church of the Good Shepherd, Memphis. 4/15/1942-9/16/1949.	The Rev. Eric Greenwood, Rector, Holy Communion, Memphis (a member of Memphis Boys' Town Board)

Memphis Boys' Town started in March 1939 when Judge Camille Kelly, Juvenile Court, placed two boys in the custody of the Rev. Vernon Lane, Rector, Good Shepherd.

Public interest was created. Arranged by Judge Kelly, a benefit performance was given by Mary Pickford, star of stage and screen, and $84,000 was raised in one night. Acreage (27.2) was purchased for $70,000 on Summer Avenue. The first chapel was a renovated old barn on the property. Numerous civic minded citizens have given generously in many ways to the worthy cause of Memphis Boys' Town. Addison W. Harris has been the administrator since Feb. 5, 1962.

NAME OF CHURCH	LOCATION	DATE ORGANIZED	DATE ADMITTED TO DIOCESE	DATE OF FIRST CHURCH-HOUSE	FIRST RECTOR (DATE)	PRESENT RECTOR (SINCE, DATE)
St. Andrew (moved to Nashville area)	New Johnsonville	11/17/1957 Camden, Tennessee		1960 (First service Easter Sunday)	The Rev. Jack Arthur 11/17/1957- Sept. 1958	The Rev. W. Harold Pauley 2/15/1959-

Organized in Masonic Bldg., Camden, Tenn. Moved to New Johnsonville Easter Sunday, 1960. Land purchased by congregation. There are 42 communicants at present. Admitted as Organized Mission, 1962.

NAME OF CHURCH	LOCATION	DATE ORGANIZED	DATE ADMITTED TO DIOCESE	DATE OF FIRST CHURCH-HOUSE	FIRST RECTOR (DATE)	PRESENT RECTOR (SINCE, DATE)
St. Ann	Woodstock (near Millington) Shelby County	Spring 1897	1898 (Self-supporting until 1918. A mission of St. Mary's; later of Calvary Church.)	Started 1898 Consecrated 11/12/1906	The Rev. Porter McCullough 1897. Followed by the Rev. Northrup and the Rev. Windiate	The Rev. Peter Keese, Jr. July, 1962

First services were held under an arbor at Rembert Town Springs (about 2 miles from present church). Ben. F. Hawkins in 1896 gave one acre of land at Woodstock to the Diocese. His daughter, Permelia Hawkins (Mrs. James Wheeler) Cocke helped to raise the money to build the church and is one of its oldest members. A new church built on a new site located at 4063 Sykes Road was dedicated by Bishop John Vander Horst on March 15, 1964.

NAME OF CHURCH	LOCATION	DATE ORGANIZED	DATE ADMITTED TO DIOCESE	DATE OF FIRST CHURCH-HOUSE	FIRST RECTOR (DATE)	PRESENT RECTOR (SINCE, DATE)
St. Elisabeth	Raleigh Shelby County	7/3/1960	(a mission)	10/14/1962 (dedication)	The Rev. John Walter R. Thomas 7/3/1960- 11/30/1962.	The Rev. John Turner Whaley (Spring) 1963

Land purchased by St. Mary's Cathedral. Ground broken for church May 14, 1961. Present communicants 114.

NAME OF CHURCH	LOCATION	DATE ORGANIZED	DATE ADMITTED TO DIOCESE	DATE OF FIRST CHURCH-HOUSE	FIRST RECTOR (DATE)	PRESENT RECTOR (SINCE, DATE)
St. George	Germantown Shelby County	6/13/1934	1940	10/6/1936	The Rev. Guy S. Usher 1940-1942 The Rev. Charles Widney 1942-1952	The Rev. David Babin 1962-

Church was named in memory of George Hanks and George Bennett, who died when small children; their parents were among the founders. Early ministers were Sterling Tracy, Charles Seymour, Prentice Pugh. John Scruggs, Lay Reader, assisted. First services held in homes and in Presbyterian Church. New church built on Poplar Pike, 1954. First church building presently used as Germantown Library. Church began with 17 communicants; at present there are over 200 adult members.

NAME OF CHURCH	LOCATION	DATE ORGANIZED	DATE ADMITTED TO DIOCESE	DATE OF FIRST CHURCH-HOUSE	FIRST RECTOR (DATE)	PRESENT RECTOR (SINCE, DATE)
St. Gregory	(near) Brownsville Haywood County	Prior to 1837		1837	The Rev. John Chilton 1837-	

The church served as both a church and school house. (No longer in existence.)

NAME OF CHURCH	LOCATION	DATE ORGANIZED	DATE ADMITTED TO DIOCESE	DATE OF FIRST CHURCH-HOUSE	FIRST RECTOR (DATE)	PRESENT RECTOR (SINCE, DATE)
St. James	Bolivar Hardeman County	4/17/1834	1834	1845 (consecrated) Present church 1869	Dr. Daniel Stevens 1834-1848 The Rev. Lewis Jansen 1848 Dr. Wm. Crane Gray 12/25/1860- 4/24/1881	The Rev. W. Joe Moore 1961-
St. James	Union City Obion County	(about) 1900	1906	1906	The Rev. Geo. W. Whitmeyer 1929- The Rev. George W. Goodson until 1941.	The Rev. Richard W. Clark

Organized by Bishop Otey and Dr. Daniel Stevens; 37 signed the Articles of Association. Services were held in Court House until 1840. The first church cost $375.00, of brick, 32' x 44'. Present church built 1869, cost $11,500, Gothic; 48' x 70'. The architect was Fletcher Sloan. St. James Cook Book, compiled by the Women of St. James Church, Bolivar, contains ink sketches of many old homes and the choice recipes of many of the best "cooks" of the town.

Church prospered for several years, then closed for many years. Church reopened in 1929. Since 1941 a Parish House has been erected, also a Rectory.

NAME OF CHURCH	LOCATION	DATE ORGANIZED	DATE ADMITTED TO DIOCESE	DATE OF FIRST CHURCH-HOUSE	FIRST RECTOR (DATE)	PRESENT RECTOR (SINCE, DATE)
						The Rev. L. A. Wilson 1942-
St. James	Memphis Shelby County	1/29/1939	1939	1942 (1440 Central Ave.)	The Rev. Israel Harding Noe 1/29/1939-7/3/1960	The Rev. Warren H. Steele 1/26/1961
St. John	Martin Weakley County	Nov. 1956	Jan. 1957	October 1958 (first service held in new church)	The Rev. Sidney Sanders 1956-May 1958 The Rev. Clark Baker July 1958-May 1961	The Rev. Richard W. Clark July 1961-

"The Diocesan Convention (1939) granted 107 men the right to start a parish where they might find a true church home and live a full, free life in Christ. . . . St. James regards itself as a pioneer unit to help in ushering in the universal Church." The Rev. Israel H. Noe (*Commercial Appeal*, 1/1/1940 Centennial Edition.)

Church was dedicated by Bishop Barth 5/3/1959. First services were held in buildings at University of Tennessee Junior College in town of Martin. Ten communicants in beginning; present number 16.

NAME OF CHURCH	LOCATION	DATE ORGANIZED	DATE ADMITTED TO DIOCESE	DATE OF FIRST CHURCH-HOUSE	FIRST RECTOR (DATE)	PRESENT RECTOR (SINCE, DATE)
St. John	Memphis (Buntyn) Shelby County	1867 1898 Reorganized 1928 Reorganized	1871 1929	1869 1939 (in Buntyn) 1949 (on Central Avenue)	The Rev. Peter Wager 1871- The Rev. Alfred Loaring-Clark 1929-1952	The Rev. Wallace M. Pennepacker Associate 10/1/1950- Feb. 1952 Rector since 1952

Peter Wager, a layman of St. Mary's, aided in organization of church. Shortly after 1871, chapel was burned. Mr. Wager revived the church in 1898.

St. Lazarus	Memphis Shelby County	1865	1867	about 1866	The Rev. James Rogers. The Rev. John West	

Jefferson Davis was a vestryman of St. Lazarus. In February, 1877, St. Lazarus and Grace Church combined. In 1878 St. Lazarus was dropped from the name. (No longer in existence.)

St. Luke	Jackson Madison County	7/23/1832	1833	1844	The Rev. John Chilton 8/6/1832- Dec., 1834.	The Rev. Frank Newcomb Butler 10/1/1954- Aug., 1963 The Rev. Frank S. Cerveny Oct., 1963-

Organized by the Rev. Thomas Wright. A history of the old church has recently been published by Mrs. D. B. James, Jackson, Tenn.—"Historic St. Luke's Episcopal Church."

NAME OF CHURCH	LOCATION	DATE ORGANIZED	DATE ADMITTED TO DIOCESE	DATE OF FIRST CHURCH-HOUSE	FIRST RECTOR (DATE)	PRESENT RECTOR (SINCE, DATE)
St. Mary	Dyersburg Dyer County	1889 (Started by Bishop Quintard)	First mention in Diocesan Journal of 1896	1903	The Rev. A. C. McCabe 1910-1927.	The Rev. Warren E. Haynes 7/1956-7/1960. The Rev. Sam Ashford Boney 7/1960

The land for the church was given between 1889 and 1896 by Mr. Charley Clark. Bishop Gailor consecrated the church in 1904. There are 100 communicants at the present time.

NAME OF CHURCH	LOCATION	DATE ORGANIZED	DATE ADMITTED TO DIOCESE	DATE OF FIRST CHURCH-HOUSE	FIRST RECTOR (DATE)	PRESENT RECTOR (SINCE, DATE)
St. Mary's Cathedral	Memphis Shelby County	1853-1858 1858	(Diocesan Convention met at La Grange, 5/26-28)	Fall 1857 (Church consecarted 1858)	The Rev. Richard Hines, D.D. 5/26/1857-1871 Dean Richard Hines 1871-1872	Dean William E. Sanders consecrated Bp. Coadjutor, 4/4/1962; William A. Dimmick succeeded him and was Installed as Dean 10/7/1962.

(Continued, p. 192)

"The Ladies Educational and Missionary Society," suggested by Bishop Otey, was organized at Calvary in 1852. Through the effort of this group St. Mary's Church was started, 1853. St. Mary's was consecrated by Bishop Otey, 5/13/1858. Land for church given (1856) by Robert Campbell Brinkley. St. Mary's became the Cathedral of the Diocese of Tenn., 1/1/1871. On 1/19/1926 the Cathedral was completed as "Gailor Memorial." Dr. John H. Davis published in 1958, "History of St. Mary's Cathedral, Memphis."

NAME OF CHURCH	LOCATION	DATE ORGANIZED	DATE ADMITTED TO DIOCESE	DATE OF FIRST CHURCH-HOUSE	FIRST RECTOR (DATE)	PRESENT RECTOR (SINCE, DATE)
St. Matthew	Covington Tipton County	1846	1866	1858	The Rev. James W. Rogers 1846	The Rev. H. Sheldon Davis 1956- (first Director of Quintard House, U. of T. 1954-1956)

"Mission work of the ante-bellum period developed St. Matthew." (Noll, p. 195) Quintard Parish.

NAME OF CHURCH	LOCATION	DATE ORGANIZED	DATE ADMITTED TO DIOCESE	DATE OF FIRST CHURCH-HOUSE	FIRST RECTOR (DATE)	PRESENT RECTOR (SINCE, DATE)
St. Paul	Randolph Tipton County	Fall 1832 (First vestry meeting held 9/30/1832)	1833	3/27/1837	The Rev. Thomas Wright 6/26/1833- 4/28/1835 The Rev. James W. Rogers 1846	

Organized by the Rev. Thomas Wright. Charles T. Quintard, D.D., was a delegate from St. Paul's to Diocesan Convention, 1854. Church burned during Civil War. (No longer in existence.)

NAME OF CHURCH	LOCATION	DATE ORGANIZED	DATE ADMITTED TO DIOCESE	DATE OF FIRST CHURCH-HOUSE	FIRST RECTOR (DATE)	PRESENT (SINCE, DATE)
St. Paul	(near) Mason Tipton County	1873	1873	Cornerstone laid 2/8/1873	The Rev. Henderson Maclin, Deacon-in-charge	(Rector of Emmanuel in-charge)

Dr. Honesty of Emmanuel gave aid in getting new church-house. Old church razed and moved to ground of Gailor School. 40 communicants.

NAME OF CHURCH	LOCATION	DATE ORGANIZED	DATE ADMITTED TO DIOCESE	DATE OF FIRST CHURCH-HOUSE	FIRST RECTOR (DATE)	PRESENT (SINCE, DATE)
St. Paul's Chapel of Calvary Episcopal Church	Frayser (Memphis) Shelby County	8/2/1959 by Dr. Donald Henning	(a mission of Calvary Church)	June-August 1961	First Vicar, The Rev. Robert N. Lockard	The Rev. Robert N. Lockard. Vicar 9/11/1960-March 3, 1964 The Rev. Thomas M. Hutson, Vicar, May 1964-

Land given for church by Miss Mary and Miss Octavia Love. St. Paul's was founded and sponsored by Calvary Church. Calvary gave $100,000 on building.

NAME OF CHURCH	LOCATION	DATE ORGANIZED	DATE ADMITTED TO DIOCESE	DATE OF FIRST CHURCH-HOUSE	FIRST RECTOR (DATE)	PRESENT (SINCE, DATE)
St. Stephen's Mission	Burlison Tipton County	1866	A mission in 1898		Deacon Ossian Alston (Dioc. Jl. 1887)	
(No longer in existence.)						
St. Thomas the Apostle	Humboldt Gibson County	8/30/1959	1960	Fall 1960		The Rev. Armand T. Eyler 1961-

Fourteen communicants.

CHURCH NAME OF	LOCATION	DATE ORGANIZED	DATE ADMITTED TO DIOCESE	DATE OF FIRST CHURCH-HOUSE	FIRST RECTOR (DATE)	PRESENT RECTOR (SINCE, DATE)
St. Thomas	Somerville Fayette County	1834	1835	1858- 11/5/1859 Consecrated 1861 when Diocesan Convention met in church 5/15-19/1861	The Rev. Samuel George Litton	The Rev. Canon Morgan C. Nichols Sept. 1962

Cornerstone laid by Bishop Otey, Nov. 5, 1859.

CHURCH NAME OF	LOCATION	DATE ORGANIZED	DATE ADMITTED TO DIOCESE	DATE OF FIRST CHURCH-HOUSE	FIRST RECTOR (DATE)	PRESENT RECTOR (SINCE, DATE)
St. Thomas	Jackson (570 North Hale) Madison County	July 1894		1897	The Rev. Joseph A. Brown 2/25/1898- 9/7/1900	The Rev. W. A. Bruce 3/10/1912 The Rev. Cecil Marshall 1963-

Organized by Dr. Joseph E. Martin, Rector, St. Luke's, Jackson, Tennessee. The family most influential in keeping the church alive is that of Joe Merry.

CHURCH NAME OF	LOCATION	DATE ORGANIZED	DATE ADMITTED TO DIOCESE	DATE OF FIRST CHURCH-HOUSE	FIRST RECTOR (DATE)	PRESENT RECTOR (SINCE, DATE)
Trinity	Mason Tipton County	1869	1871	3/30/1871	The Rev. Charles Francis Collins 1869-1874.	The Rev. Ben H. Shawhan, Jr. The Rev. Canon Morgan C. Nichols since Sept. 1962

Cornerstone laid by Bishop Quintard; the new church-house in Mason 12/8/1869. Among the founders of the church were Col. George T. Taylor and Col. John F. Jett. The Rev. Troy Beatty and the Rev. Charles Thomas Wright served as rectors.

CHAPTER X

THREE CHURCHES, EMMANUEL

Previously, in this writing, the influence of Emmanuel Church, Warrenton, North Carolina, has been acclaimed in the founding of the church in La Grange, Tennessee, and much of its history related. Yet, there is another church, the history of which should be included, as the romance of the Episcopal Church in West Tennessee is narrated.

Emmanuel Church, Episcopal, in La Grange, Illinois, was, genealogically speaking in church-family history, the "daughter" of Immanuel Church, La Grange, Tennessee, and therefore, the "granddaughter" of Emmanuel Church, Warrenton, North Carolina.

It is earnestly believed that the founding of few churches in our nation's history can be traced to beginnings more deeply steeped in the romance of religion than were these "Three Churches, Emmanuel!" The first in the threesome was founded in 1821, Warrenton, Warren County, North Carolina; the second founded in 1832, in La Grange, Fayette County, Tennessee, and the third founded in 1875, in La Grange, Cook County, Illinois.

The fact must not be overlooked that among the vestry and congregation of Emmanuel Church, Warrenton, were many of the foremost and vigilant spirits of our Southland. Notably among these were members of the families of Anderson, Bragg, Gloster, Otey and Alston.[1]

As it was in Warrenton, Warren County, North Carolina, that the chain of romance began which bound together, within half a century, three churches of the Episcopal faith, it seems well to take a glimpse of the town's notable history. Probably of greater consequence is the fact that it

---

[1] Emmanuel Church, Warrenton, N. C. "One Hundred Forty Years in Brief, 1821-1961" by Charles A. Tucker. (In manuscript form.)

Author's Note: In June, 1961, the Hestyr Shortridge Chapter of Calvary Church, Memphis, met at Davies Manor, Brunswick, Tennessee. Among the members present was Mrs. Charles Pinckney (Cravens Hollenberg) Reid. In conversation Mrs. Reid told me that her daughter, Mrs. Frederick W. (Jean Reid) Walker, Jr., lived in La Grange, Illinois, and that Mr. Walker was a vestryman of Emmanuel Church in La Grange. Also she spoke of the fact that Mr. Cossitt from La Grange, Tennessee, founded La Grange, Illinois. Interesting, rewarding research followed, which resulted in the writing of "Three Churches, Emmanuel!"

was in Warrenton that James Hervey Otey dedicated his life and talent to the advancement of his beloved church.

Warrenton was incorporated in 1779, following the creation of Warren and Franklin Counties from the old county of Bute.

Appropriately, Warrenton once was called, "The Town That Owns Itself."[2] Around 1877 the citizens built three miles of railroad to connect with the Seaboard. The establishment of the Warrenton Hotel was made possible by a local bond issue. The people also owned for many years an ice plant, electric power plant and other progressive public utilities.

Early, plantation owners of wealth and culture built homes in the town and an atmosphere of superior citizens became prevalent.

The Warrenton Male Academy, the Warrenton Female Academy, the Mordecai School for Girls and the Warrenton Female College attracted students from a number of the surrounding counties. Students came also from the best homes of not too distant Virginia.

In 1796, Marcus George, an Irishman became the efficient headmaster of the Male Academy. He was a school-master who believed in strict discipline and sound learning. In Latin, Greek, illustrated geography and pure science he drilled his youthful charges! During the more than a century of the Academy's existence, it was a great power in the educational circles of North Carolina. Such students as these were its graduates: William Eaton, Judge John Hall, Chief Justice Thomas Ruffin, Governor Thomas Bragg, General Braxton Bragg, Judge Matthew W. Ransom, Judge Walter A. Montgomery and Judge Alston Cook.

It is to be recalled that James Hervey Otey went as a teacher from Tennessee to Warrenton to head the Male Academy. There two distinguished brothers were his pupils, Braxton and Thomas Bragg.

In 1802 the Warrenton Female Academy was headed by Professor and Mrs. William Falkener of England. Thorough instruction was offered in English, French, music, dancing and drawing. Professor Falkener was a penmanship expert. Mrs. Falkener was an authority on sewing and on the fancy handwork of the time. To the young ladies of the area, who enrolled in the popular school, she taught the art of making a fine seam as well as the artistry of fancy stitches. Pieces wrought in eyelet holes, strawberry cross-stitch and as samplers, yet belong to old families in the town. These are preserved as precious heirlooms of a leisurely era of grace and courtesy.

The Mordecai School for Girls was organized by Jacob Mordecai in 1809 as a rival of Prof. Falkener's Academy. His wife, Judith, supervised the dormitory of the institution and their four children—Rachel, Ellen,

---

[2] *The Warren Record,* Warrenton, North Carolina, Sept. 13, 1946.

Carolina and Solomon—assisted Professor Mordecai in teaching. The school prospered and was sold in 1818 prior to the family's moving to Virginia.

The Warrenton Female College was established in 1840 and the Female Collegiate Institute in 1848.

Many beautiful old homes are to be found in Warrenton. One of the oldest houses is known as the "Doctor Gloster House," as it became the home of Dr. Thomas Benn Gloster and Mary Hayes Willis Gloster after their marriage in 1795. Dr. Gloster died there on January 1, 1819, and Mrs. Gloster moved to La Grange, Tennessee, eight years later.

Among the other historic houses in Warrenton are: The Bragg House, erected about 1800, first the home of Thomas Bragg, father of Governor Thomas Bragg, Judge John Bragg of Alabama and General Braxton Bragg of the Confederate Army—for whom Fort Bragg was named; the Judge John Hall Place, built in 1810; the Eaton Place, built by William Eaton, a wealthy planter, as a beautiful setting in which his very shy young daughter might more easily entertain her friends—she married Peter Hansborough Bell, a Virginian and Governor of Texas; the Tasker Polk House, built in 1850 by Major Nat Green and the John White House, "Ingleside," where General Robert E. Lee visited in 1870, when he came to visit the grave of his daughter in Warren County.

It was during the late summer of 1862 that Mrs. Robert E. (Mary Custis) Lee and her daughters, Annie Carter Lee and Agnes Lee, were guests at Jones' White Sulphur Springs, Warren County. While there, Annie Carter Lee died of typhoid fever at the age of twenty-three years. She was buried in the family burying ground of the proprietor, William Duke Jones. In 1923, the General Assembly of North Carolina appropriated funds with which to build a road from the highway, about eight miles, to her grave.

In this volume, reference has been made to the marriage of Horace Greeley and Miss Mary Cheney in Emmanuel Episcopal Church, Warrenton. Their romance had begun in New York on the occasion of their meeting at a vegetarian boarding house. Mr. Greeley was enamored by several facets of the young lady's personality, her manners, appearance, her strict adherence to a meatless diet, and her very liberal social views. During Miss Cheney's teaching days in Mrs. Allen's School she freely expressed her views in favor of the abolitionists! Her views were not happily received by the Warrentonians. Eventually the school was closed for lack of pupils. Therefore, the people of Warrenton were quite pleased when the New York publisher and future presidential candidate had married the very opinionated Yankee school-teacher and had removed her influence from the community.

From among the many persons who distinguished themselves in the civic, educational and political life of Warren County these are named in this sketch of history: Nathaniel Macon, John Macon, Benjamin, Joseph and Philemon Hawkins, Jethro Sumner, Robert H. Jones, John Hall, Kemp Plummer, William Miller, Oliver Fitts, James Turner, Edward Hall, Weldon N. Edwards, Jacob Mordecai, Matt W. Ransom, Daniel Turner, George E. Badger, William A. Graham, William Eaton, Jr., William Alston, Phillip Alston, Walter A. Montgomery, William A. Jenkins, Charles A. Cook, John H. Kerr, Josiah W. Bailey, John B. Batchelor.[3]

"Warrenton is an enduring monument to its own ancient greatness."[4]

Immanuel Church, La Grange, Tennessee, inherited from her mother church of Warrenton, a facsimile in construction, a name and several of her most devout parishioners. As has been written, John and Elizabeth Willis Gloster Anderson, their children, George Anderson and Mary Hayes Willis Gloster came in 1827 to La Grange.

Major George Germain Cossitt[5] and his family were among the early communicants of Immanuel, La Grange. The stately, spacious house in which the Cossitt family lived in La Grange, became known as "Cossitt Castle." Into this home, Major Cossitt took his two young nephews to live as members of his family. There the two boys, Connecticut born, Frederick Henry Cossitt and Franklin Dwight Cossitt, grew to manhood. They, too, worshipped at Immanuel Church. And, significantly, time alone held the secret of the ultimate material expression of the faithfulness of one of these young men to the Episcopal Church.

First to Memphis, Frederick Henry Cossitt went and later to New York, where he engaged in a prosperous dry goods business. Because of his appreciation of Memphis and of West Tennessee, he gave Cossitt Library to the City of Memphis. In keeping with the generosity of her distinguished father, Helen Cossitt (Mrs. A. D.) Julliard sponsored the well-known Julliard School of Music in New York City.

Franklin Dwight Cossitt was ever a lover of land. He continued to make his home in "Cossitt Castle" and was a cotton planter with extensive interests.

When the ravages of the Civil War were experienced by the peace-loving citizens of La Grange, "Cossitt Castle" was taken over by General Grant and used as his headquarters. Mrs. Grant accompanied the General. Mem-

---

[3] (a)*The County of Warren, North Carolina, 1586-1917,* Manly Wade Wellman, 1959. (b) *The Warren Record,* Warrenton, North Carolina.

[4] Wellman, "Foreword."

[5] Notes on Cossitt Family, courtesy of: George Marshall Cossitt, La Grange, Illinois; Florence Sillers (Mrs. Harry C.) Ogden, Rosedale, Mississippi.

Franklin Dwight Cossitt
Founder of La Grange, Illinois

bers of the Cossitt family were chased by the vandals to the upstairs rooms of their home and required to live there during the occupation by the Yankee troops!

During the late 1860's, Franklin Dwight Cossitt left his beloved La Grange, Tennessee, and moved to Chicago, Illinois. There he established a wholesale grocery business in which he was successful. In 1870 he purchased a tract of six hundred acres of land, about fourteen miles southwest of the Chicago Loop on the Burlington Route. By the tragic Chicago fire of 1871 his grocery business was destroyed.

Immediately, Mr. Cossitt became engaged in the work which he enjoyed most—the development of land.[6] During succeeding years he inspired the laying out of two or three subdivisions near Chicago. However, the village which he personally developed was his crowning effort! He named the village La Grange for his old home in Tennessee.

In laying out the town of La Grange, Illinois, Franklin Dwight Cossitt, saved a lot in the exact center of the community, at the corner of Kensington and Elm Avenue, as the site for an Episcopal Church! And, on the very first day that ground was broken, on the rolling prairie whereon La Grange was established, attempts were made toward the organization of religious services. Other lots were saved on the original town-plat for churches of other denominations, and for schools where needed. Interesting indeed was the fact that liquor restrictions were written into the land deeds which Mr. Cossitt signed, in order that the community might not become a saloon town.

The members of the Cossitt family gave great assistance in the successful development of the town of La Grange and, as well, in the establishment of the Episcopal Church[7]—the town's first church. The six children of Franklin Dwight Cossitt were: Betty, md. Herbert Mitchell; Mary, md. David B. Lyman, a lawyer, the son of an Episcopal missionary to Hawaii; Martha, md. Wm. C. Dewitt, an Episcopal clergyman and Dean of the Seminary, Evanston, Illinois; Margaret, md. Charles Shedd; Frances, md. Mr. Lay, and Franklin Dwight Cossitt, Jr., md. Margaret Fox.

The first services of the Episcopal Church were read in La Grange in 1872 in the home of David B. and Mary Cossitt Lyman. In November 1874, twenty-seven men signed a petition to organize a parish. Among the names were David B. Lyman and Franklin D. Cossitt. Upon approval of the petition by the Standing Committee of the Diocese of Illinois, the first

---

[6] La Grange Diamond Jubilee 1879-1954 (a 100 page booklet published by Diamond Jubilee Committee.)

[7] Notes on Emmanuel Episcopal Church, courtesy of Herbert H. Mitchell (chairman, Centennial Committee of Emmanuel Church), La Grange, Illinois.

vestry was elected on December 1, 1874. They were: Senior Warden, David B. Lyman; Junior Warden, Jewell K. Philo; Vestrymen—Otis S. Lyman, A. W. Mitchell, Franklin D. Cossitt, William Charnley and Samuel Vial. The vestry voted to name the Church, Emmanuel, meaning "God With Us." Truly, it was a name dear to the heart of Franklin D. Cossitt— the name of his church in La Grange, Tennessee!

The first rector of Emmanuel Church, La Grange, Illinois, was the Reverend Frederick N. Luson, who began his service on December 15, 1874. Upon the land given by Mr. Cossitt and Mr. Lyman, in the center of La Grange, ground breaking took place in the spring of 1875. On June 5, the corner stone for the new church was laid. All of the stone for the church, of rural English-church architecture, was given by Mr. Cossitt and quarried near the village. The completed edifice was consecrated October 5, 1878.

The parish grew steadily. By February 15, 1886, the rectory had been completed at the cost of $6,000.00. The parish house was built and formally dedicated on February 9, 1893. Following May 23, 1893, a new beautiful church was erected. Tragically, the new church and parish house were completely destroyed by fire early on the morning of December 1, 1924. Tremendous effort was expended by the faithful congregation. Money was raised and the present church was completed and dedicated on May 11, 1926. The present value of the church property might well be placed at one million dollars. Of Gothic Cathedral architecture, the church is beautiful indeed. Communicants number approximately 1,150, representing about 575 families.

Emmanuel Church has continued to grow through the years. The period of the late Dr. Everett Carr comprised ten years of substantial progress. Since 1953, under the capable rectorate of the Reverend Gordon Galaty the parish has made great strides. Both of these dedicated men have represented during their time the epitome of selfless service to Emmanuel Church. In turn, each has been the recipient of the genuine appreciation and sincere respect of the communicants of the parish.

To conclude this sketch, let us return to Franklin Dwight Cossitt and give further consideration to his building of La Grange, Illinois.

Mr. Cossitt's motto was, "He that plants a tree, lives for posterity." This maxim he followed as he planned the village of La Grange. Broad streets were laid out and were bordered by plantings of elm and maple trees. Many of the towering trees stand today and are truly a trade-mark of the community. They are living memorials to the late Franklin D.

Cossitt. Among the houses which he built one was built as a home for his family.

In June, 1879, La Grange was incorporated and Franklin Dwight Cossitt was elected president of the corporation. David B. Lyman was the village attorney. An authentic source has revealed that a quarter of a million dollars was spent by Mr. Cossitt in carrying forward this cherished project of building La Grange.

Today, La Grange, Illinois, gives lasting proof of the basic, sacred trilogy on which the town was founded—homes, churches and schools.

Evident, though unsung, is the romantic heritage of the third church, Emmanuel. A church magnificent, whose setting was reserved originally in the heart of the village—because the second church, Immanuel, was held close in the affection of a Christian builder—one who always wore a silk stove pipe hat and a frock-tail coat, typical of a gentleman of the South! Thus, Franklin Dwight Cossitt achieved, as he labored to share with Illinois his cherished bits of Tennessee—the name of his town and of his church, which was "descended" from the first Emmanuel of North Carolina!

CHAPTER XI

THE OTEY FAMILY

Colonel John Otey, born 1735, New Kent, Virginia, and died 1817, Bedford County, Virginia, was in command of a company of riflemen in the Revolutionary War.[1] The company captured a British vessel on the Pamunkey River and turned over the ship with its crew to American authorities.[2]

In 1764, Colonel Otey married Mary Hopkins, born July 14, 1739. Their children were:[3]

Isaac, born October 18, 1765 (more presently);

John, married (1) Elizabeth Buford, (2) Mary C. Wainwright;

Frazier, married (1) Mildred Leftwich, (2) Mary Latham;

Walter, born February 23, 1776, married Mary Walton;

Frances, married the Rev. William Leftwich;

James;

Armistead, married (1) Sarah Gill, (2) Mary Lumpkin

When Isaac Otey, born in New Kent County, Virginia, was four years old his parents, Colonel John and Mary Hopkins Otey, moved to Bedford County, Virginia. At the time, the area was still a veritable wilderness.

On February 5, 1789, Isaac Otey married Elizabeth Mathews, born on February 22, 1767[4] in Rockbridge County, Virginia. Their children[5] were:

---

[1] *Historical Register of Virginians in the Revolution,* by John H. Gwathmey, 1938.

[2] *Roster and Soldiers, Tennessee Society D.A.R., 1894-1960,* compiled by Edythe R. Whitley, State Registrar, published by Tennessee Society D.A.R., 1961.

[3] Otey Family Records, courtesy of Miss Rosalie McClellan, Memphis, Tennessee.

Note: The record of service of Col. John Otey in the Revolutionary War has been accepted by the N.S.,D.A.R., for membership of:

Agatha L. W. (Mrs. A. M.) Penneybacker (193817), Chief John Ross Chapter, Chattanooga, Tennessee;

Minnie H. C. (Mrs. T. A.) Havron, (282761), Tullahoma Chapter, Tullahoma, Tennessee;

Effie Hale (Mrs. Robert L.) Crawford, (333956) Bonny Kate Chapter, Knoxville, Tennessee;

Leslie Cummings (Mrs. David) Browder, (402160), Rhea-Craig Chapter, Sweetwater, Tennessee.

(Ref.—State D.A.R., Regent's File 1956-1959, in possession of author.)

[4] Obituary of Mrs. Elizabeth Otey, newspaper clipping pasted in a Prayer Book which was given by Bishop James Hervey Otey to his sister-in-law, Mrs. Walter Leake Otey. Courtesy of Miss McClellan.

[5] Otey Family Records, University of the South, Sewanee, Tenn.

Isaac Otey

Elizabeth Mathews Otey

Parents of James Hervey Otey,
First Bishop of the Protestant
Episcopal Church,
Diocese of Tennessee

John Mathews, born October 2, 1792—died February 3, 1859, married Lucy Wilhelmina Norvell of Lynchburg, Virginia;

Isaac N., married Prudence Buford Otey (a first cousin);

William (died unmarried);

Robert B. (died unmarried);

Littleton W. (died unmarried);

Armistead, married (1) Susan J. Terry, of Tennessee, (2) Martha Ann Nolley of Mississippi;

Sarah Maxwell, married Maj. William Cook;

Mary,[6] married Col. Edward Gwatkin;

Mildred, married John Hopkins, Jr.;

Frances A., married Capt. Paschal Buford;

James Hervey, (more presently);

Walter Leake Otey, (more presently).[7]

Major Isaac Otey was "a well-to-do farmer, a man of sterling integrity and for thirty years a member of the Virginia Legislature."[8] He served in both Houses of the Legislature and that he never lost an election is of record![9] He lived in Bedford County, Virginia, until 1829, at which time he moved to "Sandusky," near Lynchburg, Virginia, where he died October 18, 1839.[10]

Major Otey was "a member of the Protestant Episcopal Church and lived to see one of his sons elevated to a high place within its pale—he was the father of the present distinguished Bishop of Tennessee."[11]

Elizabeth Mathews Otey, wife of Major Isaac Otey, died March 4, 1855. "Her remains were brought to Liberty, Bedford County, Virginia, and buried by her husband, Isaac."[12]

The age of James Hervey Otey in relation to the birth dates of his brothers and sisters has been a matter of comment. James Hervey was the seventh son[13] among the eight boys in the family and he was the eleventh of the twelve children[14] of Isaac and Elizabeth Mathews Otey.

Of interest is this record concerning the name of the first Bishop of the Episcopal Church in Tennessee. "The son was first named 'James Harvee' after a friend in Richmond. Afterwards when the boy was nearly grown

---

[6] Elizabeth Mathews Otey died at home of her daughter, Mary Otey Gwatkin. (Obituary.)

[7] Otey Family Records. Courtesy of Miss McClellan.

[8] Noll, p. 52.

[9] *The Churchman*, an article by the Rev. S. F. Hotchkin, May 14, 1898.

[10] Obituary of Maj. Isaac Otey, newspaper clipping. Courtesy of Miss McClellan.

[11] *Ibid.*

[12] Obituary of Mrs. Elizabeth Otey.

[13] *The Churchman.* (5-14-1898)

[14] Otey Family Records. Miss McClellan.

and had become enamored of Hervey's *Meditations* he, with the consent of his father, changed the middle name to 'Hervey'."[15]

James Hervey Otey, born January 27, 1800, Bedford County, Virginia, married on October 18, 1821.[16] Eliza Davis Pannill, whom he married, was born March 31, 1800, in Oxford, North Carolina, "whose family had removed from Petersburg (Va.) to the neighborhood of Chapel Hill (N.C.)."[17] The account continues:

"She was a lady of remarkable beauty and subsequently displayed such energy of character as made her truly a help-meet for one who in the midst of incessant labor and toil for others, was to raise and educate a large family of children."[18]

James Hervey Otey in his personal appearance was "tall, long limbed, rather slender, with delicate long hands and feet."[19] At the age of fifteen, when he entered the University of North Carolina, "he was six feet in height and far from graceful in his carriage, and of such swarthy complexion as to gain for himself from his college mates the nickname of 'Cherokee'."[20]

About his home, James Hervey Otey "did his own carpentering, gardening and jobbing. . . ."[21] He played the violin. "I rocked the cradle with one foot while I wrote (sermons)," he said.[22]

The nine children of James Hervey and Eliza Davis Pannill Otey were:[23]

1.   Virginia Maury Otey, b. 8/5/1822, Franklin, Tennessee. Bapt. by Bishop Ravenscroft, North Carolina. Md. Benjamin Blake Minor. Md. 5/26/1842 by the Rt. Rev. Leonidas Polk. Virginia Maury Otey died at Richmond, Va., 4/23/1900, age 78 years. Children: Hervey Otey, Hubbard Taylor, Benjamin B., Jr., Leonidas Cobb, Viola, Jane, William and Zelle Minor, b. 7/10/1849.

2.   Paul Hooker Otey, M.D.,[24] b. 4/3/1825, at Warrenton, N. C. Bapt. by the Rev. C. C. Brainard. Md. Mary A. Bowles of Miss. Md. 3/19/1847 in Nashville, Tenn., by the Rev. J. T. Edgar. A daughter, Kate Otey, b. 9/23/1860, d. 1/12/1919, md. Wm. A. Yerger, had daughter Melvina, b. 6/28/1886, d. 5/25/1919, md. 7/22/1902, Elbert V. Reams; their daugh-

---

[15] *American Quarterly Church Review*, N. Y., October 1863. Printed by Tuttle, Morehouse and Taylor, 221 State Street, New Haven, Conn.

[16] Otey Family Records compiled by Donna Otey Compton, a daughter of Bishop Otey. Courtesy of Mary Worthington Pearre (Mrs. R. T.) Rohrer, Bethesda, Md.

[17] *American Quarterly Church Review*, October 1863.

[18] *Ibid.*

[19] *The Churchman.* (5-14-1898).

[20] Noll, p. 53.

[21] *The Churchman.*

[22] *American Quarterly Church Review.* October, 1863.

[23] Otey Family Records, by Donna Otey Compton.

[24] Dr. Otey introduced a Camp System which saved many lives. He died of yellow fever in Memphis, 1878.

ter, Dorothy Reams, b. 11/3/1907, md. 2/3/1930, Tollie Cheek; they had a son, Tollie Cheek, Jr., b. 3/16/1947, d. 4/13/1962.

3. Henrietta Coleman Otey, b. 7/15/1826, Franklin, Tenn. Bapt. by the Rev. James H. Otey. Md. the Rev. Charles Tomes on 3/19/1846 at Columbia, Tenn., by the Rev. F. G. Smith. Henrietta Otey Tomes d. Washington, D. C., 2/22/1897. The Rev. Charles Tomes d. 7/10/1857, Nashville, Tenn. Children: Frank J., Sara, James Otey, Henrietta, Andrew, Margaret and George Tomes.

4. Reginald Heber Otey, b. 2/26/1829, Franklin, Tenn. Bapt. by Bishop Ravenscroft of N. C. d. 7/27/1830.

5. Sara McGavock Otey, b. 6/30/1830, Franklin, Tenn. Bapt. by the Rev. George Weller, confirmed by Bishop Otey, d. 5/28/1847, Columbia, Tenn., at Mercer Hall (brain fever and pleurisy).

6. Mary Fogg Otey, b. 10/27/1832, Franklin, Tenn. Bapt. by the Rev. George Weller. Md. Daniel Chevilette Govan[25] (b. 7/3/1827, N. C., d., buried Holly Springs, Miss.) on Tuesday, 12/30/1853, at Calvary Church, Memphis, Tenn., by the Rev. Dr. Page. d. 10/6/1897, Seattle, Wash. (concussion of brain, thrown from an electric car). (More presently.)

---

[25] Andrew Robison Govan, born Orangeburg District, S. C., Jan. 13, 1794, died "Snowdoun" (near Lamar, Miss., Old Salem community—burned by Yankee troops during Civil War), June 27, 1841. He was a member of U. S. Congress during the days of Clay, Webster, Calhoun—were great friends. On March 10, 1825, he and Mary Pugh (b. Jan. 8, 1802—d. July 12, 1888) were married by Bishop William Mercer Green at the home of her aunt, Mrs. Eaton Pugh (who reared her), near New Bern, N. C. Their children were: (1) Eaton Pugh Govan, married Julia Hawks (more presently); (2) Daniel Chevillette Govan, married Mary Fogg Otey; (3) William Hemphill Govan; (4) Sally Daves Govan, married (a) Christopher H. Mott (distinguished career in Civil War), (b) Maj. John Marshall Billups—three children: Joseph Pierce Billups, married Courtney Walthal (Ross), Elizabeth Govan Billups, married Willis Garth, and Mary Billups; (5) John Jones Govan; (6) Elizabeth Jones Govan; (7) Andrew Robison Govan, Jr.; (8) George Morgan Govan.
Andrew Robison Govan was the son of Daniel and Louisa Govan.
Sally Daves Govan was confirmed by Bishop Green and her three children were baptized by him in St. Paul's Episcopal Church, Columbus, Miss. Ref. Mary Pugh Govan's Bible—records courtesy of Miss Mary Billups, Columbus, Miss.
Eaton Pugh Govan, son of Andrew R. and Mary Pugh Govan, married Julia Hawks, daughter of the Rev. Francis Lister Hawks (b. New Bern, N. C., 1789, d. 1866, educated at University of N. C., founded St. Thomas Hall, Holly Springs, Miss., became an Episcopal clergyman 1827, first president of University of Louisiana, among his writings were: History of N. C.; History of the Protestant Episcopal Church in the U. S.; Constitution and Canons of the Episcopal Church; Egypt and Its Monuments; Perry's Expedition to Japan. He declined three elections to the bishopric. Ref.—*Southern Literature from 1579-1895* by Louise Manly, 1895.
Francis Hawks Govan, son of Eaton Pugh and Julia Hawks Govan, married Minnie Ford. Their four children were: (1) Betty, md. Frank N. Burke; (2) Eaton Pugh Govan, md. Evelyn Beale Derrick—two sons: Francis Hawks Govan, md. Nov. 28, 1958, Peggy Jane Watson, they have two children, Henry Watson Govan, b. Nov. 18, 1959, and Elizabeth Evelyn Govan, b. Nov. 10, 1962, living presently in Memphis, Tennessee; Henry Bradford Govan, md. Mary Alice Bradford, living presently in Little Rock, Arkansas. (3) Laura, md. William Ward; (4) Charles Ford Govan, md. Ruth Felton.

7. Eliza (Donna) R. Otey, b. 8/7/1836. Bapt. by Bishop Otey. Md. Robert King Compton (b. 10/21/1840 — d. 10/9/1881, Norfolk, Va.) of Lexington, Va., on 4/12/1866 at Cornwall, N. Y., d. 12/30/1908 at the residence of her son-in-law, Charles G. Warden. (More presently.)

8. Frances J. Otey, b. 9/23/1838, Columbia, Tenn. Bapt. by the Rev. John T. Wheat, 1/27/1839, d. 2/6/1848, at Mercer Hall (scarlet fever).

9. William Mercer Otey, b. 4/15/1842, Columbia, Tenn. Bapt. by the Rev. Thomas Worrell, d. Oakland, Cal., 12/16/1898 (buried, Mountain View Cemetery, Oakland, Cal.), md. (1) Pattie Compton, Lexington, Va., 7/27/1864, d. (with infant son) 11/1/1865; md. 6/22/1876, Geraldine Gager, b. 1849, Stamford, Conn., d. 6/11/1934, Cal. Children: (1) James Hervey, b. 3/16/1877, San Francisco, Cal., d. 4/22/1949, San Diego, Cal., md. 5/13/1900, Alma Georgianna Gooch, b. 11/17/1878, Minn., d. 5/21/1955, Milburn, N. J.; (2) Mary Eliza (Maizie), b. 8/28/1878, d. 1956, md. Ernest Mendenhall, b. 6/24/1873, d. 10/15/1960; (3) Paul Emory Otey, b. 3/12/1880, d. 8/23/1952, md. 1902, Eleanor McGowan, b. 12/5/1881; (4) Gerald, b. 10/2/1881, d. 1903; (5) Wm. Mercer, b. 10/25/1884, d. 10/28/1884; (6) Donna Edith, b. 8/16/1887, d. 1903. (See page 213, for other descendants of Wm. Mercer and Geraldine Gager Otey.)

The children of Daniel C. and Mary Otey Govan were:

1. Benjamin McCulloh Govan,[26] died June 8, 1943, Marianna, Arkansas. Married in 1883, Frances Dancey. Their children were:
   Nena Dancey Govan;
   Frank Dancey Govan (unmarried), Shreveport, La.;
   Emmie Govan, married Ray Case;
   Frances Govan,[27] married Hendrix Lackey and had children—
      Hendrix Jr., Jean, Mary and Carol Lackey;
2. Donna Govan, married Peter Dubble;
3. Julia Govan, married .... Padgett (Seattle, Wash.);
4. Etta Govan, married Paul McKellar.[28] Their children were: Donna and Paul, died in early childhood, and Mary Otey McKellar, married Roy N. Douglas;[29]
5. Helen Govan, married J. J. Sample;

[26] Descendants of Benjamin McCulloh Govan reside presently in Mountain View, Ark. Mrs. Ray Case and Miss Nena Govan have supplied much of the information concerning this branch of the Otey family.
[27] The children of Frances Govan Lackey: Hendrix Lackey, Jr., Mountain View, Ark.; Jean Lackey (Mrs. W. C.) Reynolds, Texarkana, Texas; Mary Lackey (Mrs. J. E.) Barham, Little Rock, Ark., and Carol Lackey (Mrs. J. R.) Patterson, Little Rock, Ark., living presently.
[28] Brother of U. S. Senator Kenneth D. McKellar.
[29] Son of Julius Judson and Eva Ricks Douglas, Bolton, Tennessee.

6. Daniel C. Govan, Jr.

Eliza Donna Otey married Robert King Compton and had four daughters:[30]

1. Pattie Otey Compton, b. 4/5/1868, md. Charles G. Warden, one son—Robert Bruce Warden, b. 1/18/1895, md. Elizabeth Withers[31]—children: Elizabeth, Martha and Patty Warden.

2. Elizabeth Pannill Compton, b. 11/26/1869, md. J. Graham Pearre; two daughters—(a) Mary Worthington Pearre, b. 12/21/1896, md. 9/24/1924, Robert Travers Rohrer,—a son, Robert T. Rohrer, b. 11/24/1926, md. 8/29/1960, Mary Catherine Pinson; (b) Elizabeth Otey Pearre, md. John Douglas Burnham—children: Patricia, md. James Grosholz, had Elizabeth, Patricia and Douglas Grosholz; and John Douglas, Jr., md. Gloria S., one child, John Patrick Burnham.

3. Mary Compton,[32] b. 6/20/1872, d. 1/15/1963, md. John Goode Urquhart, three sons,[33]—(a) John G., b. 10/1/1906, md. Mary Tyler Heiner, children—Robert Graham Urquhart, b. 1943 (presently enrolled at the University of the South, Sewanee, Tenn.), Jennifer Urquhart, b. 1944 and Helen Urquhart, b. 1948. (b) Robert, b. 8/17/1908, d. 3/10/1915; (c) James Otey, b. 11/21/1910, md. Adair Tompkins, one child, Ridgely Urquhart.

4. Katherine Compton[34] b. 11/8/1875, md. Philip Taylor Berry—children: (a) Donna Otey Berry, b. 1/18/1895, md. Theron Ball Clement, —children, Donna and Margaret Clement; (b) Margaret Foxhall Berry, b. 6/14/1896, d. 2/9/1910; (c) Philip T., Jr., b. 5/11/1901, d.; (d) Katherine Berry, b. 11/11/1902, md. Carleton Smith, children—Sally and Katherine Smith.

Walter Leake Otey, the youngest child of Isaac and Elizabeth Mathews Otey, was born in Bedford County, Virginia, July 9, 1806, and died in Marianna, Arkansas, October 9, 1876. On August 1, 1839, he married in Raleigh, North Carolina, Eleanor Kyle, born in Raleigh, N. C., September 17, 1820, and died in Clarksville, Tenn., October 29, 1896.

Walter Leake Otey received his appointment to West Point Military Academy "from John Randolph, a fast friend of his father."[35] He was the founder of the town of Marianna, Arkansas.

---

[30] Otey Family Records by Donna Otey Compton.

[31] In possession of Mrs. R. Bruce Warden, Arlington, Va., are many of the Otey Family Papers.

[32] Otey-Urquhart Records. Courtesy of Commander John G. Urquhart, Chevy Chase, Md., a great grandson of Bishop Otey.

[33] *Ibid.*

[34] Records by Donna Otey Compton and other Otey family records.

[35] Obituary of Walter Leake Otey. Courtesy of Miss McClellan.

The only child of Walter Leake and Eleanor Kyle Otey was Frances Elizabeth (Bettie) Otey, born August 14, 1841, and died June 17, 1917. She married Capt. Thomas Cary Anderson in Memphis, July, 1858. The marriage was solemnized by Bishop James Hervey Otey, the bride's uncle.

Captain Anderson came from Virginia about 1854. He became one of the outstanding teachers of Memphis while serving as principal of the High School. Thomas F. Gailor was one of his students. (See Chap. 8, p. 133).

The children of Thomas Cary Anderson and Bettie Otey were:

Walter Otey Anderson, married Josephine Dailey;

Thomas Cary Anderson,[36] married Mamie Lightburne;

Rosalie Anderson, married John L. McClellan;

Eleanor Anderson, married John Strickland;

Virginia Anderson, married Dr. Isham Goss.

The first daughter of Thomas Cary and Bettie Otey Anderson, Rosalie, who married John L. McClellan, had the following children:

Walter McClellan;

Francis Otey McCellan (New York City);

Rosalie McClellan (Memphis);[37]

Winston McClellan (Durham, N. C.)

Eliza Davis Pannill Otey, wife of Bishop James Hervey Otey, "fell asleep in Christ in Memphis, Tenn., June 4, 1861. . . ."[38] She was interred in the churchyard of St. John's, Ashwood, Maury County, Tennessee.

Elizabeth Mathews, the wife of Bishop Otey, was the daughter of William. (Augusta Co., Va.—d. 1772) and Frances Crowe Mathews. Their other children were: John, Joseph, James William and Anne.

William Mathews was the son of John and Anne Archer Mathews. John came (1734-37) to Augusta County and lived on an original grant of 1600 acres to him from the Crown (near Natural Bridge, Va.) He was elected to the Vestry of Augusta Parish, 1746.

John Mathews was the son of Samuel (a captain of the Colonial Militia; of St. Stephen's Parish 1706; died 1718) and his first wife, Miss Braxton.

Samuel Mathews was the son of John (born at "Danbeigh" near Blunt Point) and Elizabeth Tavenor, whom he married in 1683.

John Mathews was the son of Samuel, the eldest son of Gov. Samuel Mathews (elected Governor of the Colony by the House of Burgesses, Dec.

---

[36] Daughters of Mr. and Mrs. Thomas C. Anderson, Jr.—Miss Louise Cary Anderson; Miss Geraldine Anderson, Memphis, Tenn.

[37] Miss Rosalie McClellan, former teacher in South Side High School, Memphis, makes her home at 4780 Stage Road near Bartlett, Tennessee.

[38] Gravestone inscription. Copied by Mrs. Arthur B. Chitty, University of the South, Sewanee.

1656) born 1592—died 3/13/1660. He was sent to Virginia by King James I, in 1622 as a commissioner to examine the condition of the colony. He liked Virginia and remained! He married a daughter of Sir Thomas Hinton, who was the mother of his sons. The landed possessions of Gov. Mathews were large—one plantation was called "Fleur de Hundred," another "Mathews Manor"—later called "Danbeigh." His two sons were Samuel and Francis.

Governor Samuel Mathews was the son of Tobias Mathews (b. 1546, d. 1628) and his wife, Frances Barlow. Tobias Mathews became the 56th Archbishop of York, Sept. 11, 1606.

Archbishop Tobias Mathews was the son of John Mathews of Bristol and his wife, Eleanor Crofton Mathews of Ludlow, England. The family line goes back in Wales to Gwaetfoed, Prince of Cardiganshire.[39]

The first member of the Otey family of record in America is that of John Otey, who came from Yorkshire, England, about 1625 and settled in New Kent County, Virginia. He was a member of the Virginia Grand Assembly in 1632. The Otey family of Virginia, like their English forebears, were of the Church of England, and Major Isaac Otey for years was a vestryman.[40]

In 1851 Bishop Otey visited in England. He wrote in his Diary:

"Responding to a special invitation from the Bishop of London to the Royal Chapel of Saint James, on arising from Communion, I perceived the Duke of Wellington had been kneeling next to me . . . .

I was seated on the platform not more than eight feet from Prince Albert. I never saw a more perfect man. His form is noble and symmetrical; his countenance is grave and dignified without severity, and his whole bearing that of a well bred and accomplished gentleman."

The following is quoted from Bishop Otey's address in England:

"May it please your Royal Highness, I beg leave to express my deep sense of the kindness which allows me of addressing a few words to this large and respected assembly. Believe me, sir, that this feeling of kindly regard is warmly reciprocated and carefully cherished towards the Church of England by the members of that Communion of which I am the representative here today. We can scarcely forget that it will be 36 years tomorrow (Battle of Waterloo) since the meteor flag of Britain floated in the air amidst triumphant shouts of victory. I take occasion, however, to bear testimony to the deep interest which is felt in America toward the people and the Church of England. I believe it is reciprocal. Why should it not be so? . . ."

The Archbishop of Canterbury cordially thanked Bishop Otey for his address.

---

[39] Mathews Records compiled by H. M. Frost (unpublished).
[40] Old newspaper clipping—"James H. Otey, Bedford Born, at 'Fancy Farm'." Courtesy of Mrs. Rohrer.

Bishop Otey's diary records that he sat for his portrait by Sully, the renowned artist, on November 17, 1844. It is recorded that the portrait was a gift from Bishop Otey's close friend, Dr. Mercer. It was in 1844 that Bishop Otey established "Mercer Hall" in Columbia, Tenn., and named the school for his "friend and benefactor, Dr. William Newton Mercer, of New Orleans."[41]

Evidently, soon after the writing of his will on March 22, 1862, Bishop Otey left his home in Memphis and went to visit his son in Mobile. That he placed the will in a stout wooden box and deposited the box in a secret closet is plausible.[42] During the months of his absence from his home, Memphis had been taken by Yankee forces. "He returned in October . . . to discover that his own household had been ransacked of most of its furniture and clothing by his departing slaves."[43]

In 1957 in a dilapidated building on Memphis' waterfront on the Mississippi, a well preserved wooden box virtually sealed off between ceiling and roof was found by a demolition crew wrecking old buildings. The box contained papers of early Memphis business firms and the "yellowed, almost tattered document written almost a century ago by the first Bishop of the Episcopal Diocese of Tennessee." The "last will and testament" of Bishop Otey bore the date, March 22, 1862, and consisted of five handwritten pages. The will listed certain property in Memphis and Chattanooga, Tenn., in Arkansas and North Carolina, little cash, several Bibles, Prayer Books and other church literature. To his children the will charged:

> "I exhort and earnestly beseech my children to read, mark, learn and inwardly digest what is contained in these books, and to make them wise unto salvation, useful in life and happy in death."

Bishop Otey made this bequest concerning his six slaves:

> "I especially enjoin that these servants shall not be sold out of the family and that they all be allowed the blessings of Christian worship and instruction."[44]

At the time of Bishop Otey's death in 1863, he was survived by six children—Virginia, Dr. Paul, Henrietta, Mary Fogg, Eliza (Donna) and William Mercer Otey. All of the children had died by 1900 except Eliza (Donna) Otey Compton. As the last surviving child she recorded, in her

---

[41] See p. 116, this volume.

[42] Bishop Otey's Will is in possession of Mrs. Tollie Cheek, Ripley, Tenn., a descendant.

[43] Davis, p. 37.

[44] *Commercial Appeal* (Memphis U.P.) article by Leo Sorosa. *The New York Times,* Sunday, March 3, 1957. "Bishop's 1862 Will Found in Tennessee." (Memphis U.P.)

own handwriting, the names, births and death dates, baptisms and marriages of her brothers and sisters. Through the courtesy of Mary Worthington Pearre (Mrs. Robert Travers) Rohrer, a granddaughter of Donna Otey (Mrs. Robert King) Compton, these authentic records are used in this chapter and set in print for the first time.[45]

A sturdy log house, built in the 1850's at Beersheba Springs, Tennessee, was enjoyed by Bishop Otey and his family as a summer home. The house stands today in a good state of preservation and is used as a guest house at the Springs.

At the passing of Bishop Otey, Charles Todd Quintard served as chairman of a Council to formulate appropriate resolutions. Significantly, the Council resolved that "as long as honesty and patient endurance of privation . . . shall be valued among men, the name of *Otey* will be repeated from father to son, from generation to generation."[46]

---

[45] In June 1964, Mrs. Rohrer accompanied Commander and Mrs. Urquhart to Sewanee. Mrs. Chitty discovered that Mrs. Rohrer had these valuable Otey records and arranged for the records to be sent to the author for use in this volume.

[46] *The Churchman* (May 14, 1898).

Note: Other descendants of Wm. Mercer Otey, ninth child of Bishop Otey: (1) James Hervey Otey md. Alma Gooch, had two children, (a) James Hervey, b. 2/22/1901, d. 1945, md. Mabel Frances Johnson, had one daughter, Geraldine, md. 6/17/1956, Robert H. Phitts, 3 children, James Ernest, Thomas Otey and Barbara Phitts; (b) Donna, b. 7/29/1903, md. 9/26/1931, Joseph D. Beane, one daughter Dorothy Anne Beane, b. 1/6/1937; (2) Mary Eliza (Maizie) and Ernest Mendenhall had two sons, Lee, d. at 18; Ernest D. Mendenhall, Jr., md. Barbara Spalding, children, Christopher, Lee, Barbara and Elizabeth Mendenhall; (3) Paul E. Otey and Eleanor McGowan had two children, (a) Gerald L. Otey, b. 1903, md. Reba Eves, one son, Robert Lee Otey, (b) Paul E. Otey, Jr., b. 1905, md. Genevieve Mary Murphy, children, Esther and Peter Otey, and Carl Campbell (foster son).

CONCLUSION

He who reads may ask, "What is the romance of the Episcopal Church in Tennessee's grand division on the west?"

The romance of the Church in West Tennessee represents a composite functioning of far-reaching influences and of many lives spent in consecrated effort in the cause of Christianity, through the establishment of the Protestant Episcopal Church. Wherever the movement was experienced there were enduring evidences of faith, of prayer and of devoted, gratifying service to God and to Jesus Christ, his only Son, our Lord.

The Church, characterized by influences of England, planted on American soil at Jamestown, later functioned vitally in the nation's expression of independence. Such was the heritage which she brought through the sisterhood of states to Tennessee and thence to the state's Western District. These broad strides are a part of the legendary accomplishment of the Protestant Episcopal Church of today. Each step has been a contributing factor in the romance which is enthusiastically shared.

And yet, vibrantly coupled with this extraordinary background is a heritage peculiarly our own—the sacrificial, pace-setting years of devoted Bishop Otey, who came to teach and determined to preach; the unique evidence of Christian consecration expressed by resolute Mrs. Gloster; the building of Ravenscroft Chapel by the dedicated Alston family—the first Episcopal Church erected in West Tennessee; the soul-stirring continuity of the Church's influence in three states—North Carolina, Tennessee and Illinois by the epochal founding of "Three Churches, Emmanuel"; the tireless first ministers who came bringing full "tidings of great joy," and the early communicants who became valiant soldiers of the Cross in deed and in truth. The message brought by each in his own particular manner was no figment of the imagination, nor was the motive one of pipe-dreaming or castle-building! Their vision, charted by their belief in God, was that of an eventual, glorious rainbow in achievement through the bringing of the Protestant Episcopal Church to eager, waiting pioneer citizens of a sparsely populated wilderness.

Yes, for all those who founded—a thrilling crusade by which was shared a faith, a form of Christian worship—a pot of gleaming gold at the foot of life's rainbow! Undoubtedly, such was their reward for participation and for achievement in this religious, romantically adventurous experience.

And for those who follow in their train, what is the challenge and where withal the recompense? To cherish the broad precepts of faith which symbolize the Protestant Episcopal Church; to believe the Holy Bible to be the Word of God; to follow the Book of Common Prayer as a source of form and rites in worship, which encourages spiritual growth and to be inspired by the messages in verse which comprise The Hymnal of our faith.

> Jesus with thy Church abide,
> Be her Saviour, Lord and Guide,
> While on earth her faith is tried.
> . . . .
>
> Judge her not for work undone,
> Judge her not for fields unwon,
> Bless her works in thee begun.
> . . . .
>
> All that she has lost, restore;
> May her strength and zeal be more
> Than in the brightest days of yore;
> We beseech thee, hear us.[1]

In such manner, we pray the privilege of being identified with the romance and cherished history of the Episcopal Church may be continuously invoked and perpetuated by the challenging ageless admonition of "go thou and do likewise."

> The Church from her dear Master
> Received the gift divine,
> And still that light she lifteth
> O'er all the world to shine.
> It is the golden casket
> Where gems of truth are stored;
> It is the heav'n drawn picture
> Of Christ, the living Word!
> . . . .
>
> It is the chart and compass
> That o'er life's surging sea,
> 'Mid mists and rocks and quick-sands
> Still guides, O Christ, to thee. Amen.[2]

---

[1] The Hymnal. Hymn 233.
[2] *Ibid.*, Hymn 402.

ACKNOWLEDGMENTS

The use of every known word expressive of appreciation, reams of paper and hours of writing would be necessary if an attempt were made to acknowledge in full measure the generous and rewarding assistance received in the writing of this volume.

Especial appreciation is expressed to the Bishop of the Diocese for his writing of the Preface and to the Rector of Calvary Church for the Introduction to this book.

To many persons the author is indebted for several reasons. Churchmen and others, whose valued opinions were sought, contributed immeasurably to the completed narrative. By correspondence much information was obtained from individuals and parishes. By telephone, local and long distance, material was gathered. Churchmen and others by encouragement and enthusiastic interest in the effort gave constructive criticism after careful reading of the manuscript.

Throughout this entire experience a devoted and tolerant family has provided understanding and inspiration.

Faithful household and plantation help, whose loyal services relieved the author of numerous duties, made possible more time for research and writing.

The generous listing of names, throughout the account, of persons identified with facts and sources has been done, in reality, by way of acknowledgment. Copious footnotes, which indicate both general and specific references, give credit to writers and their works. In many instances, notes by the author have been inserted in recognition of persons and events with bearing on the text.

To each and every person who in any way has so kindly given of time and talent toward the creation of this book, deep and lasting gratitude is sincerely expressed by the author.

INDEX